Writing and Postcolonialism
in the Early Republic

WRITING AND POSTCOLONIALISM IN THE EARLY REPUBLIC

Edward Watts

UNIVERSITY PRESS OF VIRGINIA
Charlottesville and London

The University Press of Virginia
Printed in the United States of America

First published 1998

⊗ The paper used in this publication meets the minimum
requirements of the American National Standard for
Information Sciences—Permanence of Paper for Printed
Library Materials, ANSI Z39.48-1984.

Library of Congress Cataloging-in-Publication Data
Watts, Edward.
Writing and postcolonialism in the early republic / Edward Watts.
p.   cm.
Includes bibliographical references and index.
ISBN 0-8139-1761-1 (alk. paper)
1. American literature—1783–1850—History and criticism.
2. United States—Civilization—1783–1865.
3. Decolonization in literature. I. Title.
PS208.W38 1998
810.9'002—dc21   97-33067
CIP

TO

Tony and Alex

Contents

Acknowledgments, *ix*

INTRODUCTION
The New Nation and the Limits
of Colonial Discourse, *1*

ONE
To Deceive the World:
Hugh Henry Brackenridge's *Modern Chivalry*, *27*

TWO
The Mental Commonwealth of
Judith Sargent Murray's *The Gleaner*, *51*

THREE
Royall Tyler's *The Algerine Captive* and
the Worthy Federal Citizen, *73*

FOUR
The Reputation of Literature and Opulence:
Charles Brockden Brown's *Arthur Mervyn*, *95*

FIVE

The Peculiar Birthright of Every American:
George Watterston's *The Lawyer*, 122

SIX

The Syllogistically Fatal World of
Washington Irving's Diedrich Knickerbocker, 144

EPILOGUE

The Vagrant Inclination, 169

Notes, 181

Works Consulted, 203

Index, 219

Acknowledgments

THIS PROJECT BEGAN AS a dissertation at Indiana University. It was directed by James Justus and its readers were Terence Martin, Raymond Hedin, and David Nordloh. Wallace Williams was present at its inception as well. To all of them I owe a great debt of gratitude; they taught me how to develop an idea. At Indiana as well I was introduced to postcolonial studies by Albert Wertheim. His encouragement, and the forum provided me by the American Association for Australian Literary Studies, allowed me to learn about a subject that was not then taught in graduate school.

This project was completed without external funding. However, colleagues· and friends at Indiana, Toledo, and Michigan State always provided encouragement and asked the right questions. I would like to thank as well anonymous readers at various university presses whose comments were always helpful even as their verdicts were devastating. My reader at Virginia provided the final impetus to make the book all it should be. My editors there, Cathie Brettschneider and Gerald Trett, provided the necessary encouragement and scrutiny to make the book better than it might have been.

My greatest debt is owed to my family. My mother, Emily Stipes Watts, provided insightful readings and commentary. She also represents to me the proper balance between scholarship, teaching, and family. I always keep my father, Robert Watts, in mind as I write because, as a great reader in history, he reminds me that it is more important to be read and understood by all educated and thoughtful people, and not just by other academics. My wife, Stephanie, is simply a wonderful partner in all ways. Her support and love make everything possible, probable, and fun. Alex was patient enough to wait for me to finish copyediting before arriving. Finally, I thank my son Tony, who teaches me every day more about courage and hope than I ever thought I could know.

A version of chapter 5 was published in 1995 as "The Peculiar Birthright of Every American: George Watterston's *The Lawyer*" in *Studies in Amerian Fiction*.

Writing and Postcolonialism
in the Early Republic

✣

The New Nation and
the Limits of Colonial Discourse

HISTORIES OF AMERICAN WRITING often leap from the "Colonial" period, which ends with the Revolution, straight to the "Early National," or something along those lines. The implicit supposition is that there is a clean break between when a community loses its status as "colony" and becomes a "nation." However, reading the texts under either heading reveals a plethora of "national" characteristics before independence and "colonial" ones lurking long after. Clearly, there is anything but a clean leap from one period to the next. How, then, might we approach this transition as we attempt to rewrite the history of American writing?

The field of inquiry that studies the transition of former outposts of empire from colony to nation, postcolonial studies, might be of some use. Although the circumstances of independence differ in the United States, can we not reverse Melville's reference to Australia as "that great America on the other side of the sphere" and use ideas drawn from places like Australia to improve our understanding of America? Many scholars of postcolonialism would resist this assignment: the United States is more often viewed as part of the colonizing world than part of the colonized. Indeed, the United States has always pursued imperial ambitions. The European origins of many of its cultural institutions have been studied at length.

But the debate about the nation's ambivalence toward this legacy has never been resolved. In 1996 Stuart Hall wrote that the United States' "current 'culture wars', conducted throughout with reference to some mythicised Eurocentric conception of high civilization, are literally unintelligible outside the framework of America's colonial past" (246). Perhaps the nation's constant anxiety over the issue of its colonial origins is the hallmark of the postcolonial condition. So far, this ambivalence has been little studied. The United States is a former colony and still often looks across the Atlantic for cultural, artistic, and educational leadership. I believe a case can be made for suggesting that a country can be both colonizer and colonized at once. This book applies postcolonial methodologies to writing in the American early republic to study the origins of this tension in American culture.

One reason for doing so is that the nation's obsession with words such as *empire* and *representation*—the phraseology of current postcolonial studies—has been present since Independence; the terms that frame my discussion are drawn as much from the early republic itself as from contemporary theory, a convergence which suggests that decolonization was as much a concern then as it is now. In 1788, responding to the proposed federal constitution at the Virginia ratifying convention, Patrick Henry made some crucial distinctions about transitions in American politics since the Revolution: "But now, sir, the American spirit, assisted by the ropes and chains of consolidation, is about to convert this country into a powerful and mighty empire. If you make the citizens of this country agree to become the subjects of one great consolidated empire of America, your government will not have sufficient energy to keep them together. . . . I wish not to go to violence, but will wait with hopes that the spirit which predominated in the Revolution is not yet gone, nor the cause of those who are attached to the Revolution yet lost" (124–26). For Henry, citizens live in a "country" and "subjects" in empires. To him, a "country," such as that which existed before the adoption on the Constitution, houses only a vestigial government whose machinations are not "out of the sight of the common people" (124). In the constitutional "empire" he fears, the gains of the Revolution will be lost and citizens reverted to mere subjects.[1]

Henry's equation of empire and republicanism merits consideration. The republicans, in modern terms, were attempting to reintroduce a stratified social order in which the "middling and lower classes of people" (124) will be reconverted to pre-Revolutionary subjects and the nation will become an empire that, like all such entities, will operate under the rubric of the word's etiological origins: *imperium*—by command. In Henry's reckoning, the republicans are, as the

British had been, colonizing—appropriating and rearranging—other parts of society to serve the needs of a centralized metropolitan capital.

Henry's distinction, two centuries ago, eerily foreshadows modern definitions of the same words: imperialism can occur on the level of metaphor, as well as that of geopolitics, and as Edward Said has commented in *Culture and Imperialism*, colonialism is "almost always a consequence of imperialism" (9). While the proponents of the Constitution were not, in Said's terms, "implanting settlements on distant territories," they were controlling "the effective political sovereignty of another political society" (9) by displacing libertarian confederation with autocratic federalism, or so Henry feared.[2] Benedict Anderson observed a parallel tendency in former colonies: "Like the complex electrical system in any large mansion when the owner has fled, the state awaits the new owner's hand at the switch ready to be very much its old brilliant self again. One should therefore not be much surprised if revolutionary leaderships, consciously or unconsciously, come to play lord of the manor" (160). Henry shares with Anderson the fear that the basic structure of colonial dominion had survived revolution and was, in fact, being reinhabited by the "new owner"—the republicans. Their new "empire" would in turn simply carry over colonial values to make it "its old brilliant self."[3]

Albeit mistakenly, Henry identifies the presumption of the founders as essentially an act of misrepresentation and appropriation: "What right had they to say, *We, the people*? My political curiosity, exclusive of my anxious solicitude for the public welfare, leads me to ask: Who authorized them to speak the language of *We, the people*?" (122). Even though the ratifying convention had been specifically elected for that purpose, Henry objects to their claim to speak for the American states and people with one voice. He rejects their representation of "the people" as monovocal and singular rather than polyvocal and diverse.[4] In their purported silencing of "the people" themselves and the appropriation of their voice, Henry perceives the sketches of imperial designs, in a strikingly modern sense of the word. This suggests that, even then, the convergence of language, power, and representation were central issues in unformed relationship of the United States to its colonial legacy.

Henry himself misrepresented the goal of the democratically elected body to which he was speaking: the founders were first asking to use that term, not just using it without consulting the people. Nonetheless, in *William Cooper's Town*, Alan Taylor has observed that "it apppalled the Federalists that their opponents were ready to change the rules by developing the democratic shortcut to political authority, circumventing approval from the old elite. . . . They insistently preached the necessity of a hierarchical and stable social order, guided by precedent: the sort of society that America had approximated before the Revolution" (159). The proximity of this type of social stratification was also noted on the level of geopolitics: another Antifederalist, James Winthrop, commented that "large and consolidated empires may indeed dazzle the eyes of a distant spectator with their splendour, but if examined more nearly are always found to be full of misery" (133). While Henry's bombast unfairly colored Federalists as autocrats, there is testimony from both the early republic and its contemporary students that the years following the Revolution witnessed an effort to retain the imperialist cultural institutions of the colonial epoch.

If we are then to admit the early republic of the United States, as Henry and Winthrop imply we do, into debates about colonialism and empire, the literary aspects of the imperial nature of republicanism must also be considered. Current scholarship holds that modern empires create and defend themselves with words as much as with weapons: "The empire in its heyday was conceived and maintained in an array of writings" (13) writes Elleke Boehmer.[5] Much writing from the early republic deliberately implicated itself in the attempted metaphorical colonization of the reader to republican interests. In regard to the politics of literary exchange, a derivative American literature based in colonial values was proposed to further national consensus-building and homogenization.[6]

In 1805 Samuel Cooper Thacher, age twenty, criticized American writers for importing "the style and the imagery of the poets of England, as much as our merchants do its wares." Thacher continues: "But whilst we continue to receive our riches by inheritance, and not to produce them by our vigour, we shall not be able to boast of any imperishable name" (154). Thacher had never experienced the direct colonialism of the British, yet thirty years after the Revolution he observes that America is still colonial in regard to writing and self-expression, still reliant on the leadership of the colonial parent. Moreover, Thacher worries that his country will never live up to its potential—"an imperishable name"—or at least distinguish itself from European traditions, if it continues to import its language and imagery. More recently, Michael Warner has identified the limiting nature of republican self-definition: "The same rhetoric that had brought the nation-state of the United States into being now blocked the development of an American imaginary by its rigorous construction of citizenship in the public sphere" (149).

In brief, Thacher, writing in the *Monthly Anthology and Boston Review* could complain, as Emerson would echo some years later, that "we have listened too long to the courtly muses of Europe" (70).[7] Furthermore, British colonial theoretician Edward Gibbon Wakefield wrote in 1834 that "the United States are still colonies" (520).[8] Clearly, there was a feeling even in the nineteenth century that Americans and their writing were still colonial, unable to express local experience and obedient to the commands of the centralized imperial metropolis in London. While Wakefield and Emerson were probably overstating the case, an anxiety about the lingering presence of colonial political and cultural institutions persisted for decades after Independence.

How, then, did we finally arrive in the 1830s at what Lawrence Buell has called a "post-colonial" literature during the "American Renaissance"? Buell identifies five properties of postcolonialism in writing from this period: "the semi-Americanization of the English language"; "the issue of cultural hybridization"; "the expectation that artists be responsible agents for achieving national liberaton"; "the problem of confronting neocolonialism"; and "the problem of alien genres" (427–29). For something to be *post*-colonial, some process of decolonization must have occurred or at least begun between the years of the early republic and the middle of the nineteenth century. The presence of these traits in writing from the early republic suggests that the process had been underway well before 1830.

Postcolonial scholarship engages the way "in which colonized peoples seek to take their place, forcibly or otherwise, as historical subjects" (Boehmer, 3).[9] Patrick Henry and Thacher express concern, however, that the potential for the new nation to become an autonomous "historical subject" will be lost if Americans continue to imitate European traditions. They have in mind, anticipating Emerson, a decolonized national culture that allows the experimentation and plurality embraced by Emerson and identified as postcolonial by Buell. Furthermore, *postcolonial* and *post-Independence* are by no means equivalent terms, since colonial social and cultural institutions persist, as Anderson notes, in most politically decolonized communities. For example, given the colonial nature of republican writing and the republicans' dominance of the national press, as I discuss below, the early republic was, in fact, not yet "postcolonial." David Simpson notes, "It was to prove more difficult to declare independence from Samuel Johnson than it had been to reject George III" (33). Nonetheless, in the early republic, we can trace the stirrings of literary and cultural decolonization.[10]

Integral to the process of decolonizing American writing, ironically, was the attempted retention of borrowed and misapplied British literary conventions by the republican elite. John Docker's comment on late twentieth-century Australians might be applied to the republicans: "And they propagate [Anglocentric assumptions] the more tenaciously and persistently because fundamentally they are always striving to become what they cannot be" (445). Yet W. J. T. Mitchell has noted that it is this lingering tension that makes postcolonial literature so vital in the otherwise decolonized world (471). Such, as well, is the vitalizing tension I wish to identify in postcolonial writing from the early republic.

The present study engages six texts written in the early republic that do three things: first, they confirm the fears about imperial/colonial ideology in the United States; second, they chart its transference to the literary arena; third, they propose strategies for the reader to resist republican recolonization and hence participate in a process of decolonization. I will be examining Hugh Henry Brackenridge's *Modern Chivalry*, Judith Sargent Murray's *The Gleaner*, Royall Tyler's *The Algerine Captive*, Charles Brockden Brown's *Arthur Mervyn*, George Watterston's *The Lawyer*, and Washington Irving's *History of New York* as books that challenge the Anglocentric and monolithic image of the new nation set forth by republicanism. Instead they suggest a more open-minded examination of the complexities of post-Revolutionary experience.

Over the two decades between Brackenridge and Irving (1790–1810) republicanism changed shape, and young people like Thacher increasingly disregarded as anachronistic and irrelevant republican ideals, favoring more liberal and plural forms of political, economic, and literary self-definition. Their critiques of republican textuality first point out the absurdity, then the danger, and finally the self-destructive nature of the narrow construction of the post-Revolutionary national imaginary promulgated by the republicans.

My goal is twofold: to introduce the early republic to the field of postcolonial studies and to introduce postcolonial studies to the early republic.[11] Before these texts can be addressed, and the question of American literary decolonization understood, I must first address a few basic questions. (1) Were the British colonies of North America *colonized* in the modern sense of the word? (2) How did republicanism retain colonial values? (3) How are we to position the early republic within the current debates about the meaning of *postcolonial*? (4) How do these six books manifest characteristics typical of recently decolonized populations and literatures? This study offers no definitive answers; like the six books to which it addresses itself, it is meant only to continue the opening of the ways in which we talk about these subjects in American cultural history.

American historians Gordon Wood, Richard Bushman, Bernard Bailyn, Pauline Maier, and Jack P. Greene all agree that something changed after the French and Indian War. British historians J. G. A. Pocock, C. A. Bayly, Don Cook, and Klaus E. Knorr agree.[12] More importantly, the writings of Thomas Jefferson, Benjamin Franklin, Thomas Paine, and a host of their British contemporaries bear witness to a radical transformation in the form of British imperial dominion from one of benign neglect to one of exploitation after the victory over the French in both Europe and North America. While an examination of the colonies before 1763 might not result in the labeling of the colonies as *colonized* by Great Britain in the modern sense of the word, the period after the war placed the American settlers in the position of colonial subjecthood in a way not unlike what occurred in other parts of the British Empire in the nineteenth century, in places now more conventionally labeled postcolonial.

Knorr has suggested that the years 1763 to 1776 witnessed a transition between the "old" and "new" British empires. While the "old empire" was characterized by an emphasis on mercantile expansion, the "new" was framed in more authoritarian terms. During these years "there was almost a complete absence of that sentimental imperial-brotherhood idea" (131). Such statements as these were published in England during this period: "For what purpose were they [the colonists] suffered to go to that country, unless the profit of their labour should return to their masters here?" "The Colonies were acquired with no other view than to be a convenience to us; and therefore it can never be imagined that we are to consult their interests preferably to our own." The American is "not completely a foreigner [but Americans] have artfully persuaded the people of England that they are fellow-citizens, and Englishmen like ourselves. But this is altogether a fallacy" (all qtd. in Knorr, 130–31). While the British colonies of North America had been founded by the "old" empire, after 1763 they were administered by the "new," employing the same administrative policies that would subsequently colonize Australia, New Zealand, South Africa, and Canada.[13] Colonials were no longer Englishmen abroad but rather were now Others and as such unsuited to the rights of British citizenship. When Franklin wrote "Rules by which a Great Empire May Be Reduced to a Small One" (1773) and Jefferson "A Summary View of the Rights of British America" (1774), they thought they were living in the old empire that transplanted "Little Englands" (Knorr, 125); they were in fact living on the margins of the much more centralized and hierarchical new empire.

Further proof of this transition was a sense that, as the 1760s passed, the North American colonies no longer suited the needs of the new empire. No less than Adam Smith, David Hume, and Edmund Burke argued at length for releasing the colonies from their bonds. Burke claimed that one might "as well think of rocking a grown man in the cradle of an infant" (qtd. in Knorr, 133). But Smith, Burke, and Hume were defeated by imperialists more intent on maintaining the power and profitability of the colonies and the centrality of the metropolis. Subsequently, the British colonists of North America were, as Burke suggests, infantilized by new imperial policies in an attempt to reprogram colonial citizenship to imperial subjecthood. For all intents and purposes, the colonies were recolonized after 1763.

This paradigmatic shift was most visibly experienced by the American colonists by, first, maltreatment at the hands of the British during the war and, second, a vigorous enforcement of the long-neglected Navigation Acts and a series of asymmetrical taxations (the famous Stamp, Townshend, and Intolerable Acts) after the war.[14] Each was deliberately constructed to subject the British colonies to the control of the metropolitan center. Franklin's "Rules" and Jefferson's "Summary View" testify to the colonizing nature of British policy after 1763 in a way that allows us to place the future United States on the list of postcolonial "settlements" even though the later settlements became independent much later. Like colonized peoples everywhere, they were made to feel marginal, childish, and unfit to govern themselves.

Franklin's nostalgia for the old empire is evident from his second rule: "That the possibility of this separation may always exist, take special care the provinces are never incorporated with the mother country" (236). Other rules elaborate the ramifications of the subject conditions of the "settlers." Franklin's pointed satire implies that the British seem intent on alienating the colonists, on forcing them to demand freedom. Likewise, Jefferson asked King George III to "no longer persevere in sacrificing one part of the empire to the inordinate desires of another; but deal out to all equal and impartial right. Let no act be passed by any one legislature which may infringe on the rights and liberties of another" (21). These are the disappointed pleas of colonized men who thought they were citizens but were in fact subjects; who thought they were colonials but were in fact the colonized.

They were both. Alan Lawson, Steven Slemon, Helen Tiffin, Diana Brydon, Graham Huggan, and Delores Janiewski have recently employed the term *Second World*—as opposed to "First World" Europe or Third World Africa, Asia, and

South America—to describe former British colonies in Australia, New Zealand, and Canada settled primarily by whites in the nineteenth century.[15] In "A Cultural Paradigm for the Second World," Lawson writes, "In some ways, it is these 'settler' societies that have been most resistant to postcolonial definition. On the one hand, there is the resistance within these societies to acknowledge their colonial status, having only recently 'won national identity.' . . . My solution to that theoretical impasse is to seek to acknowledge the 'settler' colony—indeed the settler subject—as a site of a very particular dual inscription; a place that is colonized at the same time as it is colonizing" (156–57). "Settler" colonies resist Alfred Memmi's totalizing colonizer/colonized binary, which characterizes so much postcolonial theory, as I discuss below.[16] In regard to the changes in British policy after 1763, the North American colonies had been expelled from the First World by the emergence of the new empire. Yet, of course, they were by no means indigenes living on aboriginal lands and so could not be part of a "Third." Revolutionary Second World settlers like Franklin and Jefferson testify to the internal paradoxes of this dual inscription and eventually sought to win "national identity" as a way of escaping the margin of the British empire.

These transitions between 1763 and 1776 correspond with definitions and methodologies of colonization associated with the pinnacle of the British empire between 1815 and 1914, the crucial starting place for modern discussion of the legacies of imperialism and postcolonialism. During the nineteenth century there was no premise or promise of "imperial brotherhood" between white colonials and those who remained in England. Imperial relationships were by design asymmetrical and the empire centered in London. The roots of the peripheral identity later imposed on the other parts of the Second World are thus based in the same policies that began in North America after 1763. While the British colonies of North America had not been subjected to this form of colonial dominion from 1607 to 1763, they were afterward, a regression rejected by the colonists in Revolution only thirteen years later.

REPUBLICANISM AND RECOLONIZATION

In the efforts to identify and stabilize both nation and identity, colonialism survived in the early republic. Benjamin B. Ringer and Elinor Lawless have written that "the Founding Fathers sanctified two political models": colonial and colonialist (xiv).[17] The founders employed inherited models of both colonial subjecthood and colonialist stratification and merged the two to present a facade of national unity within an orderly social hierachy. According Anderson's observation of the retention of colonial values after the Revolution, the leaders of former colonies in the Second World choose to ignore Lawson's "dual inscription" and favor one side over the other for the sake of stability and unity. Such universalizing activity dangerously ignores the complexities and paradoxes of the postcolonial condition. The resulting gap between policy and reality, between politics and the people, often slows the process of decolonization—the exploration of local conditions and self-awareness—and creates stagnating internal struggles for predominance, alienating local experience from its more complex history.

Revolutionary rhetoric, as Patrick Henry reminded us, was virulently antiauthoritarian and anticolonial, in the modern sense of the word. Thomas Paine's "The Crisis" spearheaded a literature of liberation that helped forge a coalition from the different regions, classes, sects, ethnicities, and even French interests in the colonies strong enough to defeat the British. Anderson, Clifford Geertz, Hannah Arendt, and others have identified a similar linkage of disparate coalitions and liberationist rhetoric in the creation, violent or otherwise, of new nations from former colonies.[18] After the Revolution the coalition dissolves as an elite group rebuilds the colonial mansion into "its old brilliant self." This activity seeks to disregard, as Lawson suggests, the complexities of local post-Independence conditions and represents an aspiration to pursue a place in the First World that had previously excluded it, ignoring that part of its history.

Such was the case with the version of the new nation offered by republicanism and its accompanying embrace of British and Enlightenment political and cultural ideologies. Elisha P. Douglass observed that "the traditional British institutions inherited from the empire had been remoulded into republican forms; . . . the colonial system had weathered the leveling tendencies of the conflict" (8). More recently, Gordon Wood in *The Radicalism of the American Revolution* and James Roger Sharp document efforts by the republican elite to create a stable and unified national identity. Citing Adams's and Jefferson's embrace of the term *natural aristocrat,* Wood writes: "The eighteenth-century gentry did not describe themselves as landowners or professionals who happened to be genteel; instead they were still gentlemen who happened to be professionals or landowners. They were, in short, still aristocrats, natural aristocrats, aristocrats of virtue and talent no doubt, but aristocrats nonetheless" (196). Wood suggests that the republican elite hoped that a well-trained public would recognize and authorize that elite class in the arena of public leadership. Sharp describes the years 1789–92 as the time when this elite attempted to centralize and unify their hold on political and economic power in the new nation more completely.

Henry's worst fears seemed to be coming true. *Republicanism*—as used by modern historians such as Pocock, Joyce Appleby, Wood, and others—subsumes Federalist/Antifederalist party distinctions and has been applied to the common ideological grounding of both parties: the concept of disinterested public leadership.[19] In *The Creation of the American Republic*, Wood writes: "In this respect, republicanism with its emphasis on spartan adversity and simplicity became an ideology of social stratification. . . . Most Revolutionary leaders clung tightly to the concept of a ruling elite" (478). Republicanism, then, makes two crucial assumptions: the virtue and reliability of the elite and the willingness of the public to subject themselves within a stratified class hierarchy. As the 1790s wore on, both premises eroded, and, in response, especially under Adams's administration Sharp charges, cultural dominion became even more pronounced.

Thus in the early republic, disagreements between the parties were essentially disagreements within the elite class, and as such rarely challenged the need for an elite class; their arguments were about the shape and nature of that class. To a large degree, their debates mirrored the debates of the British Parliament between the whigs and the tories. The national imaginary was then limited to these opposed viewpoints, each based in European models of nationhood and public leadership. Robert Lawson-Peebles has referred to this process as "redcoating" (63). To "redcoat" is, as it were, to act, think, and write like the British, to impose Anglocentric standards on American subjects regardless of their appropriateness or viability.

While the power machinations of Alexander Hamilton and others sought implicitly to convert existing American citizens to imperial subjects, parallel activities demonstrate the more overtly colonizing nature of republican thought externally as well. John Seelye has discussed how the republicans' plans for the Ohio and Mississippi valleys particularly revealed imperial ambitions. Dana D. Nelson has employed the terminology of colonization to discuss the explosion of the American slave industry during these same decades. Nelson as well has discussed the republican need to erase African Americans, free and slave, from all public discussions of national identity. In both situations, Seelye and Nelson see republican activity as antidemocratic and autocratic, creating policies and propaganda that disregarded or circumvented democratic values to displace local or distinct needs or concerns with policies and plans more suited to the needs of a central federal state.

This ideology is more implicitly, but just as pervasively, documented in regard to how republicans conceived of reading and writing as ways to convert the public from their revolutionary democratic ideals to an embrace of the authority of the republican elite. They perceived literacy and literary exchange as vehicles for transforming and stabilizing the public. For example, Christopher Looby quotes Benjamin Rush as claiming in 1798 that eloquence "is the first accomplishment in a republic, and often sets the whole machine of government in motion" (21). Modern scholarship has confirmed the degree to which the early republic was a "logocracy" in which language played a central role in politicians' efforts at national self-conception. Warner, Looby, Simpson, Kenneth Cmiel, and Kramer all recognize the attempted imposition of a monovocal national language as a means of establishing authority and singularity: individual texts and men gained public trust through their demonstrated mastery of the established rules of literary eloquence.[20]

But the question of who was to determine a stable version of what constituted eloquence and what kind of eloquence was applicable to the new nation was a deeper complication. In brief, the republicans chose modes, genres, and styles leftover from the colonial era to serve their own needs. After the Revolution, in place remained the discursive methods and rituals received from the colonial literary tradition.[21] In his essay "'We Hold These Truths,'" Ferguson has commented on the republicans' privileging of Enlightenment textuality: "A choice in the forms of expression (and hence in the options of response) facilitates agreement" (25), and so readers were assailed by an endless stream of political, moral, and economic texts all of which subjected the readers to the author's authority. Equally important, republicans dominated the book, magazine, and pamphlet trades in the early republic.[22]

In these media, republicans favored a close adoption of colonial concepts of public authorship and cultural authority. K. P. Van Anglen's, Lydia Dittler Schulman's, and William C. Dowling's recent studies of poetry in New England demonstrate that notions of eloquence borrowed from the British dominated debates over language in the new nation.[23] The extensive neoclassicism in the early republic also reveals Americans looking overseas for standards of cultural legitimacy. Donald Meyer, Roger G. Kennedy, and a great number of others have discussed at length the attempted imposition of various Enlightenment schemes and models on the new nation.[24] In general, a sense of colonial marginality pervaded republicanism; products of local origin were never privileged the way imported ideas and objects were.

This importation, however, was selective. During the years of the early republic, tremendous changes were happening in British writing, changes either ignored or discredited in the new nation. American republicanism chose those modes of British textuality most suited to placate and order the turbulent American public sphere—those from the middle of the eighteenth century, before the old empire began to erode, according to Dowling and Gustafson. The republicans constructed a false stability, a chimera of metropolitan coherence and, in turn, employed that as their standard of eloquence. This action affirms their acquiescence in a fundamentally colonial position. According to Robert J. C. Young, the white colonial misidentifies the metropolis as stable to legitimize its extension and his own presence in the colonies.[25] Therefore, in the early republic, its citizens' struggle with colonialism was more with their perception of themselves as colonials than with the British themselves.

The Revolution had required a demonization of the British, a process that required the simplistic representation of British culture in monolithic terms. After the Revolution, the unification of British culture that had first served anti-British propaganda would now serve to stabilize an Anglocentic version of life in the colonies before 1763 that the republicans would resurrect. But even then their endeavor was mimicry, not creation. They had yet to conceive a noncolonial or postcolonial "repertoire of self-perceptions," in Warner's terms, and so sought a purified version of the colonial culture to legitimize themselves. In short, for many republicans the former colonies were not an extension of England but rather a refinement of it. The forms American literature would take, then, would improve on British models with no necessary commitment to express local subjects or subjectivities.

Not surprisingly, colonial mimicry has been documented as a pervasive sign of acquiescence in the marginal, subaltern role.[26] The fear of taking an original place as "historical subject," to recall Boehmer, reflects the elite's fear of the destabilizing forces they had needed and unleashed to secure independence. Mimicry aims to restabilize the community by recreating the only standards of legitimacy the populace had ever known: that of the colonizers. By "redcoating" American reading and writing, republicanism attempted to recolonize the reading public of the new nation. David Spurr and Patrick Brantlinger have defined a parallel process in later stages of the British empire.[27]

In this system, the author, a representative of stable cultural and linguistic order, has tremendous authority over the reader: literature belongs to the elite, and stability and justice result from the natural benevolence and wisdom of the upper class. Such an environment encourages readerly passivity and places tremendous responsibility in the hands of those few with the leisure, literacy, and connections to bring their work to print and publication. Emory Elliott has called this connection "associationism" (31), and has suggested that it internalized British notions of noblesse oblige. Producing texts that would instruct the public in their responsibility to accept this hierarchy was one of the elite class's obligations.

Not surprisingly, the republican elite turned to the texts and genres of a similarly hierarchical society to inform their own. Just as they were not willing to trust the public to invent its own political or economic identity, linguistic experimentation with unorthodox and untested literary and discursive modes was also discouraged. For example, Samuel Miller, Timothy Dwight, Fisher Ames, and others objected to novels for their dangerous tendency to engage the imaginations of the readers, distracting them from the business of fulfilling their role as "republican machines."[28]

Finally, republicans championed an eighteenth-century conception of authorship based in Scottish commonsense philosophy that depersonalized the process of composition yet intimately connected the author to more general forms of social authority. Following Oliver Goldsmith's 1761 charge that British writing "is converted to a mechanic trade" (qtd. in Watt, 53–54), William J. Free has noted that "writers, editors, and publishers accepted literary theories which stifled imagination and reduced literary creativity to the mechanical application of dogmatic rules" (57), all the while claiming British sources for their editorial principles. Martha Woodmansee describes this version of the author as "a craftsman whose task is to utilize the tools of his craft for their culturally determined ends" (37). Those "dogmatic rules" or "culturally determined ends" represented the role of the republican author as transmitter of ideology and legitimizer of political activities.[29] The subjection of the act of writing to a larger cultural and political program indicates a stratified public sphere atop which perches the republican author/politician/natural aristocrat and beneath which—supposedly—is the humble reader.

The implicit social stratification of this mode of textuality confused those who hoped that a democratic epoch began with the Revolution.[30] The "language of 'We, the People'" was constructed for the people, but not by the people. Potentially more meaningful possibilities of American difference went unarticulated, and American writing in 1805, as Thacher claimed, was still mostly colonial.[31] In short, republicans focused on the colonial nature of American experience and ignored the legacy of being colonized after 1763 with all its incumbent injustices and inequalities.

DEMOCRACY AND DECOLONIZATION

The same historians I have cited to support my claims of the elitist and colonial nature of republicanism—Wood, Sharp, and others—all continue to chart the dissolution of republicanism over the course of the years between 1790 and 1820 or so. In particular, Steven Watts, in *The Republic Reborn*, describes the emergence of "liberal democracy" as a political force displacing republican elitism as the Revolutionary generation faded from the scene. In *The Radicalism of the American Revolution*, Wood writes, "This new democratic society was the very opposite of the one the revolutionary leaders had envisaged" (230). This is the society that, according to Buell, finally produced a "post-colonial" literature and therefore had undergone some form of decolonization.

Nonetheless, Wood and the others maintain that the seeds of this democratic decolonization were planted in the Revolution and that it merely took forty or so years for them to come to fruit. Sharp defines post-1801 America as "an increasingly complex, market-oriented society divided into a patchwork of economic, social, and ethnic interests" (276). In other words, these historians find the early nineteenth-century United States to be diverse, heterogeneous, and very confusing. These transformations have to do with the country's internalization of its postcolonial Second World hybridity and polyvocality with its rejection of republicanism and its universalizing recreation of colonial hierarchies. Just as the republicans created a false coherence in British culture, they similarly advertised a parallel unity in republican culture itself in order to craft consensus and stifle dissensus. Over the course of the early republic, however, this rubric collapsed and the dissensus of democracy emerged as the crucible of decolonizing the nation's political self-understanding.

Moreover, the seeds of American literary decolonization were also present from the moment of Revolution and were articulated in, among others, the six books addressed in the present study. They offered a counterdiscourse to republican colonialism by embracing Second World incongruities and carefully subverting republican textual standards by chiding the new nation for not recognizing the complexity of its submerged postcolonial identity. Making this claim, however, requires a clearer identification of those parts of postcolonial studies that are relevant to the early republic: the aforementioned Second World.

Nicholas Thomas has recently dismissed the binary oppositions of most postcolonial theory: "Postcolonialism is distinguished not by a clean leap into another discourse but by its critical reaccentuation of colonial and anticolonial languages" (7). Thomas instead proposes the metaphor of "entanglement" for understanding the postcolonial legacy of the collision of cultural presences during the colonial period.[32] For the most part, he is criticizing the Third World version of postcolonialism identified by Lawson as distinct from the version relevant to postcolonial settlements such as Australia, New Zealand, or, I will argue, the American early republic. While Second and Third World versions of postcolonialism share common characteristics, because of issues of race, indigeneity, displacement, and invasion, I would second Thomas's, Huggan's, Lawson's, and Slemon's notion that they are fundamentally separate. Only on occasional points of commonality will this study employ Third World postcolonial theorists such as Homi K. Bhabha or Gayatri Spivak; my main ideas concerning settlement postcolonials are rooted in the work of scholars from the Second World.

The Foucauldian oppositions favored by Third World postcolonials are mostly inapplicable to the early republic: republicanism was always an *effort* at social, political, and cultural reorganization and never a reality. Its Anglocentric ideals always contended with other presences in American culture, and it never assembled the synthesis Alexander Hamilton or Fisher Ames may have liked. Robert Shalhope has labeled the period "a struggle for predominance between competing cultural forces" (40). As such, models of Second World postcolonial heterogeneity derived from settlement experience should be useful to understanding the processes of decolonization in the early republic. Although the other parts of the Second World gained independence decades later and did so without the violence of revolution, sufficient parallels exist on the level of cultural decolonization, a process linked to but distinct from both broader historical contexts and the circumstances of independence itself, to establish revealing connections.

For Lawson, the Second World is "the site of a very particular dual inscription; a place that is colonized at the same time as it is colonizing" (155). Writing in and for the Second World, then, must interrogate that duality. Republican writing ignored it in favor of aspirations to First World legitimacy. The six writers and books addressed in the present study, however, clung to the revolutionary coalition of diverse cultural presences, anticipating the role of the Second World writer. To define that role, Slemon contends: "The Second World writer, the Second World text, that is, have always been complicit in colonialism's territorial appropriation of land, and voice, and agency, and this has been their inescapable condition even at those moments when they have promulgated their most strident and spectacular figures of postcolonial resistance. In the Second World, anticolonialist resistances in literature must necessarily *cut across the individual subject*" (110). Readers and writers of the Second World exist in a precarious balance, then, between being the victimizer and being the victim. Slemon's contention that this split occurs within the individual consciousness gives the proponents only one honest option when it comes to self-description: acknowledging and exploring the conflicted position of the Second World community and self. Writing about William Dunlap and Royall Tyler, Gary A. Richardson has already perceived an "inevitable postcolonial double-mindedness" in early republic drama.[33]

However, Slemon's ideas are still too limiting: he demands an "anticolonial" perquisite in Second World writing. Thomas, for one, argues that the "anticolonial" and the "colonial" in fact coexist in postcolonial settlement writing. Moreover, Lawson has argued that arguments like Slemon's dangerously retain the colonizer/colonized binary and instead favors a greater plurality on both a personal and public basis in Second World writing: "What I can do at this stage is begin to demonstrate the pervasiveness, within the several parts of Second World discourse, of the preoccupation of dichotomy, disjunction, and polarity and then to suggest that the embedded polemic in postcolonial texts is such as to transform and relocate those into doubleness—collapsing the binary structure while retaining its elements, but altering the relation of power between them. The achieved modal operation, then, is not antagonism but ambivalence, a word whose roots I need to revive to insist on it as 'power of both'" (69). In other words, Lawson and Thomas employ a more complex theoretical model: to be merely anticolonial further embeds the narrow binaries of colonialism. In fact, what they argue for as the defining characteristic of Second World identity is this kind of flowing plurality in which colonialism and anticolonialism are just two of many coexisting presences in an unfixed and unfixable postcolonial blend.

How, then, to write about this paradoxical condition? The first step in achieving such a diverse "repertoire of self-perceptions" is gaining the freedom to address the issue in its complexity and adjusting the medium of writing to do so. As a result, the process of Second World self-identification has generated a group of literatures striking in their self-consciousness. Bill Ashcroft, Gareth Griffiths, and Helen Tiffin, in *The Empire Writes Back,* have noted that anxieties felt by Second World writers when trying to establish cultural differences between themselves and the departed colonial parent are expressed at the level of literary self-reflexivity: "One of the more interesting features of settler colonies, in which intellectual life is so relentlessly characterized as an extension of European culture, is that from the earliest times some of the most important theoretical writing emerged in creative texts. These texts explore, in their figures, themes, and forms, the conceptual dimensions of the act of writing itself, and the tensions and issues traversing the institution of literature in marginalized societies" (137). Metafiction, or something resembling it, is, they suggest, an important part of a postcolonial community's conversation with itself about how it is going to be something other than a mere extension of the metropolitan center, a lesser version of its grandeur. Instead, these books often wonder about how to create local centrality. Second World creative texts very deliberately live double lives, wherein secondary narratives about the act of writing itself coexist with otherwise recognizable primary narratives telling a story about something else.

Lawson has elaborated more fully on the self-reflective nature of Second World text in regard to their relationship with received forms: "Synthesis is a totalising enterprise that seeks to silence polyphony and focus double vision. The Second World, postcolonial text prefers disintegration. . . . it is the function of postcolonial texts to undo unidirectional systems of representation. . . . Among the generic formulations in which this Second World ambivalence articulates itself are those which stress bifocal narration, diachronicity, texts which are not texts ('journals,' found texts, letters), framed texts" (74). In other words, Second World texts challenge received systems of representation. Second World writers in the early republic challenge republicanism's monovocalization and synthesis of colonial forms in the new nation. At heart, as Henry observed, is a struggle over the rights of representation. Sacvan Bercovitch has argued that American literary writing has always "called into question the claims of the society to represent things as they ought to be" (644). Certain counterdiscursive and dissident writers in the early republic were doing so and, by doing so, they reveal Second World qualities in the early republic despite the First World dreams of republicanism.

If the Second World writer is not merely anticolonial, how do the texts he or she produces participate in the process of decolonization? In "Postcolonial Literature and Counter-Discourse," Tiffin writes: "Postcolonial cultures are inevitably hybridised, involving a dialectical relationship between European ontology and epistemology and the impulse to create or recreate independent local identity. Decolonisation is process, not arrival; it invokes an ongoing dialectic between hegemonic centrist systems and the peripheral subversion of them; between European or British discourses and their postcolonial dismantling" (95). The Second World text participates in the process of decolonization, then, by demanding that its readers initiate and engage the perpetual "ongoing dialectic" between the colonized and colonizing sides of their collective historical experience rather than settling for a stable, but misrepresentative, simplification of that experience such as that offered by republicanism. Moreover, the Second World text rarely aligns wholly with "nationalist" ideologies since those too often stress arrival. By accentuating and narrating the notion of becoming, not being, of transience and process, Second World texts express, reflect, and contribute to the decolonization of cultures in former colonies.

METAFICTION AND AUTHORSHIP IN THE EARLY REPUBLIC

The notion of "process, not arrival" informs my reading of the decolonization of writing in the early republic. Throughout the period addressed here, public voices questioned the republican assertion that the new nation had "arrived" as the realization of Enlightenment hopes. William Grayson, arguing against the constitution, claimed that "we are yet too young to know what we are fit for" (282). Regarding reading and writing, voices at either end of the period express fundamental disquietudes.[34]

In 1782 the narrator of Hector St. John de Crèvecoeur's *Letters from an American Farmer* complained about how Americans were writing about their crisis with the British: "Much has been said and written on both sides, but who has a judgment capacious and clear enough to decide? The great moving principles which actuate both parties are withheld from vulgar eyes, like mine; nothing but the possible and the plausible are offered to our contemplation" (204). Near the end of the period, William Jenks, in *A Memoir of the Northern Kingdom* (1808), repudiates the state of literary exchange in the new nation: texts "were mostly confined to the political and commercial diaries, those vehicles of truth and falsehood so indeterminately and promiscuously, that nothing learned from them respecting the real state of the times can be fully depended on" (26–27). These authors and others testify that something was seriously wrong in the republic of letters: rather than contributing to the unfettered exchange of ideas and information, printed materials were confusing, not enlightening, the voting public; every author claimed to have "arrived" at unchallengeable truth and had expressed it in "eloquent" terms.[35] The basic republican premises of disinterested authorship and passive readership had abjectly failed to represent the politics and power dynamics of post-Revolutionary literary exchange. A space had opened between republican models and public self-reckonings and readings.

The embedded paradoxes generated the confusion of Crèvecoeur and Jenks: forms and language that made the author an aristocrat and the citizen a subject conflicted with the remnants of the Revolution. Seemingly reliable texts intrinsically duped rather than informed, and discouraged rather than catalyzed, critical reading, thinking, and decolonization: the typical participant in the crucial experiment in representative politics grew alienated and disillusioned with the early republic public sphere and, more importantly, the viability of his meaning in the processes of politics.[36] The line between legitimate, reliable texts, and selfish, manipulative ones blurred, yet all claimed intellectual basis in republican public interest. A passive reader would accept the paradoxes and reembrace colonial subjecthood. Crèvecoeur and Jenks testify to the American readers' resistance to such pacification and advocate the continued development of an activist readership that would more persistently challenge the right of the republicans to "represent things as they ought to be," in Bercovitch's terms.

In the following pages, I address six texts from the early republic of the United States that behave very much like postcolonial materials from the Second World in that they challenge the aspiring dominance of republican/Enlightenment representations of the new nation and instead insist on a decolonization of American reading and writing. They openly join the cultural battle between the legacy of colonialism and the exploration of local, postcolonial identity by making important theoretical distinctions between the received culture and the post-Independence community. Each argues for national hybridity and plurality in their confrontation with colonial textuality as it was rephrased by republicanism. While they participate in the decolonization of American writing, they also reflect the processes of more general social decolonization and democratization documented by Wood and Sharp.

Moreover, these six books do so in a manner characteristic of Second World methodologies: by challenging the right of representation and calling into question, on a formal and linguistic level, the Enlightenment's textual forms the republicans favored and resisting their monovocalizing and unidirectional systems of representation. Specifically, these books address the republican notion of disinterested public leadership and its incumbent ascension to authorship through the deployment of colonial standards of eloquence. These often undervalued texts not only reveal the American logocracy but also tell stories about life under its tyranny. Part 1 of Brackenridge's *Modern Chivalry*, Tyler's *The Algerine Captive*, Murray's *The Gleaner*, Brown's *Arthur Mervyn*, Watterston's *The Lawyer*, and Irving's *Knickerbocker's History of New York* (de)construct texts that internalize colonial authorial constructions and standards. All six contain "diachronic" narratives, to recall Lawson, that engage and challenge not just orthodox narratives about America but also colonial authorial and epistemological practices. I call this technique the *fiction of authorship*. These books are complex literary works that tell stories about writers and readers caught up in the debates over language, colonial culture, and authorship in the new nation. In the end, they help their readers resist recolonization to explore ways of imagining that place the readers, not the author, at the center of an American experience, not on the margin of British culture. They decentralize inherited authorial identity and authority and their retention in the early republic to problematize the national imaginary in ways more likely to generate more accurate and liberating local self-understanding and expression.

In a process slightly varied by each, every writer deftly demonstrates the shortcomings and self-destructiveness of the persistence of inherited textuality by creating a fictitious American author who, by all appearances, conforms to the notion of authorial legitimacy dictated by British tradition and its republican adherents. This is done using the signifiers of authority in the accepted gestures of reliability: false title pages, dedications, introductions, and other documents compel the reader initially to think that this reading experience will occur within the boundaries of the republic of letters. As such, these ficticious authors are not mere narrators, passively retelling a story; rather the most integral part of their characterization is how each *writes*, how each participates, self-consciously, in debates about how Americans should read and write. For example, the persona that composes Charles Brockden Brown's *Wieland* (1798), Clara Wieland, is clearly only a *narrator*, writing within the context of a fictional private correspondence, a standard Richardsonian technique. While the nature of her act of writing is intriguing, it is categorically separate from that of Brown's Arthur Mervyn, whose act of composition, and thus authorship, is very deliberately public.

Central to this process is each book's construction of a hypothetical American reader who has been lulled by the constricted textuality of republicanism into a kind of intellectual dormancy—a reader who, in the terms of John Quincy Adams, had yielded "the guidance of the nation to the dominion of the voice" (qtd. in Looby, 32). Each fictional author addresses the reader as a coconspirator, assuming seamless the agreement of the reader to the voice of the author. As each book progresses, every purported author turns out to be not only fictitious but also unreliable. In the process, some part of the conventional literary exchange collapses: some fictional authors realize their mistake and abandon their authorship; in others, the fictional authors' exploitation or misappropriation of authorship comes through so clearly that the reading experience becomes openly irresolvable. In either case, the fictional authors come to represent the authority of the colonial regime, clothed in the garb of republican authorship. By compelling the reader to question the monovocalizing efforts of these deluded or dangerous fictitious authors, the real authors demand a decolonization of American reading and writing methods.

These false narrators are categorically separate from both Fielding's and Stern's fictional authors, although it seems likely that the American authors found these techniques a useful starting point. Gary Lee Stonum has noted that "what is native in its European context and avows itself to be the subversive underside of dominant cultural traditions, appears strangely central to the American canon" (3). The subversive voices crafted by Fielding, Sterne, and their imitators contributed to a sense of readerly skepticism of authorial pretension in the late eighteenth-century Atlantic world. However, the characters of the British writers announce themselves as outsiders excluded from direct social meaning from the start.

On the other hand, the American fictional authors I mean to address do nearly the reverse: they announce themselves as informed insiders, only to move toward either absurdity or corruption. Instead of revealing the deeper order beneath apparent chaos, as does Tristram Shandy, they reveal the deeper American chaos beneath the facade of order, both political and linguistic, thrown up by republican textuality.[37] By compelling the reader to participate in the unmasking of an illegitimate symbol of republican authority—a conventional author—the real authors challenge Americans to seek means of communication and expression that centralize the needs of the new community and decentralize lingering Anglocentric preferences.

When we view the texts not as the compositions of the real authors but rather as the fictitious compositions of their contrived characters, the original authors must be revalued for their sophisticated self-reflexivity and accomplished (re)creations of complex processes of readership and authorship. Viewing them as Second World authors who are more concerned with subverting a tradition than creating one, we can measure the success of the real authors in the failures of the fictional ones. Essentially, the logocracy sought to limit available modes of dissent, monopolizing the terms of representation and disrupting inherited modes of representation.

By withholding or denying the authorial guidance that dictated interpretive acts in the republican public sphere, these authors cut the reader adrift from the institutionalized forms of authority imposed by the republican elite. Without externally imposed textual meaning, the reader must trust and empower his or her own interpretive skills. This liberation of the reader—or rather this implication that the reader free him or her self—parallels the growth of democratic individualism chronicled by Sharp, Wood, and Steven Watts. Their focus on individual authorial voice, then, allows their texts to become microcosms for the larger conflicts over the nature of American identity taking place around them.

Through these six texts, moreover, I trace a transition in the nature of republican authorship as republicanism's internal coherence and external control disintegrated between 1790 and 1810. This is seen in the increasingly selfish and interested nature of the fictional authors. For example, in 1792, Brackenridge's author-narrator is benevolent but absurd; in 1808, Watterston's Morcell is corrupt and corrupting. The change represents the increasing desperation of the elite's hopes for a centralized and stratified American identity that was clearly slipping from their grasp. Finally, Irving's Knickerbocker in 1809 collapses and, ultimately, is laid to rest just as members of the Revolutionary generation itself, the last one to come of age as colonials, were expiring.

While the six books I address rarely achieve a language of their own, their adept disputation of the colonial legacy represents an accomplishment unto itself, an initiation of "process, not arrival." By engaging the debate over language and authority, they reveal the scope and the intricacies of the task of decolonization, suggesting that republicanism is a step in the wrong direction. They bring to the surface the problems of authorship and readership in the post-Independence community by interrupting the relationship between author and audience, exploring the darker edges of the republican public sphere. They explore what Slemon describes as being "cut across"—neither colonist nor colonizer, neither British nor yet American.

This process resembles what the authors of *The Empire Writes Back* call "abrogation," "a refusal of the categories of the imperial culture" (38). To abrogate a site of literary exchange, a writer from the margin disrupts the orthodoxy of inherited texts through parody, mimicry, and burlesque.[38] Often this occurs within the limits of colonial discourse, eroding its integrity and contributing to its eventual collapse. Fictions of authorship occur within British textuality but abrogate its terms to remove a crucial barrier blocking the creation of a less derivative and decolonized American culture.

To establish the breadth of this phenomenon, I have selected books that deliberately dramatize how distinct inherited genres were retained after the Revolution to further republican ideological ends.[39] Then I document how the received techniques are deconstructed and decolonization demanded. In each chapter, I also address other texts by each real author that reveal nascent experiments in less restrained modes of writing than those that shackled their fictional authors.

In part 1 of *Modern Chivalry*, the subject of chapter 1, Brackenridge pretends to write a picaresque novel of American experience. But the growing eccentricities of the author-narrator as he interrupts the story to comment on various subjects reveal a space between Brackenridge and the presumptive authorial voice. This allows Brackenridge to expose the inadequacies of a number of modes of public communication, not the least of which is his own role as a public figure.

In chapter 2, I address Judith Sargent Murray's disguised entry into the American public sphere as a male author in her essays in the *Massachusetts Magazine*, presumably the work of an Addisonian figure calling himself the Gleaner. By themselves, these essays demonstrate that the fiction of authorship could also be employed in periodical literature. They were collected as a literary miscellany in 1798 as *The Gleaner*. Murray knew that her republican readers would take her more seriously as a man and so exploited their biases to force them to confront their sexism and other prejudicial ways of thinking.

In chapter 3, my subject is Royall Tyler's faux captivity narrative, *The Algerine Captive*. Updike Underhill, his fictional author, is presented as a long-suffering American doctor recently returned from Algeria, where he had been enslaved. However, Tyler's use of this presumably reliable figure to write a broad satire of American manners is employed to dramatize the broader failure of Americans to explore alternatives to European modes of action, thought, and literary exchange. Furthermore, Updike realizes how authorship qualifies the author for elite status and sycophantically conceals self-interest in a purportedly disinterested republican authorial identity.

As I discuss in chapter 4, the issue of authorship in Charles Brockden Brown's *Arthur Mervyn* is clouded by layers of voices, although it does announce itself as a novel. The voice finally emerging, however, is that of Arthur, who presents himself as a Franklinian figure whose popularity represented a genre unto itself in the early republic. However, Brown endlessly complicates the issue of Arthur's reliability to the degree that he cannot be fully known or trusted. In the end, the simple platitudes offered by both the ironic Brown and the slippery Arthur sound hollow and simpleminded, and the reader presumably is left more wary and less gullible.

The gullibility of the colonized public is also the subject of Watterston's fabulation of the authorship of a didactic confession in *The Lawyer*, the subject of chapter 5. Morcell, its presumptive author, means to use his text as a vehicle for repenting the sins he committed as a lawyer, a profession granted extraordinary public power. It becomes clear, however, that Morcell has become an author only to further his corrupt career and so banks on his eloquence to gain forgiveness and reinstatement. Watterston thus critiques how the passivity of a subjugated audience works against democratic exchange.

In chapter 6, my subject is Washington Irving's *History of New York* and its fictional author, Diedrich Knickerbocker. Knickerbocker means to write a conventional history and scrupulously models himself on English historical models. Yet when subject and method diverge, Knickerbocker allows Irving to express profound doubts about the Eurocentric view of the world and its inevitable difference from American subjects. Knickerbocker recognizes the deception central to his role and confesses his final failure.

In my Epilogue I discuss Irving's transition from early republic to postcolonial author during the 1810s as the realization of larger changes in the American public sphere implicitly demanded by the fictions of authorship: a less restrained

environment for literary experimentation, allowing writers to forgo the colonial past and explore more expressive means of national self-definition. Looking
ahead to the American Renaissance Buell has identified as postcolonial, Irving's
The Sketch-Book of Geoffrey Crayon (1819) openly explores the plurality of choices
and options available to American readers and writers in the more decolonized
public sphere of Jacksonian America.

The achievement of these writers is that their work exposes the reintroduction of British colonialism in republican ideology and textuality. By reminding
Americans of their responsibility to read and think critically, to challenge institutionalized authority, they wrote fictions that revive revolutionary sensibilities
of freedom of thought and expression, virtues of plurality that remind prosperous white Americans of their obligation to be inclusive. Not coincidentally, each
includes a plea for the acceptance of the new community's racial and ethnic heterogeneity, not to mention its women.

This study makes no claims to examine the early republic comprehensively
and announce it *postcolonial*, in the modern, theoretical sense of the word. By no
means do all early republic texts reflect Second World qualities; I mean to identify one aspect of a complex and intricate moment in American literary history
as resembling the literary politics of other former settlement colonies of the
British Empire. Simultaneously, I argue that the inclusion of the early republic
in the theoretical construction of the Second World expands our definition of
it and our understanding of the entangled nature of postcolonial experience:
postcolonialism is not exclusively a twentieth-century phenomenon and represents a more complex condition than is usually formulated because this study
explores how one former colony could be both colonized and colonizer at once.

The creators of early republic fictions of authorship by no means invented
American fiction—as Irving later admitted—nor were they the first to exhibit
tendencies we might label postcolonial. In fact, their response to any such scholarly endeavor to universalize an American technique in fiction or writing might
have been met with the same satire and subversion they used to confront similar monovocalizing efforts in the shape of republicanism. Nonetheless, their activity makes a crucial demand: the creation of a new society would be far more
culturally complex than originally thought, and it would take longer. By challenging American readers to expect more from their writers and representatives
than the inherited patterns of British life, these writers participated in and celebrated the decolonization of American culture and writing.

ONE

To Deceive the World:
Hugh Henry Brackenridge's *Modern Chivalry*

IN THE introduction to Hugh Henry Brackenridge's *Modern Chivalry* (1792–1815), the presumptive author ponders "what would be the best means to fix the English language." He subsequently claims that "I shall consider language only" (3) in order to "give a model of perfect stile in writing" (5). This self-imposed task overtly declares its colonial mission and marginal status: the author means to do nothing more original than improving on colonial modes, never exploring American difference or his own centrality. A previous generation of scholars has dismissed this remark as Brackenridge's nod to eighteenth-century British satirists such as Fielding, Sterne, and Swift, and instead concentrated on the book's encyclopedic collection of anecdotes and recreations of conditions on the American frontier in the late eighteenth century.[1]

As such, *Modern Chivalry* has often been classed as subliterary, more important as historical document than for its literary value. Recently, however, Emory Elliott and William Hoffa separately reconsidered this same passage in reference to Brackenridge's use of the conventions of narrative technique.[2] Elliott differentiates the "author-narrator" from Brackenridge: "The story of the author-narrator-hero emerges as the most important with the theme of the struggle of the writer in American society . . . as the central issue of the larger composite narrative" (184). Hoffa recognizes that it satirizes "the ultimate foolishness of those who assume that there is fixed, natural, logical correspondence between *words* and the *world*" (290).[3] Grantland S. Rice has combined these to suggest that *Mod-*

ern Chivalry "scrutinizes and demystifies the nation's uncritical faith in print" (261) to teach its readers to resist the homogenizing textuality of republicanism. Furthermore, Christopher Looby has observed the complexity of the situation into which *Modern Chivalry* was thrust by Brackenridge: "Born into the modern polyglot world, this nation of emigrants immediately sought to establish a monolingual standard to aid in its attempted national self-constitution. Hugh Henry Brackenridge's *Modern Chivalry* is probably the best textual witness we have to the contradictions and ironies of this simultaneous exogenous pluralization and endogenous standardization" (204). Looby reads the book as a series of "textual ruptures produced by these formal anomalies" (210) and argues that the author-narrator "repeats endlessly the formulas of an ideology of static, closed, hierarchical social relations" (246) rephrasing republicanism as "an ideology of economic privilege" (249). Essentially Looby brings together both generations of scholarship. His hybridized reading and his observation of the early republic's internal contradictions I would take one step further.

My reading adds the suggestion that Brackenridge's observation of these phenomena is not only antirepublican but also postcolonial: he writes as a Second Worlder, resisting, through eight hundred pages, the "standardizations" and reinscribed hierarchies that would reverse Revolutionary liberties. The "author-narrator's" ambition to "fix" a language representative of the "world" becomes the ultimate target of Brackenridge's linguistic satire, and his narrative becomes the act of a colonial eager to please his betters in the metropolitan center.[4] Given the complex and heterogeneous nature of the post-Revolutionary and Second World new nation, "fixing" any American subject within English boundaries enacts a process of colonization, "a disabling master discourse . . . which silences" the colonized people, according to Homi K. Bhabha (126). A colonizing language depends upon an enforced stability of uniform meaning and a subjugation of local variation and change. Moreover, meaning derives from the metropolis, not the colony; in fact local variations are seen as disruptive and degenerate.

Any "fixing," especially one that embraced the Anglophilic legacy, positions Americans as colonizers, erasing and ignoring the anticolonialism of the Revolution. Steven Slemon, however, has noted that since the experience of the Second World settler "cuts across . . . the individual subject" (110) the only path to accurate self-identification lies through an exploration of both sides of the bisected post-Independence experience. The author-narrator and republicans like him ignore what Laura Murray has called "the multiplicities of this [early republic] social and discursive context" (2). The solution embraced by Brack-enridge, and the other writers in this study was, in the words of Alan Lawson, to "challenge the power of language to make boundaries, to speak forever with one voice" (72). Although Lawson was addressing Australian and Canadian texts, he might have been addressing the American early republic in general and *Modern Chivalry* in particular.

Modern Chivalry can be read as a fiction telling the story of how an author colonizes and monopolizes the American subject by imposing rephrased and misrepresented British notions of authority and propriety on a heterogeneous language and populace. The author-narrator's subsequent chaotic and overbur-dened text, failure, and final abandonment by Brackenridge in the later volumes of *Modern Chivalry* manifest the real author's rejection of the lingering ortho-doxies of the colonial period and his attempted decolonization of both subject and reader. As Elliott and William Lenz have recognized, in part 2 of *Modern Chivalry*, the distance between author and author-narrator fades until it is nonex-istent. Because part 2 is not, then, a fiction of authorship and thus does not ad-dress how republicanism recolonized the new nation, I will limit my reading of *Modern Chivalry* to part 1, the four installments published between 1792 and 1797.[5] In these, Brackenridge reveals the inadequacy of colonial language and gen-res to express and represent American subjects. When the author-narrator is compelled to treat his reader, the American citizen, as a colonial subject, Brack-enridge exposes the self-destructive nature of the persistent counterrevolution-ary and recolonizing ideology increasingly embraced during the 1790s by the emergent republican elite.[6]

Part 1 can thus be approached as a complicated narrative self-consciously aimed at disrupting its audience. Although the fictional author wishes *Modern Chivalry* to participate in what Michael Warner calls the "republican paradigm," the text inverts and refracts the republic of letters and its latent recolonization of the Revolutionary public. It emerges as an important and sophisticated compo-sition in which the real author deftly manipulates his fictional author and real audience to craft an organic and original commentary on the shifting dynamics of reading and writing in the early republic.

Part 1 of *Modern Chivalry* was published in the 1790s, a decade when issues of language, culture, and colonialism were subjects of intense and constant public controversy in the republican public sphere.[7] However, its machinations reveal the republicanism shared by both parties to be a general program to conform the new nation to one received model or another and to discourage the development of local difference. The sides of these debates were determined by different reckonings of the relationship of the new American culture to the older English one. One side argued that the new nation was a child of the old, improving upon its elder, but still part of English culture. Adherents to this cause were generally Hamiltonians. On the other side, Jeffersonians argued that the nation was obligated to seek a different path and so suggested a broader amalgamation of European culture and Enlightenment models—a hybrid of established cultural institutions. Nonetheless, by 1806 even the formerly radical Jeffersonian Noah Webster "proposed only modest revisions to [Samuel] Johnson's orthography," according to Gilbert Youmans and Greg Stratham (148), revealing the creeping Anglophilia of the republican elite.

Although each party favored different forms of linguistic authority, both desired to institutionalize American culture: to "fix" a static entity representative of reliable authority based on some form of received models. Colonial culture works on the supposition of the stable metropolitan center: Americans had been asked to submit to British culture during the colonial period. Such self-misrepresentation by the British is typical of colonizing methodology. After the Revolution, however, republican figures, such as the author-narrator of *Modern Chivalry*, typically retain the fiction of the metropolis's singularity for the purposes of reinscribing colonial hierarchies, now with themselves in the privileged position. Ignoring the plurality of British culture in the 1790s allowed the republicans to present a more ordered model of the ideal culture than the one that existed.[8]

Furthermore, this impulse to confine the American subject represents the broader ideology of republicanism to check the unrestrained and presumably dangerous antiauthoritarian passions of the Revolution. Richard D. Brown identifies the Sedition Act of 1798 as particularly representative of republican efforts to contain the access of the populace to materials that might corrupt their "virtues." Therefore, neither party was concerned with how language was genuinely used but rather focused on how it *should* be used, a prioritization that reflects a desire to colonize the American public through control of the choices of cultural characteristics made available for their selection. Such a limitation necessarily cripples the imagination of both readers and writers, as Brackenridge suggests in his orthodox but dysfunctional author-narrator. The author-narrator, as he begins, appears to be an eager colonial subject. However, as he records the speech of his American subjects, he understands the vast space between what Europe and the republicans would like America to be and what it actually is and observes how passive readership reconverts revolutionary citizens into colonial subjects.

The picaresque which the book seemingly becomes but which the author-narrator twice disavows (43, 195) formally reflects Brackenridge's organic alternative to the author-narrator's static formats and inorganic, "fixed" language. Ian Watt praised the picaresque for its expansive ability to express the inevitable variety in human experience: "a stimulating wealth of suggestion and challenge on almost every topic of human interest" (288)—hardly an appropriate vehicle for "fixing." Like the Australian Joseph Furphy in *Such Is Life*, Brackenridge finds the picaresque particularly suited to expressing the plurality and dichotomous nature of Second World life: the tension between the stability and safety of reverting to established colonial structures and the danger and risky proposition of defining genuine difference.

The disavowal of the picaresque makes *Modern Chivalry* a fiction of the authorship of early republic prose in general. Rice has catalogued this process as a deliberately constructed warning to early republic readers not to trust their leaders. However, my concern is about what Brackenridge was warning his readers against: not just the elite's abuse of power but their abuse of power through their reformulation of colonial hierarchies. Nonetheless, this broad format allows Brackenridge to investigate a wide spectrum of textual authorities in a protean fiction, depicting the many forms of authorship present in the early republic. In the narrative of Captain Farrago and his Irish servant Teague O'Regan, authority figures are fictionalized as they existed daily in the early republic, giving speeches garbed in authorized language to manipulate the guileless public.[9] More importantly, in the introductions and the conclusions of each volume and in chapters when the author-narrator addresses the reader directly, Brackenridge lampoons a variety of written forms of authorized rhetoric. As the text moves beyond the merely picaresque, it blends a metafictive element not accounted for in European versions of the genre. This self-reflexivity demonstrates its Second World hybridity.

In these sections, by attempting to exhibit his mastery of an assortment of English genres to reveal the breadth of his knowledge of the English language, the author-narrator betrays the ignorance that his creator identifies as weakening the integrity of revolutionary freedoms, a hangover from the colonial epoch. Brackenridge dramatizes conventional modes of public writing as shifting, deceptive, and inevitably corruptible, threatening whatever ingenuity and genuine freedom may be available to the nascent American community. This secondary narrative binds together part 1 as a coherent critique of the effort to "fix" any American subject, demanding that any attempt to "fix" something old prevents the invention of something "new."

※

Modern Chivalry is the only text addressed in this study to which the real author signed his name, hiding behind neither anonymity nor a pseudonym. The title page of each of the four installments that compose part 1 is relatively uncomplicated, and authorship is attributed to "H. H. Brackenridge," a name with which Brackenridge could be sure his readers were fairly familiar. He was trained at Princeton under John Witherspoon, the expatriate Scotsman who trained students in classical styles and forms of writing.

Starting with the famous poem "The Rising Glory of America," coauthored with Philip Freneau in 1771, Brackenridge published extensively in this mode. His plays included *The Battle of Bunkers Hill* (1776) and *The Death of General Montgomery* (1777); his journalism the editorship of the *United States Magazine* (1779) and the *Pittsburgh Gazette* (1786); and his fiction *Father Bombo's Pilgrimage to Mecca* (1770) and "The Cave of VanHest" (1779). As a minister, Brackenridge published occasional sermons and, as a lawyer, legal papers.[10] In short, he demonstrated all the authorial signs of joining the republican elite. His mastery of this wide array of British forms was typical of the early republic's notion of a "lettered" man, a literary aristocrat writing to enlighten the public through his language's representation of order and propriety.

In 1787 his exclusion from the Constitutional Convention alienated Brackenridge from mainstream American politics, although he did campaign in western Pennsylvania for the Constitution's ratification. Subsequently, his writing changed radically: like a homegrown Paine, he remained loyal to democratic revolutionary ideals while his republican contemporaries moved toward political and cultural "redcoatism." The difficulty he had with the first piece he attempted to write after his public defeats demonstrates his shifting and unsettled approach. In 1788 he tried to write a mock-epic, "The Modern Chevalier," which had earlier versions of the adventures of Teague and Farrago. Its neoclassical pretensions speak to the lingering colonialism of his earlier work.

However, the incompatibility of the chaotic American subject and the ordered form and line of the genre caused him to cease composition: the imposition of a fictitious order on the new nation ring false, and Brackenridge went in search of more expressive words and formats better suited to American subjects. The result was *Modern Chivalry*. A fragment of this poem appeared as the work of a fictional and failed author, M'Comas, in the introduction to the 1797 installment of *Modern Chivalry*, discussed below. Brackenridge's abandonment of "The Modern Chevalier" and his initiation of the generically imprecise yet unified *Modern Chivalry* can be seen as the textual reflection of Brackenridge's rejection of the dominant modes of political discourse.[11] No longer welcome or functional within republican political or literary contexts, Brackenridge, now living on the frontier in Pittsburgh, embraced a geographical, political, and authorial exile from the recolonized eastern seaboard.

To Brackenridge, each political party offered only its own version of recolonizing the United States, and neither explored difference. In 1798 Brackenridge joined Jefferson's Antifederalists but only to be appointed to the Pennsylvania Supreme Court by the incoming Antifederalist administration in that state, a position from which he, like Royall Tyler on the Vermont bench, would consistently defy party instructions. Part 1 of *Modern Chivalry* was written by a man who, during the nation's most vehement period of party politics, stood on the outside, content with neither of the opposing factions.[12] His efforts to mediate the Whiskey Rebellion of 1794 reflect his precarious position. The rebels saw Brackenridge as part of the government and the government saw him as one of the rebels.

He explained this in *Incidents of the Insurrection* (1795), an unadorned narrative that further articulates the difference between Brackenridge's voice and the author-narrator's in *Modern Chivalry*. As a denizen of the Ohio valley, Brackenridge had a real sense of republican colonization, as opposed to the more figurative and metaphorical forms of recolonization depicted and deposed by the other authors addressed in this study. Following the Revolution, the eastern states gazed west with dreams of empire, according to John Seelye. Empire, as Edward Said has remarked, "almost always" employs "colonialism . . . the implanting of settlements on distant territory" (9). The East's colonization of the Ohio valley in the 1790s represented its embrace of the imperial, colonizing role. Brackenridge's sympathy with the Whiskey Rebels demonstrates his loyalty to the anticolonial and decentralized values lost in the East.

Part 1 of *Modern Chivalry* reflects Brackenridge's personal sense of displacement in its use of an author-narrator whose ambition to create a text acceptable to both sides engenders his final absurdity. The author-narrator's inability to produce a successful text is less a personal failure than it is Brackenridge's observation of a national failure to overcome the polarized, factional rhetoric of the two parties. Like all colonizers, according to Abdul R. JanMohamed, republicans facilitated their colonizing energies through the imposition of oppositional binaries: us/them, East/West, Federalist/Antifederalist.[13] Second World writing, among other things, attacks these oversimplifications to explore the more entangled post-independence realities. In *Modern Chivalry*, just as in his political career, Brackenridge stands outside the mainstream of American events, alienated from its menu of choices and unwilling to be implicated in the colonizing rhetoric of republicanism, outside the binaries. He can then be viewed as exhorting the American public to purge the colonizing republican rhetoric and seek other words and formats expressive of a less restricted national character, exploring the multiple possibilities implicit in their local communities.

To extend Elliott's point, then, the "H. H. Brackenridge" affixed to part 1 of *Modern Chivalry* is a mask employed by the alienated Brackenridge of the 1790s to undermine writers like the "H. H. Brackenridge" of the 1770s and 1780s who intended to impose a single image on the new nation. To begin the process of disruption, this misdirection served to ensnare the readers who recognized and trusted that name as a reliable and authorized source of legitimate commentary on national and cultural issues. Brackenridge constructs his earlier literary identity as pompous, aristocratic, and, above all, colonizing by discrediting the modes of writing he had used successfully as a younger man.

To establish this position in the introduction to the first volume of *Modern Chivalry,* Brackenridge crafts an author-narrator whose ambitions allow the reader to recognize an aspirant to the republic of letters. As such, Brackenridge can be seen placing his text before the public in a way that indicts two standard functions of public rhetoric: the desire to "fix" the new nation; and the inevitable failure of any static, transplanted perspective to express American experience. By contextualizing his own work in the same intellectual traditions of standard texts, the author-narrator openly announces his wish to contribute to the recolonization of the American reader.

In the opening paragraph the author-narrator claims an authority in the tradition of the departed colonizers whose language, it is tacitly understood, is the same on both sides of the Atlantic. He states that he means "to fix the orthography, choice of words, idioms of phrase, and structure of sentence, than all the Dictionaries and Institutes than have ever been made." Soon thereafter, he makes an absurd claim regarding the relation of language to subject: "So here culing out the choicest flowers of diction, I shall pay no regard to the idea; for it is not in the power of human ingenuity to attain two things perfectly at once . . . so to expect good language and good sense, at the same time, is absurd" (3). The author-narrator's befuddled attempt to make sense satirizes the aristocratic British notion that literary writing is merely a leisurely occupation of a gentleman. Other poorly conceived digressions from the story of Farrago and Teague throughout *Modern Chivalry* further undermine the legitimacy of the voice of the author-narrator.

The fictional author next assumes that his work will find its way into the republic of letters and merit critical attention: "It will be needless for me to say any thing about the critics; for as this work is intended as a model or rule of good writing, it cannot be the subject of criticism . . . because in a model there can be no defects" (4). This tautology reinforces the absurdity of this voice. In the final sentence of this paragraph, Brackenridge extends his commentary to the viability of language in general: "I have no objections, therefore, to any praise that may be given to this work; but to censure or blame must appear absurd; because it cannot be doubted that it will perfectly answer to the end proposed" (4).

The author-narrator also assumes a detachment of "stile" from "sense." According to his logic, then, what makes sense cannot be good style and what is good style cannot make sense. Any future texts following this code would be ridiculous—language would lose its social viability and beauty would be excluded from everyday life. In either case, Brackenridge suggests that voices such as those of the author-narrator, when publicly accepted, threaten the future of language in America, both political and literary, by constricting its ability to adapt and grow with the new nation. Brackenridge silently recognizes that all language bears rhetorical weight: to claim otherwise is to delude oneself, as is shown when the author-narrator fails, almost immediately, to create a text lifted above the demands of "sense."

When concluding, by explicitly discussing the social role he would have his text play, the author-narrator implicitly makes "sense" by applying the text to his specific context.[14] He claims a purpose that, again, allows the real author to comment on more than the author-narrator could ever know: "Being a book without thought, or the smallest degree of sense, it will be useful to young minds, not fatiguing their understandings, and easily introducing a love of reading and study. . . . It will be useful especially for men of light minds intended for the bar or the pulpit" (4). A "fixed" language will make it very easy for the unqualified and the ill-prepared to ascend to positions of social authority, the bar or the pulpit, the real author suggests, because a "fixed" language is easy to duplicate and wield as an instrument of demagogic power. An unfixed language is ultimately more demanding, but more likely to produce minds capable of adapting themselves to the changing and flexible needs of the new nation.

The introduction as a whole exposes the flimsy machinery required of any text seeking a role in the public sphere: an authorial voice and genre cast in enlightenment intellectual traditions and therefore capable of expressing the character and needs of the specific context of the republic. Entry into this sphere of authorization required a self-destructive hubris, representative of a parallel republican failure to seek freedom and plurality. The author-narrator seeks to improve natural language: his subsequent failure to adhere to his plan testifies to Brackenridge's disgust with the solipsism and stagnation of the early republic.

Volume 1 of *Modern Chivalry*, the first work of creative literature written west of the Appalachians, was published in February 1792. The episodic narrative of Farrago and Teague reflects a broad range of conditions on the transappalachian frontier. The episodes focus on the verbal battles fought over social power. Farrago and other educated men constantly deceive the uneducated public and the uneducated public always disregards the lies. In every instance, neither group really offers a solution to any specific problem, expressing more interest in internecine disputes than genuine activity and progress. In volume 1 Brackenridge also establishes a relation between the fiction of Farrago and Teague and the fiction of the author-narrator's composition.

The first chapter opens with an anecdote about horse racing. This vignette, which introduces Farrago and Teague, dramatizes the absurd arguments and misundestandings that figure so largely throughout *Modern Chivalry*. Brackenridge wastes no time in ridiculing the precise terminology of the introduction. Like the author-narrator, Farrago is first characterized by "his greater knowledge of books than of the world." Farrago should be the ideal result of the reading program suggested in the introduction. Instead, he has established a way of thinking wholly separate from actual events—like the author-narrator's notion of language, he is all "stile" and no "sense." Teague is described as an "Irishman," a term for which the author-narrator assumes his audience has a definition: "I shall say nothing of the character of this man, because the very name imports what he was" (6). If so, the author-narrator's "perfect stile" involves a poverty of specific description, so becoming an explicit vehicle for simpleminded racism.[15] Robert Secor has observed that the type of humor deployed by the author-narrator in Teague's depiction was typical of republican strategies for consolidating national identity around an Anglophilic model: "Stereotypes of the Irish, Scottish, Germans, Dutch, and Jews, different as they were, all served to mark these groups as outside the boundaries of the dominant culture" (189). Such a technique protected republican monoculturalism from both the plurality of European cultures leftover from the colonial period and from the influx of new groups after the Revolution.

The anecdote itself, as Hoffa and Barry Grant have suggested, is a farce involving the impossibility of communication in the early republic. Farrago and Teague come upon some low characters preparing for a horse race, and Farrago's horse is suggested for an entry. As Farrago begins a lengthy and informed discourse on various aspects of heredity, the men think he is merely bluffing, trying to build up his odds. When Farrago continues to spout information, "the Jockeys thought the man a fool, and gave themselves no more trouble about him" (8). In the commotion, Farrago is knocked off his horse and falls on his head. The author-narrator takes this opportunity to discuss all available treatments of head injuries while Farrago and his doctor argue about his case.

Throughout the chapter, different versions of language conflict with each other. The jockeys do not understand Farrago, Farrago misinterprets the jockeys, and the doctor only befuddles Farrago. These conflicts occur both within and without representations of authority, making the formation of any meaningful authority impossible: the intellectual authority of Farrago is irrelevant to the jockeys, and the scientific jargon of the doctor irritates Farrago. These failures occur because each speaker assumes that his way of speaking is the only reliable means of communication. More important than the internal problems of each of these dialects is the inflexibility and intolerance of each speaker to other uses of English. That is, each imposes a monophonic version of proper speech. Since none is held in common, chaos reigns. An open admission of the polyphonic nature of American speech and life, one that embraced its Second World heterogeneity, might have prevented the conclusion.

During the subsequent "Observations" chapter, the author-narrator, despite his initial disclaimer, makes "sense" of the events of the text. The changing tone and self-consciousness of the "Observations" chapters throughout part 1 maintain the continuity of the fiction of authorship. As volume 1 opens, the author-narrator seeks to maintain the function he had claimed in the introduction. To instruct the "weak and visionary," he reflects, the "great secret of preserving respect, is the cultivating and shewing to the best advantage the powers that we possess, and the not going beyond them" (11). In betraying the enormity of his own task, the author-narrator stands revealed as his own negative example: in assuming to "fix" the entire language as a unified entity, he, more than any of his characters, goes "beyond" his abilities.

However, the author-narrator also concedes that Farrago's overexposure to reading had generated his "simplicity." In addition, despite his dismissal of the jockeys—"there are no people who are by education of less philosophic turn of mind" (11)—they at least recognize Farrago as a fool while neither the author-narrator nor Farrago himself is capable of such a simple observation. The chapter ends with the author-narrator's failure to recognize the true worth of his writing: "I have to declare, that it is with no attempt at wit that the terms are set down" (11). Brackenridge thus dons a straight-faced mask: the episodes throughout the book are often funny, as the real author deploys a vast array of devices and modes to reveal the balkanized nature of American society: language creates division, not unity, by privileging anachronistic modes of discourse and suppressing the nascent inventiveness of other classes and ethnicities.[16]

The pattern established in the first two chapters structures the remainder of volume 1. As Farrago and Teague travel through an undescribed American landscape, they stumble upon political writing (19–22), legal writing (35–37), religious discourse (41–44), and the language of treaties (61–62). Farrago, Teague, and the motley Americans they find never really change: Farrago continues to try to instruct the ignorant, the ignorant ignore him, and Teague is forever frustrated in his attempts at social mobility. The most consistent abuse of language is Farrago's constant deception of Teague. For example, Teague is offered positions in politics, the ministry, and in the American Philosophical Society. In each case, Farrago concocts lies concerning what each would expect of the "poor bog-trotter," motivated by the interchangeable excuses of self- and public interest. The language of paternal authority, revealed as duplicitous in the hands of an untrustworthy elite, is undermined.

This trend is also identified as having specific racial dimensions. Book 5 of volume 1 describes how two white Americans attempt to hire Teague to pose as a Kickapoo chief to validate a treaty justifying the theft of Indian lands. Teague's inability to speak proper English qualifies him for the job. In this episode, English is used a vehicle for the exclusion and exploitation of two marginalized groups: indigene and Irish. Concepts of plurality and inclusiveness are foregone in favor of reimplementing the monovocalism of British colonial culture and the displacement of the multivocal American scene. Similarly, in volume 2, African Americans and women will be silenced by the same policy of linguistic exclusion based on colonizing hierarchies.

One small voice appears in volume 1 that, by its integrity, reveals the dishonesty of all the other American voices. Following the oft-noted episode involving the farcical election when an Antifederalist weaver defeats a Federalist lawyer despite Farrago's support of the latter (an episode based in Brackenridge's own experience), Farrago and Teague visit a "Conjurer" (18). When queried as to the problematic nature of the election, the Conjurer replies by suggesting the duplicity of both parties: "And hence a perpetual war: the aristocrats endeavouring to detrude the people, and the people contending to detrude themselves. And it is right it should be so; for by this fermentation, the spirit of democracy is kept alive" (19). In a 1789 essay, Brackenridge similarly compared democracy to "wrestling" (129) and "a double-geared mill" (131).[17] As such, the Conjuror may be said to represent Brackenridge himself. Both character and author realize that democracy is a political instrument of flexibility and chance whose dangers are far preferable to the stagnating stability of other systems. Democracy acknowledges the occasional anarchy and chaos of the post-Independence community and, perhaps, best serves decolonization in the Second World. The Conjurer refuses payment and Farrago leaves, still unable to understand the episode.

The author-narrator's subsequent "Reflections" reveal a momentary dissatisfaction with his original mission. He concedes that a great deal of language's use is for deception and that communication involves far more than words: gestures, volume, disposition, and other contextual conditions complicate and, in a sense, remake a decolonized language as simply one of a series of available modes of discourse in a heterogeneous community. He concludes the episode by reflecting on his own text: "Now it may be said, that this is a fiction; but fiction, or no fiction, the nature of the thing will make it a reality" (22). This smudging of the criteria of textual reliability is presumably exempted by the author-narrator's claims not to make "sense."[18] Moreover, the author-narrator admits to a veiled concentration of power among the elite: access to print, not authenticity, establishes authority. Conversely, Brackenridge proposes a textuality based on more fluid and openly constructed borders between reader and writer, and text and subject, at the time radical notions.

The author-narrator soon returns to his original thickheadedness. He labels the digression a momentary lapse and, instead of perceiving the failure of his quest, suggests that he has suffered only a temporary lapse: "The truth is, I will not give myself the trouble to write sense for long. For I would as soon please fools as wise men; because the fools are the most numerous, and every prudent man will go with the majority" (37). The author-narrator thus defends his own foolishness and escapes safely into the irresponsibility of "nonsense." The next significant claim he makes allows Brackenridge to contextualize this absurdity in the early republic: "No one can attribute to me the least tincture of satire, or ridicule of individuals or public bodies" (43). Of course not: the author-narrator means for his text to elevate its author to membership in an esteemed "public body." The author-narrator then disclaims Lucian, Le Sage, Cervantes, and Swift, all antiestablishment figures, to confirm his complicity with empowered textuality: "I never knew any good come of wit and humour yet . . . I have carefully avoided everything of this nature" (43). Again, Brackenridge satirizes the self-marginalization of the many authors of the period who grimly demanded an American literature based on classical models.[19]

Volume 1 ends with a Postscript in which the author-narrator betrays his own authorial violations of the very admonitions he had suggested throughout the preceding chapters. For example, in the introduction he limited himself to "stile," not "sense," because "a Jack of all Trades, is proverbially of a bungler" (4). He mentions his plans to publish legal commentary, classical studies, zoology, botany, and Orientalism—all of which, presumably, he would do as badly as he had in writing for "stile" in volume 1. Furthermore, he says he writes to "fill up the interstices of business" (77). He also regrets not being able to stay in Philadelphia to promote the book more aggressively, "for it is of no consequence how a book becomes famous, provided that it is famous" (77). Ironically, these are meant to elevate the fictional author in the eyes of the republic of letters: he shows himself wealthy, industrious, and such a master of language that he can address any subject, as would such increasingly dubious figures as Tyler's Updike Underhill, Brown's Arthur Mervyn, and Watterston's Morcell, to be discussed in subsequent chapters. Since the author-narrator in fact cannot communicate in any of these forms, Brackenridge has deftly inverted the notion that "virtue" in one field creates it in others, undercutting the notion that all social responsibility can be placed in the hands of Jefferson's "natural aristocracy."

The author-narrator next returns to language, making two statements that reveal the inconsistency of his self-appointed task. First, he articulates the Hamiltonian position: "Language being the vestment of thought, it comes within the rules of other dress; so that as slovenliness on the one hand, or foppery, on the other, is to be avoided in our attire; so also in our speech, and writing" (77). One page later, he echoes Noah Webster: "The English language is undoubtedly written better in America than in England, especially since the time of that literary dunce, Samuel Johnson, who was totally destitute of taste for the *vrai naturelle* or simplicity of nature" (78). At once he concedes that language must adhere to "rules of dress" and acknowledges that, in the United States, language has improved by reattaching itself to the "simplicity of nature." He would have language both a contrivance of man and a natural phenomenon.

In his conclusion he retreats from both suppositions, unwilling to confront the contradictions: "I am quite out of a patience with this postscript. I have written it, the Printer informing me that he had a few pages of the last sheet to fill, which must be blank unless I add something more" (78). Brackenridge thus suggests that the republic of letters has not bothered to familiarize itself with the actual condition of language in the American community, blindly following an ideology that allows problems to go unsolved. As a result, the new nation, like the text itself, is threatened with implosion. The postscript itself then follows neither "rules" nor "nature"—hardly a demonstration of "perfect stile."

Volume 1, as whole, establishes the method for the remaining three volumes of part 1: the lampooning of authorized modes of discourse by interweaving a fiction of events with a parallel fiction of the book's composition. While Farrago and Teague constantly expose the disharmony and chaos created by Americans' inability to communicate with one another, the author-narrator consistently endeavors to reassemble a single American voice. Each of the other three volumes is less general as Brackenridge explores the various manifestations of this destructive arrangement in specific contexts of the 1790s.

The fiction of authorship in volume 2 is generally less apparent than in the other sections of part 1, reflecting the inconsistency of Brackenridge's own ideas concerning his work. Having recognized the inability of British genres and language to express American subjects, he is left without a model: to transcend mere re-action, he must seek a new literary paradigm. But this does not weaken *Modern Chivalry*'s internal narrative: instead it only reflects his desire to explore alter-native modes. In it, the narrative of Farrago and Teague plays a larger role and reiterates many of the same subjects introduced in the first volume. Once again, Brackenridge, in the fiction of his main characters, satirizes authorized language as it muddles and confuses social mobility, natural science, manners and courtship, and, most importantly, slavery. The more general focus of this volume is the rep-resentation of how official language in the early republic extinguishes ambition, retards the emergence of local identity, and maintains an unjust status quo.

No introduction contextualizes the first episode. Volume 1 had sold quite well, and so Brackenridge could safely assume that his readers would remember the author-narrator's absurd ambition to join the elite and his equally self-consum-ing linguistic agenda. The author-narrator makes his first self-consciously au-thorial appearance to comment upon Teague's fight with a hosteler. In the manner of many of the new nation's neoclassical writers, he relates the scuffle to Livy's description of the combat of the Horatii and Curatii. However, he concludes the chapter with a passage that allows Brackenridge to enter the text: "It may be thought, that though stile is my subject, yet I might now and then bring along a thought to entertain the reader, and introduce some subject of moment, rather than the fistycuffs of two ragamuffins. I would just ask this questions; Is not the talent of the artist shewn as much in painting a fly, as a waggon-wheel. If this were intended as a book of morals, or physiology, and not a mere belles lettres composition, there might be something said;—as the case is, the critics must be silent" (90). Although the author-narrator means this remark to demonstrate the trivial nature of fiction, Brackenridge here suggests a superior power of fiction, since it can address actual subjects unfettered by the restraints of convention or the limitations of a consciousness that claims to be objective. Moreover, the author-narrator's inability to interpret this episode forces the readers to explore their own reactions reformulating the passivity of standard readership. In volume 2's most important section, this distinction between fiction's ability to be truthful and nonfiction's tendency to be fallacious is used to compel a rather vehement social activism.

One night Farrago discusses the issue of slavery with a Quaker. Speaking for the political consensus, Farrago regretfully condones the peculiar institution: "It is necessary that there be domination and subjection, in order to produce compound improvement and advantage" (137), echoing Jefferson in *Notes on the State of Virginia*.[20] In his "Remarks," the author-narrator echoes Farrago's legal defense of slavery. Nonetheless, to show off "perfect stile" in legal writing, he correctly concludes that "the holder of a negro must, therefore, look back to that act which first made him, or an ancestor, a slave; and if he cannot justify this, he cannot justify the retaining him in servitude" (138). After exploring the legal ramifications in the best language of pamphleteers, the author-narrator retreats from this contrary supposition, reverting to his unwillingness to accept the "sense" of writing whose only purpose is "stile": "I shall say no more on this head, lest I should furnish hints to pettifoggers, who may make ill use of their information" (140). Brackenridge, in control of the text as the author-narrator is not, has already "furnished" a significant statement concerning slavery's injustice.

The remainder of Farrago's and Teague's adventures in volume 2 reflect the fact that slavery in America is not restricted to specific racial divisions: Farrago's use of language enslaves Teague at every turn. For example, in regard to dialect, Teague and a slave speaking before the American Philosophical Society are both shown speaking nonstandard English and thus ridiculed by the membership. When Teague attempts to become a lawyer, Farrago whips him and harangues him in a language associated with power, not servitude. The author-narrator briefly comments that Teague's speech is "like that of a wolf at the bottom of a well, or a dog that had lost his master" (150).[21] In either case, social and racial hierarchies are perpetuated by the abuse of language—freedom defeated by an aristocracy of diction. Moreover, Brackenridge's targets are the institutions of the early republic, not those excluded from them.

Volume 2 concludes with a parodic Postscript that confirms the irony of the author-narrator. To inspire greater sales, he suggests that the government buy a large number of copies. He claims that since he is such an obvious master of "stile," if he turned to politics, all politicians, including Hamilton and Jefferson, each referred to by his position in George Washington's cabinet, would be "a great deal in my power." He bullies them by announcing that "if I should break out upon them, I know not where I might end" (157). The author-narrator's hubris here places him not among the nation's elite but atop it. He takes to its logical extreme the premise that mastery of "British" language engenders intellectual control. Brackenridge, however, is not demeaning the power of language, just that of the wrong language, such as the author-narrator's, which mistakenly values reactionary consistency above tangible uses and subjects.

Volume 3 was published in Pittsburgh in 1793. This geographic distance parallels Brackenridge's increasing separation from the power centers of the East, a development suggested in the postscript of volume 2. Now both geographically and ideologically marginalized, Brackenridge becomes increasingly critical of the closed world of republican discourse. Living in a part of the country actually being colonized, Brackenridge more acutely perceives how colonization in any form violates revolutionary principles. The episodes, reflecting the expanding scope of Brackenridge's anger, no longer describe local characters but rather move into the cities and the corridors of power, as the subjects grow from horse racing to foreign affairs and presidential politics.

Volume 3 opens with a long introduction that reaffirms *Modern Chivalry*'s fiction of authorship.[22] In it, the author-narrator clarifies his deceptive purpose: "I acknowledge that no man will ever possess a good stile that has not well studied, and exercised himself in writing, selecting with a most perfect delicacy, in all cases; the proper term; but he must go beyond this and be able to deceive the world, and, never let it come into their heads that he has spent a great deal of thought on the subject" (161). The author-narrator carefully creates the writer as an aristocrat of language, a colonial overlord leisurely dispensing his power for his own purposes upon the relatively powerless populace. The phrase "to deceive the world," reflects the innate power of established language to create a false reality, removed from truth and the real problems of the new nation.

The author-narrator next presents a review of the first two volumes to confirm his place in that inner circle. The review from a nonexistent "Young's Magazine," is, of course, glowing and confirms that the book's exaltation of "stile" is comprehensive and totally free of "sense." The author-narrator's excursion into the republic of letters represents the real author's alienation from false notions of American paradises. Like the author-narrator, the fictional reviewer considers language only as it *should* be used, and not as something *actually* used, and so easily overlooks real problems and ambiguities.

Encouraged by such a favorable notice, the author-narrator includes other pieces of his writing. After some fifty lines of hudibrastic verse so imitative of Butler that its derivativeness would be transparent to any eighteenth-century reader, he claims to be the "superior" of Swift, "for I can rise to the swell of the highest pipe of diction" (167). To prove that claim, the author-narrator includes a recent "speech" that echoes the standard Antifederalist reactionary approval of the French Revolution (168–71) by cloaking it in the legacy of classical mod-els.[23] That is, the same author-narrator who claimed that "the people detrude themselves," now celebrates a populist revolution. Brackenridge thus identifies the lack of any means of intelligent distinction among the authorized genres and languages: both the Hamiltonians and the Jeffersonians claim a monopoly on linguistic, and thus social, authority. However, the author-narrator is so busy cel-ebrating both that he neglects the vast majority of events in his community en-compassed by neither. Because both sides claim the exclusive truth and seem eloquent, the hapless author-narrator can make no distinctions and resorts to endless contradiction.

Next, the author-narrator recalls his visit to the apartment of the late M'Comas, a fictional Scottish immigrant whose writing had often appeared in magazines and newspapers around Philadelphia. M'Comas is characterized by his landlady as an eccentric intellectual: "I would rather have a person that would sit still, and hold his tongue, and sleep in my house, than a raving crazy brained like him, that made more noise than the rats" (172). The author-narrator next includes nearly a thousand lines of M'Comas's hudibrastic verse in which a member of the post-Revolutionary Society of Cincinnati is harangued by his American countrymen for his aristocratic pretensions.

The poem itself, "Cincinnatus," is in fact a fragment of "The Modern Cheva-lier," which Brackenridge tried and failed to write before *Modern Chivalry*. As such it reflects Brackenridge in a transition from insider to outsider. It consists of a rather repetitive sequence of arguments, all of which recreate the inability of the aristocratic "Cincinnat" to communicate with the small-minded townsmen. Brackenridge clearly sides with the dogmatic vehemence of neither, and both sides look foolish. The author-narrator, however, gushes over the lines to the de-gree that he offers his endorsement of their significance to America: "The bro-kenness and disjointings of the verses, one line running into, and interlaced with another, carries it beyond the monotonous, though . . . more musical imitators of Butler: amongst whom, Trumbull, of Connecticut, easily deserves the first place; yet though his similes, and other excellences of his composition he may surpass the Cincinnatus of M'Comas; nevertheless I must give the Scotch bard the praise of greater variety in the structure of his verses" (195). The landlady's remark, however, haunts the author-narrator, M'Comas, and now also John Trumbull and the rest of the Connecticut Wits: the writing they do may bear in-tellectual credentials, but, in the acquisition of literary authority, each writer has lost touch with the language and issues of the community around him.[24] Brackenridge clearly conflates his author-narrator with Trumbull and others like him, such as his own earlier authorial persona, in a monolith of literary colonialism.

The remainder of volume 3 seems almost an afterthought. Appropriately, it ends with an appendix subtitled "Containing Thoughts on Some Preceding Subjects" (247). This time, even within paragraphs, the author-narrator contradicts himself. For example, after explaining that he did not mean "a burlesque on the President," he suggests that the president demonstrates that "not all men are philosophers," a title he more proudly assumes for himself. Even if he is not genuinely apologetic, he is a terrible writer, in this instance. He concludes by addressing the conflicts with Indians on the western frontier: "It would be a pity that all this expence in raising troops, and exertions in training them, should evaporate in the smoke of a treaty" (249). This statement uses empowered language to justify genocide, successfully "deceiving the world" into thinking it had no other option. Once again, Brackenridge's critique of the early republic's policies toward the frontier bases itself in the logocratic empowerment of official language and its component neocolonialism.

These ever-growing contradictions, representing the chaos of voices within the logocracy of the early republic, represent how, to recall Slemon, Second World self-identification bisects the "individual subject" (110). Brackenridge suggests that republican textuality aspires to be all things to all people, or perhaps to fool all of the people all of the time. Brackenridge recognizes the Americans' complicity in the annihilation of American indigenes yet also perceives how the retention of British cultural norms threatens a parallel cultural genocide: the destruction of any promise of creating a new national identity. In this case, reinscribing the colonizing binary has a very dark effect. Not acknowledging that Americans were *both* colonizer and colonized becomes more than self-deception: such an admission might soften policies toward natives while simultaneously revaluing national identity. If the nation, then, does not decolonize itself by admitting and exploring both sides of its identity, it will both kill the indigenes and reverse the Revolution. While *Modern Chivalry* by no means provides a solution to these paradoxes, it observes the complexity of the problem and demands steps be taken to create a forum for discussing them more honestly.

Brackenridge implicitly connects the failure of American language to a more general social fragility, a development that became very real to him in the years between the publication of volume 3 and his composition of volume 4. In many ways the same tensions he identified in his writing erupted in western Pennsylvania. The East's imposition of an unfair excise tax initiated a smoldering conflict during which neither side was able to articulate its needs clearly to the other. The Rebels found themselves treated unjustly by a government they found distant, both geographically and politicaly from its needs; the Federalist government responded with twelve thousand armed troops. Brackenridge, as mentioned above, was left to mediate.[25] His efforts were largely unsuccessful, and the ensuing frustration affected his composition of volume 4 in 1797, the darkest, least hopeful section of part 1.

In the first three volumes of part 1, slapstick humor and the foolishness of the author-narrator seem to hold out hope for correction: as if to say, this is mere buffoonery, easily repaired if both political parties and the author-narrator would stop being so dogmatic and inflexible about how language. In volume 4, the problem seems deeper: language represents only the superficial manifestation of more profound and intractable flaws in human character. Brackenridge's experience in the Whiskey Rebellion seems to have removed his final illusions concerning the "correspondence between *words* and the *world*," or as least the English/republican version of that correspondence that had characterized the Sternian satire of the first volumes. Completing his deconstruction of the master discourse, Brackenridge now wonders how English can ever be freed of its colonizing and divisive tendencies.

To mark that moment, the author-narrator begins to disappear from the text, a development completed in part 2. He himself notes his gradual disappearance from his own text: "It may be observed, that as I advance my book, I make fewer chapters, by way of commentary, and occupy myself chiefly with the narrative" (295).[26] In volume 4 there seems little point in satirizing official modes of discourse in the person of an inept author-narrator: such critique still occurs within the boundaries dictated by the lingering colonial culture. Freed from the metanarrative and the author-narrator, the text begins to chart new territory, abandoning the strictures of colonial paradigms.

As a result, volume 4 looks the most like a novel, and the least like a fiction of authorship. Brackenridge moved from testing the limits of official discourse to transcending its boundaries in an age when fiction was publicly condemned.[27] Volume 4 mostly describes, not surprisingly, the adventures of Teague, Farrago, and Duncan, an articulate Scottish servant who temporarily replaces Teague as

Farrago's footman as they come into contact with a popular crowd-action closely resembling the Whiskey Rebellion. Like Brackenridge, they are thus thrust into the middle of a conflict in which the distance from dogmatic rhetoric to gunfire is remarkably short. As was the case in the actual Whiskey Rebellion, the multivocality of the nation was forced to conform to monovocal standards, and the result is violence. Brackenridge's point is that language that depends upon the construction of hierarchical arrangements between author and audience is grounded in fear and subjugation.

At the end of volume 4, Farrago for the first time "returns to his home" (326). It seems likely that *Modern Chivalry* as a project to critique the republic of letters from within had outlived its usefulness—it was no longer worth salvaging, according to Brackenridge. Some type of new beginning was required, and he waited seven years before resuming the book. In part 1, Brackenridge had explored virtually every mode of written discourse authorized by the early republic's literary establishment. Finding these modes inconsistent, closed-minded, against the interest of freedom, and, ultimately, capable of justifying slavery and violence, Brackenridge knew he either had to stop writing or start exploring other ways of using language. He had demonstrated the corruptibility of the colonial/republican intellectual tradition to such a degree that, when he wrote fiction again, he could look only outside its narrow constraints.

Part 2 of *Modern Chivalry* (1804–15) presents a text radically different in narrative voice, tone, and scope. In it, Brackenridge abandons the fiction of authorship, adopting a voice more reflective of the growing surrealism of Farrago's and Teague's adventures. Anticipating the heroes of James Fenimore Cooper's *The Monikens* (1832), Poe's *Narrative of Arthur Gordon Pym* (1839), and Melville's *Mardi* (1849), Brackenridge's protagonists move just beyond reality into a symbolic universe characterized by abstracted versions of real events. Brackenridge's leap into an imaginative world also reveals his increasing inability to restrict himself to eighteenth-century forms of language. Elliott has likened the new narrative voice to that of a "prophet-sage" whose power of imaginative conceptualization "stands in direct opposition to the demagogue as well as the aristocrat" (209). It represents Brackenridge's exploratory experiments with a decolonized American voice. Unfortunately, part 2 is overlong, repetitious, and, at times, almost unreadable.

While Brackenridge was not content with standard means of understanding, imagining, and writing, he was unable to conceive of a coherent alternative. Brackenridge's place between the colonial epoch and the decolonized literary democracy places him at the crux of the awkward moment of decolonization: with one foot in each, he must straddle both as he seeks the right balance between retention and revolution. This is not to say that, having finished part 1, Brackenridge was unable to compose worthwhile and important fiction—he just did not do it in *Modern Chivalry*. His short story "The Trial of Mamachtaga" (1806) relates, in a barren style suited to its subject, the defense, condemnation, and execution of a Delaware tribesman in western Pennsylvania in 1785. Mamachtaga is human and honorable—he did get drunk and kill a fellow drinking companion who happened to be white—but uncompromised by the *noble savage* ideal that hampers Cooper's representation of native Americans.

In Brackenridge's story, the racial tolerance, imaginative expansiveness, and linguistic broad-mindedness implicit in *Modern Chivalry*'s critique of early republic writing and language are explicit, the triumph of what Looby calls "exogenous pluralization." The white lawyer who defends Mamachtaga represents a favorable alternative to the prospective American leaders targeted in the *Modern Chivalry*. His voice and his mind never measure his client, experience, or language against inherited standards or hierarchies. Instead, he comprehends the complexities of Second World American life and improvises a compassion whose depth reflects a paradigmatic shift from the closed ideology of the republic of letters. Moreover, before Mamachtaga's death, he is allowed to search the forest for cures for the illness of the jailer's son and for paints to wear at his execution. On neither occasion does he escape.

The jailer accompanied Mamachtaga on these ventures but went only because, had Mamachtaga escaped, "the jailer himself would have fallen sacrifice to the resentment of the people" (364). At once the reader feels a loss at Mamachtaga's execution and wonder at the lawyer's admiration and the jailer's trust. This moment of frontier plurality and heterogeneity, however, is trumped by the suspicions of the conventional crowd, schooled in less creative means of formulating social identity and less willing to rethink standard notions of race and character. While Brackenridge drafted this story in 1785, he rewrote and published it in 1806, perhaps only then recognizing its significance.

Furthermore, in his Conclusion to the volume in which "Mamachtaga" appeared, *Gazette Publications* (1806), Brackenridge further distinguished his own ideas about language from the petty tyranny of *Modern Chivalry*'s fictional author: "A man of very moderate parts can fill an office, perhaps the better for being moderate; but it is but one in many that can show a single spark of the celestial fire that distinguishes the orator, the philosopher, or the rapt poet" (376).[28] There are certain figures capable of using language not "to deceive the world" but rather to express truths unfettered by overt political or factional motivations. Brackenridge realized that the "spark of celestial fire" was extinguished in too many typical early republic texts.

The dowsing had succeeded: Americans had limited themselves to the menu of linguistic, textual, social, and political choices with which they had been raised during the colonial era rather than exploring decolonized alternatives. Part 1 of *Modern Chivalry* was the first of a series of early republic texts that attempted to remind the post-Revolutionary citizenry of their plurality, polyphony, and of their anticolonialist origin. On the whole, Brackenridge's author-narrator is the most colonial of the fictional authors addressed in this study: he writes sincerely, if ineptly, in an effort to recolonize the United States through stabilizing and confining its language within known forms. He never grows or exploits the standards he champions for overt personal gain. Later figures would increasingly and overtly question or manipulate the colonial standards he hopes against hope to preserve.

❧

TWO

The Mental Commonwealth of
Judith Sargent Murray's *The Gleaner*

POSTCOLONIAL "WOMEN WRITERS' uses of oral traditions and their revisions of Western literary forms are integrally and dialectically related to the kinds of content and the themes they treat" (257).[1] Ketu Katrak's linkage of generic and linguistic experimentation to antipatriarchal and postcolonial struggles could inform our reading of any number of early republic women writers who challenged the narrow strictures in which they were forced to operate. Anna Eliza Bleeker, Mercy Otis Warren, Phillis Wheatley, and dozens of others have been studied for their linguistic and social feminisms.[2] This chapter will address Judith Sargent Murray's *The Gleaner* because Murray both confronts patriarchy in the manner of her female colleagues and along with the male writers addressed in this study attacks colonialism through the fictional recreation of a diverse series of genres and authorships.[3] Perhaps better than anyone else of the era, Murray succeeded in replicating the plurality of the unofficial and discouraged spoken and written languages of common usage in the new nation to confront both leftover colonialism and its component inscriptions of marginality and sexism.

In 1993 Stanley Elkins and Eric McKitrick published *The Age of Federalism: The Early American Republic, 1788–1800*. As a resource for the political affairs of the new nation during this crucial decade, it is invaluable. Yet every woman listed in the index is there because she was married to a Federalist politician or is a late twentieth-century historian. In 925 pages, the authors could find virtually no significant political activity by women in regard to the formation of Federalist policies. Whether this omission reflects the historians' biases does not matter. Women were simply excluded from early republic public life.

Moreover, Ian Watt and others have documented a striking gender divergence in the writing of the time. Men wrote for other men about business and politics; women wrote for other women about morality and the necessity of not crossing into the world of men.[4] Not incidentally, the continuation of female domesticity and generic segregation suited the needs of the recolonizing republicans at the close of the American Revolution. Even before the Revolution, John Adams grouped women with the other problematic minorities that represented a potential threat to republican order. He blamed the ministry for this antiauthoritarian activity: "Depend on it. We know better than to repeal our masculine systems. . . . After stirring up Tories, Landjobbers, Trimmers, Bigots, Canadians, Negroes, Hanoverians, Hessians, Russians, Irish Roman Catholicks, Scotch Renegadoes, at last they have stimulated the [Ladies] to demand new privileges and threaten to rebel" (24). Nathan O. Hatch has documented the egalitarian anticolonialism of revolutionary ministers.[5] Adams here, in a letter to his wife, reflects the republican awareness that the heterogeneity of the American community was a further source of destabilization and decentralization he and his compatriots meant to check. The republican paradigm, as Cathy Davidson and many others have documented, therefore actively sought a master discourse of female enclosure.[6]

In Massachusetts, Judith Sargent Murray, whose second husband was John Murray, one of these controversial ministers, was aware that texts that advertised a female author were usually restricted to a female readership and denied access to the network of publishers, editors, and critics who nourished the distribution and promulgation of texts in the early republic.[7] To enter surreptitiously and thereby critique its exclusivity, Murray assumed a man's name for her publications: a fictional author whose ultimate unmasking reveals the tangible social loss caused by the exclusion of any group from the democratic process.

Murray's *The Gleaner*, both as a series of articles in the *Massachusetts Magazine* (1792–95) and as a book unto itself (1798), revealed and confronted the gender bias of the reinscripted British cultural institutions in the early republic. Importantly, sexism is just one of a series of oppressive and antidemocratic developments Murray observes and undermines. The pieces that became *The Gleaner* announced themselves as occasional essays written by an aging and prosperous white male with the necessary time and access to education and public places to form and articulate worthwhile recommendations for the improvement of the community.[8] Murray's fictional author calls himself the Gleaner, but he also reveals himself as one Mr. Vigillius, a comfortable New England merchant.

Like Brackenridge's author-narrator in *Modern Chivalry*, Vigillius addresses a broad range of subjects and experiments with a series of diverse genres. This form of authorship was typical of early republic authors and grounded in the received British models favored in republican textuality. Michael Warner, Emory Elliott, and Thomas Gustafson have discussed this characteristic of the republic of letters as part of an effort to craft an image of the social leader able to transfer his eloquence to all places where authority was needed: all genres of writing and all potential aspects of public leadership could be successfully managed by the rational and eloquent leader/author.[9]

Acts of authorship were understood as acts of leadership that at once explicitly, through direct address, and implicitly, through a demonstrated mastery of ordered language and text, compelled the reader to accept the intellectual guidance of the author and to apply the textual orderliness more broadly to external public behavior and citizenship.[10] The example of the Addisonian miscellany serves to reveal how republicanism transformed and rephrased British culture to serve its own needs. While the English miscellany was a form suited to experimentation, challenging aristocratic hierarchies but defying classical unity, in the post-Revolutionary United States the same genre served to exhibit the multiple abilities of an eloquent elite.

Although it was proposed that such an arrangement would create a leveled meritocracy, the association of authorship and authority with other forms of public success in fact rewarded the merely derivative and complacent—those fitting into, rather than rejecting or improving, the received model—excluding others based not on quality of thought but rather on difference in gender, race, language, or technique. Readership, like justice, was supposed to be blind to everything but the evidence at hand: the predominance of Anglophilic white male authors suggests otherwise. Not surprisingly, the language and range of generic options employed in the republic of letters to address and express American topics was constricted to those selected from the colonial regime.[11] By imposing this "logocracy" on the post-Revolutionary public, republicanism threatened to recolonize the new nation by perpetuating a national culture rooted in the exclusionary and undemocratic ideology of the colonial epoch.[12]

The Revolution's radicalism was checked by a fear that its rhetoric might become real, especially in light of the violence of the French Revolution, which initially made reference to many of the same democratic ideals. Republicans used the negative example of the French to justify their own departure from the aspirations of 1776 and their reintroduction of colonizing discourse. In pre-Revolutionary discourse such as Thomas Paine's, post-Revolutionary inclusivity was promised. Based on that promise, women contributed to the cause with their lives, property, and energy.[13] However, as the new nation came together, excluding them, women felt alienated, betrayed by a post-Independence return to their place on the margin. As is true in most decolonized communities, the coalition built to repel the colonial regime was dissolved, and the accompanying rhetoric of consensus abandoned.[14] In the United States, Revolutionary discourse had promised a politic based on rational individuality. After the Revolution, in order to maintain their place atop the community, early republic males decided that, while women were not necessarily disqualified from political meaning because they were women, they were irrational and, as such, unreliable participants in public decision-making, as John Adams's letter to Abigail makes clear.

In Gayatri Spivak's terms, early republic women were thus "doubly-colonized": first on account of their subject role as passive members of the recolonized, republican state, and second through their gender.[15] Linda Kerber, Davidson, and Nancy Cott have discussed how this double exclusion compelled the creation of a separate "women's sphere" in post-Revolutionary New England in which women established their own literature and culture separate from the world of men protected by the republic of letters.[16] Kerber notes that this sphere was characterized by a discourse of disappointment: "Women had indeed served in and supported the American Revolution . . . but in 1787 were not in a strong position to make collective demands as a group" (250). Denied access to the public means of appeal available to men, women had to "destabilize and then renegotiate their relationships with men" (251). Because literary exchange was considered central to the formation of national character, resisting women made elaborate efforts to enter the republic of letters to demonstrate not only their rationality but also the autocratic and recolonizing nature of republicanism in general.[17]

Such is the case in *The Gleaner*: by finally revealing herself as a female, Murray disrupts those readers who had, following the norm, taken seriously this identifiably male authority figure in ways they would not a female. As a series of essays, *The Gleaner* features a conventional male voice gradually advocating women's significance through Vigillius's recognition of his wife's abilities. As a book presumably written by an equally fictitious female author, one Constantia, who finally reveals Vigillius as her mask, it challenges the republic's exclusion of women by demonstrating the ability of one woman to enter and contribute to the male world of authorship.

Murray's use of two fictional authors, as well as a series of smaller voices, not only assured her of both male and female readers—a rare early republic phenomenon—but also reminds Americans of their common interests, transcending the class and gender distinctions of her day. In that sense Murray's book coincides with current feminist critiques of the "public sphere": the atmosphere of rational intellectual exchange identified by Jürgen Habermas as having reached its clearest expression in the late eighteenth-century North Atlantic community. Despite republicanism's claim to inclusivity and rationality, the public sphere irrationally excluded potential female participants.[18]

Murray's dramatization of female rationality and literacy is doubly accomplished by her introducing a covert feminism to her writing after the reader has become comfortable with Vigillius.[19] In fact, Vigillius often becomes merely an editor for the women in his life—his wife, ward, and correspondents—all more capable of creating an interesting text than he. Nonetheless, his male presence, however invisible, frames and validates the women's writings in the minds of the readers prior to Murray's unmasking. As the text is repeatedly interrupted and disrupted by equally fictitious correspondents and references to other texts, *The Gleaner* not only allows a women to join the republic of letters but also *represents* a textual alternative: multivocal, heteroglossic, and diverse—a pastiche of presences that dramatizes Murray's notion of the community in general.

This disruption is possible only after the character of Vigillius and his place in the republic of letters is assured. Hence, in both the series and the book, Murray was careful to initiate the reading experience as an event within republican culture. Her use of the term *miscellany* also contributes to this internal fiction. It refers to a genre in European writing that pretends to dismiss literature as secondary activity of public men, all the while confirming the seemingly unassailable authority of the articulate leisure class. While Vigillius means to write in this occasional manner, Murray's almost metafictive narrative of her book's authorship reveals far greater unity than the received genre suggested. The book finally reveals itself as a unified and sequential narrative about the alienation and dis-

placement of a conventional male author: its claim to be a miscellany is Vigillius's—not Murray's. Through the diminution of his character, her book is far
more unified than his. This embedded narrative reveals a progressive and sequential accumulation of voices that ultimately challenge the reader to explore
his or her own interpretive skills. Therefore, my reading of *The Gleaner* will center on those sections where the issue of authorship muddies the interpretive
norms to challenge the early republic's constructions of reliable social and cultural authority.

For purposes of brevity, I shall address three particularly revealing sequences:
the embedded novella "The Story of Margaretta" and its accompanying commentary on American authorship (essays 2 through 16), Mrs. Vigillius's history
of gender politics (43 through 56), and the later essays on literature and politics
in the United States (69 and 94). By the end, Vigillius himself actualizes a gradual transition from complicit republican to decentered dissident by shifting from
a British mode of authorship to Murray's more appropriately American mode of
democratic and decolonizing literary production.

When the essays that became *The Gleaner* first appeared in 1792, Vigillius presented himself as a typical Addisonian, using a voice and assuming an authority
left over from the British dominion. While this technique may have been an unstable vehicle for challenging traditional forms of writing in England, in the new
nation, it was clearly representative of a stable and stabilizing vehicle for the textual self-creation of the literary and social elite, as Murray's use of it reveals. However, by the time the book was published in 1798, Murray's secret had long been
out: her readers knew the Gleaner was a female, though not necessarily Murray,
and that Vigillius was more than a pseudonym: he was a *character*.[20] By showing how easily a woman could write in a man's voice and how easily an objective author can become a character in a subjective fiction, Murray blurs both the
colonialist and sexist distinctions that defined the republican pubic sphere, starting in the prefatory materials.

In the book, she introduces another fictional author, Constantia, who appears
to acquiesce to the marginal role granted women authors in the republic of letters. On the title page of the three-volume set, beneath the title was an inscription
that reveals Murray's suggestion that her book represents a text in compliance with
the didactic public discourse of the period:

Slow to *condemn,* and seeking to *commend,*
Good *sense* will with deliberation scan;
To *trivial* faults unwilling to descend,
If *Virtue* gave, and form'd the general plan. (1)

The references to authorial humility suggest the fictional author's awareness that
she is a guest in male territory, welcome only so long as she recognizes her status as guest. "Constantia" was a name used by Murray on various occasional writings she published during the 1780s.[21] It was also known to the public because
it had also been employed by Sarah Wentworth Morton, and the subsequent clar-
ification of the two Constantias was a public event. The name itself, rooted in
constant, implies loyalty and consistency, passive qualities rather than assertive
strengths.

The subsequent dedication and preface maintain this deferential tone. The
dedication is to John Adams, at the time president and, in fact, ironically one of
The Gleaner's original subscribers. First, Constantia is careful to distinguish a republican leader from a royal patron on the grounds of his "meritorious" achievements:

The homage we yield to eminent abilities, and luminous rectitude, can
never involve the charge of singularity; for genius, elevated by virtue and
unimpeached integrity, adorned by literature, elegance and taste, have in
all ages commanded the esteem and veneration of mankind; but although
I might plead the sanction of numerous and respectable examples, I cannot, however, discern the utility of essaying to prove, that the majesty of
the day illumines our world, or that his salutary influence, like some glad-
dening deity, diffuses over the face of nature, consistency, harmony, and
unrivalled beauty. (12)

To this point, Constantia is heroically anticolonialist in distinguishing the sycophantic hyperbole of European patronage from American discourse. Soon thereafter, however, she mentions that Adams is "another Elisha, clothed in the sacred
vestments of authority" capable of leading the country through the "emergen-
cies and dangers of a FREE GOVERNMENT" (12). Such is typical of republican
rhetoric: leadership occupies an unsettled space between aristocracy and democracy, as Adams himself admitted.[22]

That said, Constantia recognizes the de facto power of republican leaders to
exert broader cultural influence: "Yes, Sir, I indulge a hope that your name may

not only shield me from the oblivion I dread, but possibly confer a degree of celebrity, to which my own merit might not furnish a title" (12). Here Constantia reveals that the republic is not the straightforward meritocracy it advertised itself to be: the politics of reputation and patronage still carry weight, and she means to exploit the system to her advantage.

This tone is continued in the Preface to the Reader. In it, Constantia again reveals the self-serving and self-referential nature of the early republic public sphere: "A lover of humanity, I do not remember the period when I was not solicitous to render myself acceptable to all those who were naturally or adventitiously my associates. . . . Yet this is my *ruling passion* a fondness to stand well in the opinion of the world, . . . to become a candidate for that complacency we naturally feel toward those persons, or that performance, which hath contributed to our emolument, or even amusement" (13). Like Brackenridge's author-narrator, Constantia makes reference to an inner circle of "associates," a limited group whose taste and judgment is presumably superior to that of the general public, that she would use her authorship to join. By recognizing the connection between the authorship of a conventional text and social advancement, Murray implicitly recognizes the unmeritorious nature and hierarchical nature of republican textuality—an arrangement that subjugated the reader to the author, colonizing the public to the interests of the elite.

Having gained access to the republic of letters, Constantia recognizes and concedes that her contributions as an author, on account of her gender, must be trivial and marginal. Contrasting her work with that of her male counterparts, she confesses: "had I been mistress of talents for an achievement so meritori-ous, my first object in writing would have been the information and improvement of my readers. . . . But vanity, in the most extravagant moments of her triumph, having never flattered me with the capability of conveying instruction to those, whose understandings have passed the age of adolescence, my view has been only to amuse; and if I can do this without offending, I shall be honoured with a place in the gentle bosom where I should else been unknown" (13). Given the extensive commentary on adult subjects in the subsequent eight-hundred pages, the hollowness of this confession is apparent: Constantia's and Murray's self-definitions as writers are very different. Whereas Constantia seems content with her place on the margin, Murray rejects it and reveals the hazardous situation of women like Constantia who concede the cultural center to men.

Near the end of the preface, Murray indirectly identifies her fictional narrators as characters in a more general narrative, a fact she openly concedes in the conclusion: "Having, in the concluding essay, given my reasons for assuming the masculine character, I have only further to observe, that those who admit the utility of conveying instruction and amusement by allegory or metaphor . . . will not object to the liberty I have taken" (14). This would be nonsensical were she not referring to the Gleaner as a character in a larger dramatization of the act of authorship, nodding to the careful reader that Vigillius will be manipulated like any other role in a fiction. Moreover, the difference between the Constantia who writes the preface and that who writes the conclusion, as I note below, is significant: the latter rejects the marginality embraced by the former. The intervening narrative prepares the reader for the disruptive conclusion by forcing the recognition of the tangible social value of women's contributions to the public sphere. Nonetheless, in the preface, while Constantia means to trivialize the masculine voice, Murray's deliberate smudging of the character's presence unsettles his introduction, implying a complexity casual readers would overlook.

In the first Gleaner essay, Vigillius (a male version Constantia) presents himself with the proper humility of a public man dabbling in authorship. From this point, the project of *The Gleaner* is underway: the initial fiction of compliance established, Murray may commence disruption. Jay Fliegelman observes that early republic authorship disowned creativity to "take refuge from the responsibility and visibility of authorship behind [English writers'] models" (174).[23] Given both his own and his wife's subsequent disparagement of how Americans rely too heavily upon borrowed cultural standards, Vigillius is established by his status in the public sphere, as well as his gender, before he starts writing: Murray is setting up the straw man of the conventional male author.

The first essay then ends the introduction of Murray's internal fiction of her book's authorship. The next ninety-eight essays, before the hundredth, in which Constantia returns, compose Vigillius's book. Like all miscellanies, it responds to events that occurred in the course of its composition and employs a sequence of genres and their appropriate languages. The one purported constant is Vigillius, who intends, like his English forefathers, to control and guide the creation of a text that will sate his "insatiable thirst for applause" (16). In Murray's hands, however, his calculated lack of consistency gradually destabilizes the entire text.

❧

Murray begins by setting *The Gleaner* in Vigillius's home. His ward, Margaretta, represents Murray's typical female reader, whose experience comes to serve as a model for the readers. Vigillius carefully introduces Margaretta first as a reader.

Reading through the *Massachusetts Magazine* looking for a poem from Morton, Margaretta stumbles upon the first Gleaner essay. This nod confirms women's readership of public documents, as well as their understanding of them, the first of Murray's seemingly accidental entries into debates over women's rights and skills.

Essay 3 opens by recalling Margaretta's readership but then diverges into a whimsical Franklinian discussion of punctuality. This, however, leads him to a discussion of the politics of his time. Unintentionally, he objects to the recolonizing effect of classicism in political discourse: "This fond predilection for, and preference of, the ancients is, in reality, altogether unaccountable" (33). Instead "an order of nobility is instituted, an order, to which all our worthies may pretend—the order of Virtue—which, in truth, is alone ennobling; and since the career being open to all, we may with democratical equity pursue the splendid prize" (36). Placed so close to the first essay and Constantia's dedication, which suggests a means to power other than merit, Vigillius has already strayed from obsequiousness into a more honest democratic self-conception. But he cannot maintain it. He soon becomes anecdotal and then, in essay 5, moralistic. At this point, he realizes that his short attention span compromises his authorship and wonders "whether it may not be well to account for [the Gleaner's] being induced to wander, in a field, where, the soil having been so often trod, he could expect to glean so little" (41). Implicitly, following the models offered by Addison and Swift have led this American writer to a dead end: staying the course means stagnation and repetition.

He starts again with an anecdote about how a young American doctor had proved superior to British ones during the Revolution. This doctor succeeds through his willingness to take chances and experiment with his discipline. Although Vigillius is not sure of what to do with this story ("what shall we say?"), Murray is: the doctor personifies a liberated and decolonized intellect. Unlike Vigillius, he represents hope through the purgation, not the continuation, of the leftover British practices used by the republicans for their own purposes. By recalling the anticolonialism of the Revolution, Murray reminds her reader of the legacy of antiauthoritarian thought and action that she found central to the difference between the new nation and England.

Not sure of the literary analogue to the doctor's genius, Vigillius begins to allow other voices to occupy space on his pages. All of the letters that interrupt the text, of course, like those that appear in Brackenridge's *Modern Chivalry*, represent fictional characters in Murray's internal narrative. The first calls for public funding of the arts, "providing for the establishment of real genius, whether it be found in the male or female world" (45). This voice, although male (Modestus Mildmay), seems to represent Murray's own, albeit momentarily. The proposed fund would encourage American writing to decolonize itself, until "a mute inglorious Milton would no more be found" (46). This new Milton, or, rather, these new Miltons, could be either male or female; Murray retains the gender-blind rhetoric of Revolution and rejects the colonizing aspects of female enclosure.

The need for such decolonization is made clear in essay 4, when the Gleaner overhears a discussion of American authors. The critics he hears, like most commentators on American writers at this time, uniformly disparage current conditions: "They summoned before their imperious tribunal, the candidates for fame, which, in this younger world, distinguish the present day: Trumbull, Barlow, Humphreys, Warren, Morton, Belknap, & &-these all passed before them; and as they seemed determined to set no bounds to their invidious censures" (47). The Gleaner himself becomes their next target, allowing Murray to reflect on the nature of public authorship. Murray's seemingly thoughtless inclusion of Warren and Morton observes the neglected presence of women writers. That is, Americans speaking casually accepted female authors; it was only the recolonizing elite that excluded them. This compels Vigillius to reconsider his ambition to join the republic of letters. Now out of things to say and skeptical of the only ways he had known in which to say them, Vigillius seems out of options.

The remainder of essay 6 provides a rescue for the text from an unlikely source. Readers write in and request to hear the whole story of Margaretta. These letters contain colloquialisms and show few signs of refinement, yet they seem more promising than the small-minded literary critics from the first part of the essay. They represent a curious and protean American public, still bearing the potential for decolonization and intellectual self-liberation. Bored and alienated by Vigillius's routine demonstration of his mastery of British forms of authorship, they want something more challenging, something less sermonizing and condescending. By allowing readers to join in the creation of the text, Murray and, significantly, Vigillius, deconstruct British authorship and open the text to more appropriate language and themes.

To his credit, Vigillius follows their advice and in essays 7 through 14 relates Margaretta's courtship and eventual engagement. Through this sequence, Vigillius's wife, Mary, becomes the dominant figure in the text. Her voice is contrasted to her husband's through his inclusion of her letters to Margaretta, and the clarity of her prose outweighs the comfortable paternalism of his.[24] The crucible for Margaretta's education involves the oldest of sentimental settings: courtship. Mary prepares her protégé for this trial through rigorous training in the liberal arts. The development of critical thought is privileged over the indoctrination of platitudes; Margaretta is taught how, not what, to think, and trained in self-reliance: "We are daily assuring her, that every thing in her future depends upon her own exertions" (63). Aware of his less liberal readership, Vigillius responds, "No, Mr. Pedant, she was not unfitted for her proper sphere; and your stomach, however critical it may be, never digested finer puddings" (61). While Vigillius concedes male domination, Mary (and Murray) mourn these domestic imbalances. In the end, Mary instructs Margaretta to marry a man who will not interfere with her intellectual autonomy and development.

Margaretta spends some time in New Haven, where she is courted by one Sinisterius Courtland, who attempts to seduce Margaretta with his mastery of language and allusion: he aspires to meet the stereotype of republican respectability, even claiming the authorship of a love poem written by a rival suitor. All the while, Vigillius and Mary know Courtland for what he is: a seducer. Instead of interfering, however, they trust in their ward's capacity for intelligent decision-making: "We well knew, that could *she herself* make the discovery we wished, such an event would operate more propitiously than any information, however important, which might be handed her from any other quarter" (75). Vigillius recognizes that guidance that disallows the participation of the guided is pointless: genuine growth is prevented and the subject only becomes alienated. Instead, he and Mary trust in Margaretta's intellect.

Acting on her own, not under the domineering rein of a patriarchal authority figure like so many other sentimental heroines, Margaretta discovers Courtland's deception and instead marries Edward Hamilton, a young minister. Throughout the episode, Mary's letters encourage Margaretta to exercise her capacity for decoding the words of others. Margaretta successfully avoids danger by seeing through the empty words of the seducer, just as Murray instructs her reader to challenge conventional texts.[25] By desentimentalizing the genre, Murray's novella disrupts expectation and implies that useful reading and writing need not follow established form.

Murray internalizes the colonizing role of didactic fiction that consolidates patriarchy by instructing young women to stay within emotional, intellectual, and political boundaries set by men. Didacticists make the reading experience appear conventional by employing the language and plot structure established by William Hill Brown in the States: a young woman choosing among potential husbands. All then identify heroines *not* as those who learn their place, as the genre demands, but rather as those capable of overcoming convention and developing skills traditionally denied women. Resisting colonialism, then, has to do with thinking independently, or, for women, resisting enclosure. In regard to Murray's framing narrative of Vigillius, this departure from convention inspires the previously complacent male writer to question a system that made men like Courtland attractive.

Vigillius, like the revolutionary doctor who ventured to expand his discipline, now openly "wanders" upon fields fruitless by the standards of British textuality. Destroying "all arrogant distinctions," he alights upon a democratic alternative, citing Paine as his model: "The avenues to the goal of wisdom, being more widely expanded, proficients of every description may throng her ample courts, and to every member of the mental *Commonwealth*, the road to literary honours may be alike open" (126). A mental commonwealth, as opposed to a republic of letters, becomes the quest of the remainder of *The Gleaner*. Such a commonwealth would necessarily be more improvised, heterogeneous, and mobile and would, therefore, openly acknowledge the complexities of Second World experience. This sequence also reveals Vigillius as a character. However, although he is a character, Vigillius still purportedly represents a stable authority figure within the book. Subsequent developments undercut not only the prestige of authorship but also the stability of his authority.

Vigillius soon recognizes that the largest obstacle preventing the realization of the mental commonwealth, both political and textual, is the exclusion of women. While his own home is a commonwealth of intelligence both male and female, most Americans were not so lucky. Throughout the middle essays of *The Gleaner*, Murray discusses both the marginalized condition of women in America and republicanism's more general divisiveness, a topic also discussed by Charles Brockden Brown in *Alcuin* (1797). This discussion begins with Vigillius's evolving views on female education, that eventually result in Mary's manifesto on the necessity of female autonomy and empowerment.

Recalling the trap that almost ensnared Margaretta, Vigillius embarks on a sequence of commentaries on how republicanism has balkanized American society. In reference to elitism, he observes: "Prejudices so absurd are particularly ludicrous in a government, the genius of which is, to cultivate as great a degree of equality as will exist within the requisite order and well being of the Commonwealth; and yet, strange to tell, perhaps there is no part of the world, where these unnatural distinctions, so humiliating to the mechanic, and so elevating to the *suppositious* gentleman, or exist more forcibly, than in some of these American States" (134). Later in this same essay, he recognizes that social elitism particularly victimizes women: "An old maid [American children] are from infancy taught, at least indirectly, to consider as a contemptible being; and [women] have no means of advancing themselves except in the matrimonial line" (139). Vigillius argues then that the exclusion of women is representative primarily of a larger exclusion of other groups from social meaning. Essays 26 and 27 particularly expound this idea, reminding the readers of the democratic foundation of the Revolution and the Constitution. He particularly attacks party politics and factionalism as forcing Americans to choose between English and French allegiances. Implicitly, Murray recognizes that allegiance to either compromises autonomy and recolonizes American goals to foreign interests.

By having Vigillius come around to this view, Murray has initiated dissident political commentary from a female perspective, demanding the expansion of the limited choices available in the constrictive public sphere. Through this sequence, Vigillius shows signs of the same inconsistencies that almost made him stop writing after four essays. In essay 32, he interrupts his political commentaries to rhapsodize on the beauties of winter. In it, he demonstrates a striking, but normally suppressed, artistic sensibility, revealing the covert worth of another excluded mode of authorship. This interruption complete, Vigillius returns to what he considers to be more important subjects and is flattered to respond when a reader asks about his religion.

The erratic and stuttering nature of this section demonstrates the transitional nature of Vigillius through this part of Murray's book. Without an English or French model, Vigillius seems lost, and his paradoxical behavior mirrors that of the republican fathers who would also reject colonial patriarchy while reinscribing their own. Vigillius is intimidated by the entangled complexities of his compromised and bifurcated identity in the Second World. While he cannot and would not wholly disavow his English cultural origins, he recognizes its ability to corrupt and preclude the exploration and development of more appropriate local self-definitions and identities.

Again, his readers rescue him by reining in his inflated pretensions in essay 34 and by personifying the less inhibited linguistic freedom he fears. Corrected, he returns to the subject of female education. This time he recognizes that reactionary imitation is the sign of an untutored intellect and that the American nation deserves better: "National attachment should, therefore, dictate the studious cultivation of a national language" (296). But Vigillius can only observe the ideals he espouses: a product of the republic, he cannot realize them, and writes in narrow Addisonian tones. Murray, excluded by gender, is free to explore that natural and perhaps national tongue as it grows away from its British origin. The accumulating and irregular letters that interrupt the Gleaner represent still more alternatives to Vigillius's colonial mode of authorship and articulation. Like Brackenridge's *Modern Chivalry*, Murray's book has become multivocal and polyphonic, with the voice of the conventional author among the least interesting.

Essay 34 was the last number to appear in the *Massachusetts Magazine*. Freed from deadlines and the limitations of serial publication, Murray's own text becomes increasingly diverse and complex. Primarily, the emergence of female voices forces Vigillius to share the podium of authorship, formally embodying a more inclusive cultural milieu. However, these transitions do not disrupt the book's unity; rather they allow Murray to make Vigillius and Mary's story even more central.

With Vigillius increasingly unsure of his role as author, in essay 43, at the request of a fictional female reader, he hands the series over to Mary. Mary presumably writes a series of letters to Margaretta on the history of gender issues, focusing on the suppressed and foreshortened contributions of women to civilization. In total, more than half of the second part of *The Gleaner* is monopolized by women's voices. While Vigillius is still present, he is increasingly marginal in his own book. Moreover, when he does venture forth, his focus is now almost entirely related to women's rights.

The dialogue between Mary and Margaretta begins with a literary discussion about a novel read each had read. Margaretta asks for Mary's interpretation and the discussion grows into a larger extrapolation of the surrounding embedded issues of sexual politics. In essay 44, she outlines her plan of subjects in an organized and sequential fashion toward the end of celebrating women's heroism through the ages (364–65). After forty essays from the male Gleaner, however, even the most conservative reader most likely trusted Vigillius's whimsical guidance and would not question his inclusion of his wife's letters, so long as their publication occurs within his general authorship.

The next ten letters represent Murray's most obvious appearance in the text. In them, Vigillius's self-consciousness falls away and a powerful voice emerges. Mary begins by summarizing and commenting upon Plutarch and moves into a discussion of Alfred the Great, leading up to the figure of Mary, Queen of Scots. At this point, she introduces Dido, the Carthaginian queen, as a missing member of the canon of revered historical models. She specifically blames the sexist historiography of Virgil for excluding her from significance: "She is precipitated from the sublime height upon which her achievements and her merit hath placed her, and described in an immortal poem, which hath been, and will be read by thousands who never look into history, as a lascivious wanton!" (387). Mary's (and Murray's) critique of the gendered canon is done with the intent of making her early republic readers understand the biased nature of male-dominated society and the emptiness of its claims to objectivity. Control of the past and control of the text then become control of the present. Mary's taking over her husband's book represents, then, a dual moment in historical decolonization and feminist revisionism.

The subsequent history of Mary Stuart dramatizes the processes by which the same means of misrepresentation and deception victimized and silenced not just a valuable woman but a valuable *person* whose potential contributions to civilization were suppressed and plotted against. In contrast, the villain of the narrative is Elizabeth Tudor. Elizabeth's treachery is based in "unsexual" behavior (406). That is, women who merely emulate men contribute nothing original and, in fact, make it worse for more daring women; they merely perpetuate the cruelty and exclusivity of the male world. Next, Mary Vigillius moves on to male leaders who represent the type of inclusive leadership she would seek in America. This sequence concludes with a discussion of William Penn and centers around his humane treatment of "American aborigines" (443). Mary's history lesson ceases abruptly in essay 53 when Vigillius reappears and apologizes for remaining absent for too long. But the damage has been done: Mary's voice has become the more important, and the reader can only be sorry to see her depart.

Murray's female readers at this point are shown that their participation in debates on issues of culture and history is not only permissible but required. Silence is not only inappropriate but also unpatriotic. Mary's eloquence displays a comprehensive education and courageous original thought. Her model of achievement and authorship dramatizes the powerful discourse occurring within the hidden "women's sphere" of the early republic. The enclosure of Mary's discourse in domestic correspondence reminds the reader of women's absence from American public life. Murray's employment of the fiction of authorship allows their concealed entry into the republic of letters, demonstrating the absurdity of its exclusionary ideology.

Nonetheless, Murray is aware that Mary's achievements, no matter how great and regardless of their power to move American readers, will be forever lost, like Mary Stuart's, without the transformation of the male-dominated public sphere. Once activated, American women faced another obstacle: American men. Murray's conception of the "new man" of the 1790s is suggested by the return of a chastened Vigillius.

The Gleaner who returns seems aware of how his wife had raised the stakes of the discussion. Mary has broached the issue of how republican culture misrepresents and shapes the truth for its own ends. Like so many other fictional authors in this study, Vigillius is now compelled to question the rules and assumptions that governed his authorship at its initiation and does so in and around essays 57, 69, and 94. The power of Mary's interruption thus effects both Vigillius and reader, opening the path for Murray to extend her critique of the society that had dictated the now inadequate means of reading and writing to which the Gleaner and the reader had initially covenanted within the republic of letters.

In essay 57 he responds to an apparent accusation of plagiarism. He ends by reflecting on the self-referential world of publication and distribution he had entered and by recognizing how a lack of experimental or alternative ideas necessarily leads to accidental repetition. Later, in essay 60, he comments on the nature of derivative customs in America: "It is a common practice to arraign the despotism of custom; and, lovers of liberty, we revolt from every thing which would begirt us with the lines of necessity" (483). To evaluate specific customs, including those of his own authorship, he now adopts Mary's critical method, questioning accepted norms and venturing dissident opinions. Hereafter much more open to suggestion and less compelled by convention, Vigillius experiments with an authorship representative of an inclusive mental commonwealth.

As his voice more and more resembles Mary's, the lines of gender distinction blur. But that is Murray's point: intelligence and compassion, while traditionally gendered traits, are now available to all. She means the reader to perceive the fallacy of their division and the potential for all Americans—male and female—to achieve both. Readers "of every description" are encouraged to "store [the] mind with ideas, to invigorate the intellectual powers, and to habituate [themselves] to reasoning, comparing, investigating and concluding." Neglecting to do so has "defrauded society of that assistance which mankind hath a right to reckon on from [their] abilities" (499). Murray's challenge is to readers of both genders: their ignorance is only a symptom of a more general colonial self-limitation. Central to the process of decolonization, then, is an opening of the order that perpetuated colonizing hierarchies such as sexism.

The theme of challenging texts and authors continues in Murray's inclusion of her two plays in *The Gleaner*. These are introduced in essay 69 where Murray, through Vigillius, reintroduces the subject of national literature. Holding up Morton's Philenia as a model, Murray, through the reformed Vigillius, establishes a model of "American literary genius." Morton, however, is identified as an exception. Other American writers are anonymously derided for too narrowly following British models. To discredit their decentering of American subjects and language, she applies a critical reading to their models—Homer, Addison, Pope, and Reynal—and finds them all antithetical to the unencumbered exchange of reliable information and insights.

Vigillius is aware of his deviance from expected norms: he suggests that he may "stand accused of incoherence." His goal, however, is no longer the closed, resolved textuality of republican prose but rather a place in the mental commonwealth, and he asks only that the readers "open the votaries of genius" (543). Murray here indicts the republic of letters for its slavish perpetuation of inherited colonial marginality and challenges her readers to explore national difference. Perhaps Murray's personal experience in the republic of letters impelled this condemnation of it as well: the critical rejection of her plays in 1795.[26] Trusting in the reader's becoming open-minded, Murray includes her two plays, "Virtue Triumphant" (essays 70 through 75) and "The Traveller Returned" (essays 80 through 84). Like Mary's letters, they allow Vigillius to escape from the possibility of authorial impropriety and allow Murray to introduce a female alternative to the male voice of Vigillius. In the fiction of authorship, another male voice, "Philo Americanus," asks the Gleaner to include these plays in his miscellany. Doubly authorized then by male editorship, the plays enter the text.

Even with such protection, drama was a controversial genre in the early republic: without the stability of the printed page or the pulpit, the stage was difficult to restrain and was thus viewed as dangerous in the republic of letters. Mary Anne Schofield's discussion of Murray's plays recalls Vigillius's abstract defense of the stage in essay 24.[27] Vigillius admits that drama might have a negative influence on the uncritical consciousness. But between essays 24 and 70 a more skeptical mode of readership has been defended, demonstrated, and actualized as the reader sorted through the shifting voices. The plays themselves mirror the internal drama of *The Gleaner*: "Male perception is inaccurate throughout, and the women take it upon themselves to educate the male properly" (Schofield, 266).

By now Vigillius sees nothing amiss in this inversion of the usual gender politics: Mary had already instructed both Vigillius and the readers. Murray's goal, then, has been the activation of readers, compelling them to decolonize their reading positions: the texts themselves are not dangerous—uncritical readers are.[28] At this point, Murray is making unusual demands on her reader. However, these demands—the shifting genres, the fleeting voices—make the reader work harder to discern the course of the narrative: when Vigillius steps offstage, both text and reader are compelled to seek new means of literary exchange.

In essay 87 Murray, with whom Vigillius can now be almost identified, demands that gender-blind open-mindedness must be part of American difference: "Be neither Englishmen nor Frenchmen—be Americans" (701). In essay 88 she reconnects this sentiment to women's equality in public affairs. She recalls the abandoned promises of post-Revolutionary equity and harangues the forces enclosing women: "I may be accused of enthusiasm; but such is my confidence in THE SEX, that I expect to see our young women forming a new era in female history. They will oppose themselves to every trivial and unworthy monopolizer of time. The noble expansion conferred by a liberal education will teach them humility; for it will give them a glance at those vast tracts of knowledge which they can never explore, until they are accommodated with far other powers than those at present assigned to them" (703). Now quoting Mary Wollstonecraft instead of Addison, Vigillius's transformation is complete, and the remainder of essays 88 and 89 through 91 consist of his rephrasing of his wife's message of the sexist imbalance of British cultural institutions.

All that is left for Vigillius to do is apply his now-decolonized intellect to the subject of authorship, as he does essay 91. Appropriately, correction comes from the women's sphere, "a circle of ladies in the next room" who criticize the reactionary privileging of things foreign (762). Using the example of Mercy Otis Warren, Murray distinguishes American themes from English ones. The inclusion of Warren as a representative American writer, despite her gender, represents the mental commonwealth: the more inclusive alternative to the republic of letters in which both sexes are equally represented and welcome.

Murray concludes Vigillius's authorship with another barrage of letters from American readers (essays 93 through 99). Again, they are unpolished and awkward, but they are rigorous and lively, and therefore merit a place in American publications. In fact, through the use of dialect and local color, Murray seems fifty years ahead of her time, foreshadowing James Russell Lowell and others who employed nonstandard dialects to demonstrate the diversity of American life. Their final displacement of the former republican of letters symbolizes Murray's rupture of the closed textuality of republican modes and her initiation of a more democratic and egalitarian relationship between reader and writer.

In the last number of *The Gleaner*, Constantia reappears. This time she identifies herself as the same Constantia who had filled "some pages" of the *Boston Magazine* during the 1780s, a figure acknowledged to be Murray. By coming forth as herself to the readers of her book, Murray's disruptive text is completed. In language far more direct than Vigillius's, and with the frankness and forthrightness of Mary, Murray comments on the gender politics of the republic of letters: "Observing, in a variety of instances, the indifference, not to say contempt, with which female productions are regarded, and seeking to arrest attention, at least for a time, I was thus furnished with a very powerful motive for an assumption, which I flattered myself would prove favourable to my aspiring wishes. I anticipate on this occasion, the significant shrug and expressive smile of the *pedantic petit-maitres*; . . . and it will be affirmed, that the effeminacy and tinsel glitter of my style could not fail of betraying me at every sentence which I uttered" (804). Her contempt for the "*petit-maitres*" of the republic of letters is here stated directly. After belittling their hypocrisy, she comments on her intent and method: "Having conceived, that in my borrowed character I should become abundantly more useful, I felt assured that this consideration was in reality sufficient to justify this measure" (804). Since her stated intent is to disrupt—"to arrest attention"—her goal can only be revealing the torpidity of the recolonized American public sphere.

Subsequently, Murray notes that her disguise was so successful as to fool her husband for over three years. Clearly the unmasking would redouble the text's already disruptive impact. Later she reveals that she has written a unified text, not a miscellany: "If the manner in which my dramatic essays are introduced, should require an apology, it may be sufficient to observe that it was requisite to the uniformity of my plan" (807). The book itself, then, resists generic categorization, at least according to any genre established in England or republican America. Instead the text is organic, the genuine product of a decolonized American pen. In one important moment, she reveals the ultimate goal of her fiction of authorship. Not surprisingly, it relates to gender: "I was ambitious of being considered *independent as a writer*; if I possessed merit, I was solicitous that it remain undiminished. . . . Rousseau has said, that although a female may ostensibly wield the pen, yet it is certain some man of letters sits behind the curtain to guide its movements" (805).

✤

Murray's demand for independence as a writer culminates her efforts at double decolonization. First, her declaration of autonomy reflects her suggestion that Americans are never truly independent until they have understood the need to purge the unoriginal textuality that had subjected their interests to British needs and republican power structures. Second, she means to free women from the domestic imprisonment imposed on them on both systemic and personal levels to explore their own value in a democratic society. In both instances, Mary Vigillius serves as the new hero/author ready to supplant men like her husband as authority figures in the early republic just as she had in the book.

By abrogating notions of authorial convention, Murray's medium becomes her message: only by compelling readers to sift through a protean assemblage of authorial voices can she disabuse them of their self-destructive and compulsive quest for English-style authority figures. Her manipulation of the British genre of the miscellany demonstrates an alternative American textuality as inclusive and broad-minded as the society Mary demands. The book Murray created embraces a plurality of voices and formats within a unified whole, serving as a model for the truly decolonized and democratized American community republicanism suppressed, clearing the way for otherwise marginalized writers like Morton and Warren.

Murray was, then, as much anticolonialist democrat as feminist: by her reckoning, feminism, or even gender equality, was impossible without democracy. Republicanism thus becomes an ideology of exclusion, robbing the new nation of both its genius and the valuable potential contributions of the silenced. By giving space on the page to the otherwise marginalized, *The Gleaner* embodies the joyous plurality of American life. By creating the failed authorship of a presumably exclusionary text, Murray calls for a more general questioning of the forces that were constricting the public sphere in the early republic.

Her efforts at pluralizing American life extended beyond her career as a writer. In 1785 Murray wrote to her brother about her recent frustrations in finding a job for a young friend: "I expatiated upon the capacity of the Boy, for the business for which he was proposed, with many etceteras—But these kind of people are very obstinate, and very ignorant as well as very proud—To all I could urge, a single objection was, in their opinion, sufficient—He was a *Negro*" (95). In the ideal meritocracy, or in any public sphere truly governed by reason, all that should matter is "capacity." However, just as gender limited Mary to a domestic role, here race limits this young man to destitution. Murray's opinion of the range of American diversity relates to all forms of exclusion. Her demand for decolonization has to do with race, gender, and any other means of stratification and exclusion.

Like Brackenridge, Murray wrote an enormous and layered book, even by eighteenth-century standards, that comes to embody, in its very bulk the diversity of its subject. Both create a reading experience that is diverse, inconsistent, self-contradicting, and, most importantly, demanding of innovative and open-minded reading. *The Gleaner* remains a more coherent text than *Modern Chivalry*. More than in *Modern Chivalry*, and perhaps more than any other in the writing of the early republic, Murray's character Mary provides the decolonized alternative to the fictional authors of the male writers. Her ability to transcend the republic of letters is something they cannot do. However, Mary's enclosure in her husband's book reveals that Murray was aware of the logocracy's dominance, even as she attacked it.

After writing *The Gleaner*, Murray largely faded into obscurity and poverty before dying on her son-in-law's Mississippi plantation in 1820. Perhaps her disappearance from the American public sphere represents the larger enclosure of American women into the separate sphere identified by Kerber and Cott. Murray attempted to forestall or combat the removal of women from American public life by proving their worth in any society that claims a foundation in equality and participation. Her recognition of republicanism's inherent reinscription of patriarchal social institutions participates in a particular pattern of decolonizing dissidence in the early republic in regard to both culture and gender.

THREE

Royall Tyler's *The Algerine Captive* and the Worthy Federal Citizen

By EMPLOYING THE Algerine Crisis as the backdrop for a satire of conventional constructions of national identity, Royall Tyler's *The Algerine Captive* critiques American texts of the 1790s that allowed American readers and writers to retreat behind derivative notions of identity—both personal and national—that discouraged more exploratory thinking and acting. More in a textual than a political context, this crisis revealed the new nation's willingness to attach itself to European culture rather than examining its own post-Revolutionary complexities or interrogating its diverse and divergent condition for signs that the homogeneity and stability required of European nation-states was missing in the United States.

From the early 1780s through 1815, the United States faced its first international challenge to prove that it could defend its interests abroad and do so in a way consistent with the democratic and antiauthoritarian values it claimed to embrace. When, following the Revolution, American ships in the Mediterranean ceased to be protected by the British navy, they became prey to pirates of the states of Algiers, Morocco, Tripoli, and Tunis. Most European nations made treaties with the pirates, usually involving some form of tribute.[1] In 1791, when this issue first reached Congress, reaction was divided, as were many conflicts during this period, strictly along party lines: the Antifederalists favored the construction of a national navy; the Federalists favored the kind of negotiation followed by European governments.

Neither represented an alternative to an established mode of response formulated in Europe. The debate was complicated in 1794, when the nascent navy was destroyed and the British made a more generous treaty with the Algerians—a treaty so conciliatory that the pirates were allowed to expand their raids beyond the Mediterranean.[2] The poet and diplomat David Humphreys finally negotiated a treaty for the United States not unlike that of the British. Thereafter, the Americans, like the Europeans, paid the demanded tribute, and the United States was merely added to the list of nations that complied with the age's standard diplomatic practice.

More important, as far as Tyler is concerned, is the cottage industry of texts published in response to the crisis. Books were published whose intent was to educate the American public about the Algerians in such a way that the government's response to the crisis seemed the only possible solution. Mathew Carey published *A Short Account of Algiers*; James Leach *A New and Easy Plan to Redeem the American Captives in Algiers*; Susanna Rowson *Slaves in Algiers*; and finally an anonymous poem called "The American in Algiers; or, The Patriot of Seventy-Six in Captivity."[3] In plays, polemics, sermons, and other forms of public speech, Americans were convinced that a policy that copied that of England was in the nation's best interest. Despite their acquiescence in extortion, the republicans still bathed their response in patriotic rhetoric. Fisher Ames, in fact, demonstrated the publicly endorsed viewpoint by claiming that the British settlement "was not less favorable for us as we could make it, if we could legislate for both sides of the Atlantic" (qtd. in Ritcheson, 296).[4] With such statements, American policy was equated with that of the British and was an accomplishment held up as a sign of legitimacy—as if the only possible standard of nationhood was that of the British. Ames here reflects the republicans' need to stabilize post-Revolutionary society through an attempted recolonization of the unpredictable public. This Anglocentric response reflects the drive of the republicans to model the new nation as a new, improved England rather than as something new.

In the 1790s American politics and society were increasingly anglicized in texts that villainized the Jacobin excesses of the French Revolution; even such traditionally pro-French Antifederalists as Jefferson had withdrawn their support of the revolutionaries by the middle of the decade.[5] Siding with the vanquished aristocracy in the French Revolution shifted America's overseas image from revolutionary firebrand to predictable role-player—as if to say, the new nation is happy conforming to the policy of its parents and is unlikely to start trouble by extending its erstwhile egalitarian domestic rhetoric overseas.

Moreover, these texts acquiesce in the European exoticizing of the pirates as Oriental Other. While the Federalists had no choice but to sign the treaty and so resolve the issue on a political level, on a textual level, the Algerine crisis brought a number of leftover colonial prejudices and imperialist rhetoric to the surface: the accompanying publications reinscribed the racism and elitism of European phraseology. In *The Algerine Captive*, Tyler confronted the (mis)labeling of the Islamic North African as Other by drawing Algeria as oddly similar to the United States in order to compel Americans to reconsider, first, their own assignment as First World imperialist and, second, their inheritance of the racist rhetoric of the colonial era.

By discussing to the Algerian crisis in European terms, the conventional texts embodied republicanism's zeal for remaking America as a nation only by European standards. John C. Miller has noted their aspirations: "the Federalists' objective was to mold the United States in accord with their vision of an established order securely protected against demagogues and democratic majorities. This vision took the form of a highly aristocratic, class-conscious society in which gentlemen knew their privileges and the lower orders knew their place" (117). Miller goes on to note that a constitution composed in 1800 "would have born little resemblance" to that the one written in 1787 (118). Therefore, the republican texts which responded to this crisis serves as a useful demonstration of how the republicanism became "an ideology of social stratification" (478) in the terms of Gordon Wood in the *Creation of the American Republic* during the course of the 1790s. Republicanism, then, sought to establish the United States as a part of the First World, foregrounding its proofs of international legitimacy and occluding the more complex struggles over identity that complicated it in ways resembling Second World communities.

The republican transformation of American society and the Algerine crisis are connected in a way that reveals the intertextuality of early republic political and literary discourses. Two of the principal diplomats during the crisis were David Humphreys and Joel Barlow. During the 1780s both had been Connecticut Wits, a group of young patrician writers set on mythologizing America in the images and language of Augustan couplets. In regard to both poetry and politics, each sought to define his nation not by what should or could be done in a revolutionary continuum but rather by doing what was done in England. Lacking any farsighted vision, the policies of both favored a definition of America as clone of England, trading revolution for superficial independence and never decentering British culture from its place at the center of the new nation's public sphere. Instead of acknowledging the complicated place of the United States, split between its European roots and its rejection by England in the decades before the Revolution, these policies and poetics opted to ignore the paradoxes and embraced only one-half of this bifurcated identity. Tyler, on the other hand, identifies and satirizes the resulting absurdities this caused in American public life.[6]

❧

Tyler's fictional author of *The Algerine Captive; or, The Life and Adventures of Doctor Updike Underhill, Six Years a Prisoner among the Algerines* (1797), Updike Underhill, dedicates his work to Humphreys and boasts that his book is "founded on FACT" (xiii). Tyler, previously a Federalist poet, lawyer, essayist, and playwright, like Humphreys and Barlow, had achieved a reputation for respectability and patriotism.[7] This text, however, demonstrates Tyler's disillusionment with republicanism's continued veneration of British modes of thought and language. He seems aware of the growing plurality of British discourse in ways republicans were not. It should be noted, then, that his attack is not on British textuality per se but rather on how republicans attempted to protect those versions of British writing suited to their purpose of legitmizing the nation. Perhaps their ex-colonial insecurity caused them to seek in British culture a stable, but chimerical, model to which they could aspire.

Moreover, by deftly interweaving the device of the "oriental letter"—a genre dating back to Montesquieu's *Persian Letters* (1721) and used in the United States by Henry Sherburne in *The Oriental Philosopher* (1800) and Washington Irving in *Salmagundi* (1807–8)—with the captivity narrative, Tyler accomplishes a sophisticated generic experiment. Like *Modern Chivalry* and *The Gleaner, The Algerine Captive* appropriates, refutes, and then recombines conventional literary forms into something more original and innovative than the more conventional texts he had written earlier in his own career.[8] The new, slippery, and hybridized text, then, represents on a stylistic level the type of Second World risk-taking originality Tyler identifies as missing from too much post-Revolutionary thought and language.

The fictional Updike writes for very personal reasons: to produce a text whose acceptance will enable him to enter the nation's semiaristocratic republican power structure. That this structure exists Tyler assumes as a given. The text itself is presumably Updike's autobiography, written upon his reentry into the public life of the early republic. He traces his Puritan ancestry, rural childhood, classical education, and subsequent adventures outside of the States. Most of the text, therefore, has little to do with his advertised title; instead, it allows him to show that his training was based on the finest of European thought and tradition. Updike is thus positioned as a colonial: anxious about pleasing the standards of the metropolis and unwilling to explore local difference.

However, Tyler soon establishes that his intent is to satirize, not celebrate, the cultural icons Updike, ever the colonial, would embrace. From the start, Updike frames his life in a world of texts, forever unable to unshackle himself from colonial master narratives. After immersing his birth in the colonizing history of his Puritan ancestor, Captain John Underhill, Updike depicts a childhood any reader would recognize as ridiculous. He is taught the classics, reads them literally, and becomes wholly unfitted to be a farmer. He embarks on a medical career only to become mired in the everyday life in the early republic. His professional and textual options in America exhausted, Updike enlists as a ship's physician on a slave ship, from which he is captured and sold into slavery in North Africa. After six years, he is ransomed by the diplomat-poets and returns to the United States to continue a career he had never started. Then, most importantly, he begins his career as author with a text that aspires to every level of social acceptance.

By all appearances, *The Algerine Captive*, published anonymously, seems to be a travel adventure of an American among the Algerines. However, the subtitle—"Life and Adventures"—recalls the picaresque novel: both terms, in tandem or singly, had been used to present the doings of such picaros as Don Quixote, Tom Jones, Humphry Clinker, and, on the American side, Jonathan Corncob and Thomas Atwood Digges's Alonso—a tactic aimed at securing high sales while not upsetting the demand for objective narrative.[9] While *Modern Chivalry* pretended not to be a picaresque but actually is, *The Algerine Captive* pretends to be a picaresque but is not: it is a character study of the shortsightedness of the typical American embracing the colonial mentality both as a person and as an author.

It also marks Updike as a *character*, blurring the lines between author, reader, and narrator that provided the superstructure for the transmission of readerly submission in the republic of letters.[10] Updike immediately pays tribute to

Humphreys and to the popular English tradition of "Life and Adventures," reflecting his hope, upon his return from captivity, to be a "worthy FEDERAL citizen" (2:228) in the book's much-discussed final passage. During the late 1790s Tyler dissociated himself from party politics, a move that suggests his recognition that the new nation had abandoned the earlier ideals that had characterized the Revolutionary and constitutional periods, threatening the integrity of the democratic process by too rigidly importing its means of self-discussion.[11] Tyler creates Updike not as an idealized American but as a typical American who, duped by the discourse of the early republic, conforms to both its politics and literary rhetoric.

Earlier criticism of *The Algerine Captive* has established the book's socially dissident activity. Cathy N. Davidson, for example, claims that in *The Algerine Captive* "the 'unwary reader' is warned that official history, like official dictates, is mostly an expression of the scotomas and the stigmatisms of the official vision of the time" (201–2). All recognize Tyler's mistrust of "official" documents and their rhetoric.[12] Unlike Davidson, John Engell rejects both the fact and the promise of the final passage in which Updike, though not Tyler, celebrates the enlightened potential of the self-proclaimed "worthy FEDERAL citizen." Engell concludes that "Updike is the consummate gull . . . one of the greatest gulls in American literature" and that if all Americans were like him, "the country would quickly descend into slavery" (31), or, in my terms, colonial subjugation. By denying that Tyler removes the veil between himself and his fictional author, Engell suggests that Updike demonstrates an unflagging incapacity for intellectual growth.

I would extend this concept to suggest that his authorial acquiescence represents the deeply colonized nature of Updike's intellect. Tyler recognizes the Janus-faced nature of colonial thinking in the Second World early republic: as a standard author, Updike endeavors to control both the reader and the Algerines. Updike can think of no terms other than those of manipulation and hierarchy. To reveal the paradoxes and self-destructive nature of colonial thinking—to decolonize his audience—Tyler internalizes the colonizing function of republican literary exchange and disrupts its subjugation of the reader and elevation of the author by having Updike fail badly at both. In their place, Tyler asks for the initiation of the type of genuine introspection from which Updike consistently retreats.

An examination of how Updike writes and presents his book to the public reveals more about the "FEDERAL citizen" than about the same character before his announced change. A closer examination of the story of how Updike wrote his narrative and meant to present it to the public—Tyler's fiction of authorship—will show the book to be a concealed narrative of rhetorical retreats from formal resolution that develop through the abandonment of a succession of literary forms. If nothing else holds the book together, it is this. The pattern of repeated flight mirrors Underhill's constant retreat from the ambiguities of decolonized freedom. Updike's fear of originality is present in all three of the book's essential elements: the prefatory materials and its two volumes.

❧

The prefatory materials—title page, dedication, and preface—not only begin the separation of Updike from Tyler; they also suggest Tyler's belief in the incapacity of European techniques to express American subjects. Updike demonstrates a consistent trust that the framing of his life in recognizable forms will automatically reveal it as a model for others to follow. Updike's consistent feeblemindedness, however, implies just the reverse: that it is possible to master literature and be a fool. Updike's frequent allusions to prominent literary figures and conventions betray a concealed commentary on the relevance of the literary canon and orthodox syntax to a recurring topic in the early republic: the creation of an American literature and language that would reflect and express national ideals and potentials.

Like most books of its time, *The Algerine Captive* had an ornate title page. A quotation from the literary canon introduces the text by at once framing the new book in a familiar context. Updike chooses a selection from Shakespeare: "By your patience / I will a round unvarnished tale deliver / Of my whole course" (1:i). While Updike alludes to the objectified textuality of British tradition by assuming that any tale can be "unvarnished," Tyler makes certain that throughout *The Algerine Captive* histories are portrayed as fictions. Nor is it "whole," since Updike ends scenes before their inevitable ambiguities overwhelm his limited and derivative interpretive or authorial skills.

This pattern of ironic allusion continues in the dedication. Updike dedicates his book to "David Humphreys, Esq. Minister of the United States at the Court of Lisbon, &c." (1:iii). Humphreys, in 1797, was American ambassador to Portugal, where many of the negotiations with the Algerines occurred. Updike continues by distinguishing what he sees as an American form of dedication from the European practice of patronage:

> In Europe, dedications have their place; and the author oftener looks to the plenitude of pockets, than the brains of his patron. The American author can hope but little pecuniary emolument from even the sale, and not any from the dedication of his work. To adorn his book with the name of some gentleman of acknowledged merit involves his whole interest. With this view will you, sir, permit a lover of the Muses, and a biographer of private life, to address to you (a poet and the biographer of a hero) a detail of those miseries of slavery, from which your public energies have principally conduced to liberate hundreds of our fellow citizens. (1:iii–iv)

Updike here demonstrates the public conflation of republican poetics and policy. This passage, presumably written at the conclusion of his adventures and self-proclaimed maturation, foreshadows a prominent irony. Updike's reference to "the miseries of slavery" makes no specific mention of Algeria. In fact, the most appalling slavery described is the American enslavement of Africans, while Updike's own miseries seem luxuriant in comparison. Tyler seems to be alluding to American slavery, an industry well protected by the treaty. This dedication, coupled with his concluding wish to become a "FEDERAL citizen," becomes a veiled request for social advancement. Raised far from the cities, Updike also seems to be attempting to use his hoped-for literary reputation as a means of social advancement.

The preface has always been read as Tyler's own statement, since its narrator refers to Updike in the third person. Given Tyler's layered text, such an association may be too hasty. The figure who writes the preface is complex and paradoxical throughout. He begins by discussing developments in American reading habits over the six years of Updike's captivity and continues to celebrate the widespread literacy of the early republic. Next, he points to the misuse of unguided literacy throughout the public: "The worthy farmer no longer fatigued himself with Bunyan's Pilgrim up the 'hill of difficulty' or through the 'slough of despond,' but quaffed wine with Brydone in the hermitage of Vesuvius, or sported with Bruce on the fairyland of Abyssinia: while Dolly the dairy maid, and Jonathan the hired man, threw aside the ballad of the cruel step mother, over which they had so often wept in concert, and now amused themselves into so agreeable a terror with the haunted houses and hobgoblins of Mrs. Ratcliffe, that they were both afraid to sleep alone" (1:vii–ix). The narrator conflates novel reading and sexual immorality, a common practice in the republican paradigm.[13] This passage allows Tyler to dramatize how such a conventional text was meant to be read: the fictional but authorized narrator would bully Dolly and Jonathan into an act of reading that is presumably rational at the same moment that he discredits more emotional responses. Reading thus becomes a performance of colonization, not creation: subjectivity is erased, and the reader is compelled to live in the world dominated by those of more sober concerns, such as Updike.

When the narrator of the preface means to teach Dolly and Jonathan more socially acceptable choices and methods for their reading, his first observation on fiction concerns not its substance but rather its nationality: "The first is, that, while so many books are vended, they are not of our own manufacture. If our wives and daughters will wear gauze and ribbands, it is a pity they are not wrought in our own looms" (1:x). Objecting not to "gauze and ribbands," the narrator suggests instead that if American morals are to be corrupted, the corruption should at least benefit American commercial publishing interests. His next objection is that novels glamorize British life: "The second misfortune is, that novels, being the picture of the times, the New England reader is insensibly taught to admire the levity, and very often the vices, of the parent country. While the fancy is enchanted, the heart is corrupted. . . . It paints the manners, customs, and habits, of a strange country; excites a fondness for false splendor; and renders the homespun habits of her own country disgusting" (1:xi). This refers to tracts that condemned fiction for these same reasons: Samuel Miller, Lord Kames, and Hugh Blair condemned fiction in these terms.[14] If *The Algerine Captive* discussed these "homespun habits" in a wholesome way, we might hear Tyler's voice in the preface. But since Updike's narrative often portrays "homespun habits" as small-minded and inane, the preface's author is a separate character; and although this writer thinks he is nationalizing the reader, he is instead merely substituting one form of dominion for another.

In the final pages of the preface, yet another voice is introduced. This "friend," like Updike and the first narrator, shares in their deluded interpretation of the inverted function of Updike's text. Nonetheless, his commentary veils Tyler's ironic inversion of those expectations. This friend says that Updike's story will "exhibit our own manners" (1:xii). Updike, encouraged by the friend, will deliver those manners not as a celebration of "homespun habits" but rather as Tyler's satire of them. The preface's final lines about "the young lady [who] borrowed Plutarch's lives, and, after reading the first volume with infinite delight, supposing it to be a novel, threw aside the others with disgust, because a man of letters had inadvertently told her the work was founded on FACT" (1:xiii) extend Tyler's joke because, after all, *The Algerine Captive* is founded on fiction.

The preface then concludes with a conversation among a few self-proclaimed "men of letters." They claim that public-spirited adventure tales such as Updike's can be used to alter the public's reading habits and so make literate citizens capable of moving beyond the illiterate masses of Europe. Tyler is conspicuously dubious of their assumptions. The preface, with the other prefatory materials, satirizes the automatic equation of literacy with liberty. Tyler ironically demonstrates how the wrong kind of literacy becomes a hermeneutic of suppression, not liberation. The fictional authors of the prefatory materials assume that Dolly and Jonathan, after reading the narrative, will be able to appropriate Updike's advertised powers of free thought and rational virtue. Once the text begins, Tyler's Updike demonstrates neither.

Instead Updike means to use their literacy and the power of the English traditions not to create freethinking voters but rather to propagate more Updikes eager to continue a derivative tradition. Like Murray, moreover, Tyler substitutes a seemingly accidental polyphony of otherwise excluded voices both to undermine the standard claims to coherence and national monovocalism and to reveal the true heterogeneity hidden beneath the weight of republican rhetoric. The preface's complexity and intertextual referentiality makes *The Algerine Captive* not just of the republican paradigm but about it as well. As such Tyler implicitly indicts his own prose and poetry in its paradoxes and contradictions. Tyler's critique then comes from within, seeking improvement in the manner of Brackenridge and Murray, and not yet the reinvention sought by Brown or Irving.

The preface mentions a series of genres, most of which had been granted a degree of repute: "biography, travels, novels, and modern romances." Volume 1, set mostly in America, contains all of these genres while also incorporating the language of the pastoral, the epic, legal prose, and histories—again, all forms guaranteed to transmit republican ideology to a passive citizen/reader. These are used to describe Updike's ancestry, birth, education, training, travels, and capture. Updike also throws in anecdotal meetings with Thomas Paine and Benjamin

Franklin. As such, the volume is purposefully disjointed and contradictory, as Engell has established.

Mentioning these genres establishes Updike as reader, providing a model, in turn, for his own reader. His passive and uncritical reading of such texts allows him to be manpulated by them, blind to both his own and his community's difference from the world they create. The numerous sections in which he flits back and forth between genres are most revealing of Updike's literary and personal shortcomings. At the end of every sequence, Updike fails to complete the discussion of his subject: the limitations of each inherited genre allow him to escape before confronting the implications of meaningful resolution.

Chapters 1 through 3 contain an extended history of the fictional Updike's historical ancestor, Capt. John Underhill, a controversial Puritan figure mentioned by Cotton Mather and Jeremy Belknap.[15] Because John, an independent-minded and courageous nonconformist, is "dedicated to protecting his freedom and the freedom of others" (1:21), he is forcibly removed from the Puritan theocracy—the decolonized mind conflicting with the colonizing settlement. At the end of the second chapter, Updike gives himself the narrative space to evade serious consideration of his ancestor's relevance to the 1790s: "Whoever reflects upon the piety of our forefathers, the noble unrestrained ardour with which they resisted oppression in England, relinquished the delights of their native country, crossed a boisterous ocean, penetrated a savage wilderness, encountered famine, pestilence, and war, and transmitted to us their sentiments of independence,— that love of liberty, which under God has enabled us to obtain our own glorious freedom,—will readily pass over those few dark spots which clouded the rising sun" (1:20). What Updike readily passes over is John and all he represents. John embodies an earlier America: a settlement rather than a colony. His alienation from the Puritans represents the difference: they become colonizers while he, by demanding his freedom, remains decolonized. As Davidson has pointed out (201–2), Tyler is clearly equating Puritan religious and Federalist political power structures in their mirroring of English models—a complication beyond the ken of the narrow-minded and befuddled Updike.

Yet Updike, like all early republic historiographers, is more eager to craft a unifying bridge between rebellious Puritans and early republic America as a singular progression toward republicanism.[16] His merging of Puritan and Revolutionary histories, a connection borrowed from other historians such as Belknap and Miller, allows his reactionary linkage of two periods to replace more serious probing of the issue. From behind Updike, Tyler favors John and thus champions nonconformity and dissidence, as opposed to Updike's compliance and slavish conformity. John was purportedly banished for saying "that the government at Boston were as zealous as the scribes and Pharisees, and as Paul before his conversion" (1:19). John refuses the institutional authority of the theocracy that was bringing order to the wilderness. To his credit, John favored freedom above conformity. Conversely, Tyler perceives an inversion of the usual formulation: a pattern of authoritarian autocracy in America that suppresses rather than promotes individual freedom and thought.

In chapter 4 Updike relates an allegorical anecdote concerning his birth reminiscent of Bunyan. His mother, while pregnant, dreamed she saw "a number of young tawny savages playing at football with my head" and assumes that "she had the native Indians in her mind, but never apprehended her poor son's suffering many years, as a slave, among barbarians more cruel than the monsters of our own woods" (1:26). Updike excuses the use of dreams "in this enlightened age" by pleading precedence "in the sacred scriptures" in which meaning is often "communicated by Providence through the intervention of dreams" (1:27). This misreading undermines the objectified self-importance in the rhetoric of the eighteenth century: the age is thus defined by pretense and self-deception, not enlightenment. Moreover, this foreshadows Updike's inability to conceive of a heterogeneity of experience: both the Indians and Algerines are Others that colonial thought teaches him to conceive as inferior and savage.

In the chapters that follow, Updike briefly discusses his miseducation at the hands of early republic pedagogues. He is trained in the classical tradition, a method directly connected to neoclassical and republican discourse. Moreover, the classical tradition was evoked directly by the Wits in *The Anarchiad, The Columbiad,* and *Greenfield Hill.* The narrative of chapter 6, which concludes Updike's childhood and begins his picaresque travels, humorously articulates Tyler's vision of the failure of these social-cultural-literary paradigms to define American experience. Significantly, Updike is a good classical scholar: he earns the praise of his teachers and correctly translates Virgil. By being taught that mere memory and recitation "as loud as I could speak" (1:30) are rewarded, however, Updike never develops patterns of independent thought or critical thinking.

While something is clearly wrong with Updike, something is also wrong with the tradition. By making a joke of this classical scholar, Tyler casts doubts on the utility of the classical model on a larger scale—that is, his parody extends beyond poor Updike to an entire way of thinking that commends slavish unoriginality and represses self-exploration. In fact, such training soon becomes dangerous and antidemocratic. On his travels, chapters 7 through 25, through northern, southern, and the mid-Atlantic states, Updike, like Brackenridge's Farrago, meets illiterates, quack doctors, violent backwoodsmen, and pretentious townspeople. Although regional variations among these diverse groups are noted, Updike can communicate with none of them. His classical education has distanced him from their language and lives.

When Updike is challenged to a duel whose prevention ironically catalyzes his social acceptance, Tyler dramatizes a tyranny of pretentious social conformity. Just as his educated man is absurd, Tyler's rustics are brutal, ignorant, selfish, and shortsighted.[17] Tyler takes advantage of this chaos to dramatize the inability of the American populace to communicate with itself: in the vortices of presumed authority and demonized mob rule, the communication needed for true self-expression is prevented. Beneath this fiction of Updike's writing his autobiography, Tyler suggests that the entire menu of ideological and linguistic choices available in the 1790s was inadequate and likely to perpetuate an even more absurd national community.

Tyler means to identify the nation's inability to communicate with itself as a barrier to the more complex merging necessary to the creation of the ideal state promised by the Revolution. An anecdote in chapter 23 concerning Benjamin Franklin reflects Tyler's views on the necessity of compromise and adjustment. This chapter resembles one of the *Spectator*-style letters that characterized Franklin's literary career before *The Autobiography*. Its final lines reflect Updike's inability to achieve the freedom of thought of either Franklin or John Underhill: "The doctor [Franklin] took an apple from a fruit basket, and presented it to a little child, who could just totter about the room. The child could scarce grasp it in his hand. He then gave it another which occupied the other hand. Then choosing a third, remarkable for its size and beauty, he presented that also. The child, after many ineffectual attempts to hold the three, dropped the last on the carpet, and burst into tears. See there, said the philosopher; there is a little man with more riches than he can enjoy" (1:134). Updike's use of the *Spectator* format allows him to leave this parable as a quaint demonstration of Franklin's wisdom. This child, small enough to be pleased by one apple, becomes obsessed with having more. When the opportunity for a single better apple comes along, his hasty greed prevents his being able to hold what is best. The inability to make decisive choices—like Updike's to settle on a single literary format—represents an immature perspective.

Updike, ever oblivious, returns to his meandering picaresque mode upon leaving Franklin, grabbing yet more apples. When he meets the same ignorance and tyranny in the South as he did in the North, he switches careers and narrative forms as he signs on as ship's doctor on a slave ship. Chapter 25 begins an adventure narrative in the style of *Robinson Crusoe*. Updike cannot even retain this narrative frame. After two adventure chapters, he relates his visit with Paine in London and further demonstrates his weakness by attaching himself to the nearest available role model. Initially, his thoughtless defense of Paine, based on Paine's patriotic past, overwhelms any capability to think critically. While there, Updike witnesses Peter Pindar, an English satirist, outwit Paine. Updike stops short of noting that he, too, has been foiled. Seeing this, however, Updike quickly changes course in a brief but vituperative and typical attack on Paine's *Age of Reason*.

This attack, of course, never really discusses the substance of the text: Updike quickly retreats behind republican reviews of the book.[18] Updike retreats from considering the meaning of his change of heart toward Paine by reverting to the language and imagery of the adventure narrative. The final three chapters of volume 1 describe Updike's experience on board a slave ship and his capture by the Algerines. Updike is horrified by the slave trade and rejects the captain's offer to ship some slaves of his own on board: "I cannot even now reflect on this transaction without shuddering. I have deplored my conduct with tears of anguish; and I pray a merciful God, the common parent of the great family of the universe, who hath made of one flesh and one blood all nations of the earth, that the miseries, the insults, and cruel woundings, I afterwards received when a slave myself may expiate for the inhumanity I was necessitated to exercise towards these MY BRETHREN OF THE HUMAN RACE" (1:170). Updike's retreat to homiletic apology is meant to cloud the complexities of the horrors of slavery. Rather than explore the ramifications of what he has thought, Updike trots out terms he seems to have memorized. Ironically, this act completes Tyler's characterization of Updike as unwitting slave to conventional thought. He is made colonial by adhering to derivative ways of thinking and writing and consistently kept from free thought or expression. Moreover, as a doctor on the slave ship, Updike is implicated in the industry. Updike dislikes slavery, but still gains his living from it. Tyler's sensitivity to this degree of implication places him on the vanguard of abolitionism.

Furthermore, since Updike is presumably writing his book after his return to America, one would think that it would be accompanied by a sense that he will work to abolish American slavery. Chapter 32 contains a promise made to himself that he would "fly to our fellow citizens in the southern states; I will on my knees conjure them, in the name of humanity, to abolish a traffic which causes it to bleed in every pore" (1:171). While this appears admirable, the pledge that concludes the book, to become a "worthy FEDERAL citizen" mentions no such mission: Updike has safely transferred his reader's attention to slavery in Algeria by then, so slavery in the United States is quietly forgotten. This episode allows Tyler to chide those ministers and journalists of the 1790s who publicly decried slavery but never moved themselves to action.

Volume 1 describes a pattern of rhetorical retreats that characterize not only the youthful Updike but also the returned and supposedly chastened Federalist. Separating his actions as a child from his literary recreation of those actions as an adult reveals a consistent weakness in Updike's character. Most importantly, it reveals Tyler's sophisticated dramatization of the small-mindedness of a colonized American author. Volume 1 features two men, John Underhill and Benjamin Franklin, whose articulate nonconformity characterizes decolonized freedom before and during the Revolution. As such, it appears that either would be better equipped to represent America on the international stage than Updike. Unlike either John or Franklin, Updike is a product of the early republic and so represents the new generation schooled in republican rhetoric. Essential to the survival of John's and Franklin's spirit is the ability of the next generation to resist new forms colonial incursions on American freedom. Volume 2 darkly contemplates that threat.

In volume 2 Tyler explores the ramifications of the self-perpetuating marginality of American thought when tested in the broader world. Critics have universally claimed that volume 2 lacks the narrative depth of volume 1.[19] However, volume 2 reveals new depths to Updike's evasion of meaning. Tyler suggests that Americans like Updike are not only poorly equipped to create a truly free American state but are also unlikely to achieve the degree of intellect necessary to spread democracy around the world. In fact, just the reverse: Updike turns colonizer, contributing to, not combating, the protoimperialist agenda and rhetoric of the British. The failure of Tyler's Updike reveals that decolonization and freedom involve more than mere political independence. Instead they require the formulation of a new and more flexible paradigm for understanding, one that recognizes the exploitative and colonizing effects of European thought. In specific, Tyler engages the issues of race and religion as each was being deployed in the early republic as a source of exclusion and stratification and throughout the world as forces of dominion and imperium. By undermining their sources, Tyler argues that freedom can never be exclusive and must in a more inclusive way acknowledge and value a variety of presences on the national scene.

In what appears to be a positive development in Updike's character, chapter 2 of volume 2 opens with a passage that would appear to demonstrate his growth. As a slave Updike is almost compelled to consider himself and his actions in ways he never had before and develop a language of compassion. Nonetheless, Tyler uses this opportunity to demonstrate Updike's inability to conceive of language or ideas he has not read elsewhere: "The higher his rank in society, the further is man removed from nature. Grandeur draws a circle round the great, and often excludes them from the finer feelings of the heart: the wretched are all of one family, and ever regard each other as brethren" (2:14). While his comments on hierarchy and freedom resonate with meaning, his claim that "our fellow citizens who set at nought the rich blessings of our federal union, [should] go like me to a land of slavery, and they will learn to appreciate the value of our free government" (2:27) reveals an equation of "our federal union" with "free government," demonstrating his inability to think past republican publicity and forgetting, conveniently, his fellow Federal citizens in the "Southern states." Moreover, Tyler's deft placement of the phrases "our federal union" and "land of slavery" so soon after Updike's commentary on American slavery suggests that Tyler has a more profound criticism in mind. The subsequent events redouble Tyler's deliberate disruption of the normal reading experience in a way that reveals his call for decolonized readership.

Soon after his capture, Updike meets an Englishman, a former slave who gained his freedom and prosperity by converting to Islam. Updike despises the disloyalty of the Englishman: "I pity you too, replied I, the tears standing in my eyes. My body is in slavery but my mind is free. Your body is at liberty, but your soul is in the most abject slavery, in the gall of bitterness and the bond of iniquity. You have sold your God for filthy lucre; and "what shall it profit you if you gain the whole world and lose your own soul, or what shall a man give in exchange for his soul?" (2:31). Volume 1 established the irony of Updike's resistance: his own freedom is often chimerical. Instead of questioning the Englishman in an articulate manner, Updike reverts to the safety of the biblical text, reciting again loudly, as he had as a schoolboy, and again mistaking volume for verity. His repetition of cant phrases and his out-of-hand condemnation of Islam typify his method: the thoughtless and captivated mind unable to take risks. Nonetheless, the stresses of slave labor over time force Updike to seek refuge in the luxurious facilities available to possible converts.

In chapter 6 Updike is transported to the "Sacred College of the Musselman Priest" and treated royally. In that chapter as well, he meets his proselytist, a converted captive Greek, whose behavior alone intimidates Updike before the theological conversation begins. The Greek begins by reassuring Updike as to the method of his evangelism: "He said the holy faith he offered to my embraces disdained the use of other powers than rational argument; that he left to the Church of Rome and its merciless inquisitors all the honour and profit of conversion by faggots, dungeons, and racks" (2:39). Here the Greek appears the one more able to think critically. By promoting himself using the one term most central to eighteenth-century thought, "rational argument," he impresses the fearful Updike: "Though I viewed his conduct as insidious, yet he no sooner retired, than, overcome by his suavity of manners, for the first time I trembled for my faith and burst into tears" (2:39–40). Considering Updike's inability to resist attractive words and ideas that require no thought on his part, his fright is justified. The muslim Greek has mastered the language and forms that were presumably the exclusive property of republican virtue. The use to which he puts them, converting Christians to Islam, reveals that they can ultimately become vehicles of manipulation, not just for the free exchange of ideas.

Chapter 7 alarmed eighteenth-century critics who misread Tyler's irony. Davidson cites a London critic who commented that "in the dialogue with the Mollah, the author too feebly defends that religion he professes to revere" (qtd. in Tanselle, 208). Tyler would agree: Updike *does* too feebly defend Christianity. That London critic erred because he identified the fictional Updike with the real author, although he correctly noted Tyler's obvious sympathy for religious and cultural tolerance. In his "Narrative Irony," Engell notes that Tyler uses the Mollah to show his anger "against the elements of American society that destroy freedom" (27). Indeed, the Mollah's comments identify many of the contradictions in American life that Updike glossed over in volume 1. His commentary on the servitude of Christian slaves in America especially defines the hypocritical practice of Christianity in America, a contradiction for which Updike cannot account.

Like Irving's Mustapha ten years later, the Mollah offers an outsider's critique of American thoughts and ideas. Tyler's Mollah, however, is complicated by the fact of his European birth: this European muslim is a hybrid, a cosmopolitan capable of merging and mixing the best of both Eastern and Western traditions. The Mollah, and, through him, Tyler, deconstructs the conventional and self-righteous rhetoric of the early republic: his commentary reveals the ultimate hollowness of so much of the language used to gloss certain hypocrisies and contradictions in the post-Revolutionary United States. The Mollah represents Tyler's rejection of the colonizing binaries of East/West and Christian/Muslim, revealing the entangled nature of all these purportedly distinct cultural presences in late eighteenth-century North Atlantic culture.[20]

Consequently, Tyler dramatizes Updike's inability to articulate an intelligent defense. As a retrospective author, Updike frames his verbal inadequacy in a form that allows him to escape from commenting on or being responsible for the content of his rhetorical defeat: the dialogue. Updike transcribes only the words said by each. The dialogue is dominated by the Mollah who, at times echoing Locke's, Paine's, and deistic critiques of Christianity, traps Updike into virtual silence by anticipating all his practiced and unoriginal defenses. Updike's defense of Christianity consists of a series of cant statements, void of substance, the products of memorization, not contemplation. Updike concludes by escaping, literally, from the Mollah's logic: "After five days' conversation, disgusted with his fables, abashed by his assurance, and almost confounded by his sophistry, I resumed my slave's attire, and sought safety in my former servitude" (2:53). "Confounded by sophistry," Updike reverts to real servitude, allowing him to retreat from considering the fact that Christianity in America serves the same hierarchical and oppressive political and social constructs as "Mahometanism" did in Algiers, this time with the white, not the African, as the slave.[21] By reversing the racial roles of slavery, Tyler hints at the ultimate similarity of Algiers to the United States, not so Other as the imperialists would like.

By having him write in a similarly cowardly way, Tyler characterizes Updike as he writes the book after returning to the States, as well as Updike in the debate, as unable to defend issues of principle and intellectual significance. Even later as an author, Updike cannot conceive the rhetorical strategies necessary to refute the Mollah's logic and instead repairs to a safe slavery in an elusive text. Both John Underhill and Franklin could have stood a better chance of defeating the Mollah since each was free to articulate more courageous and original thoughts. Specifically, Updike retreats behind an exoticizing of the non-European Other. His refusal to confront the challenge of Islam to Christendom represents the colonizer's mindset: he simply erases what he cannot defeat.

After this segment, the remainder of volume 2 seems rhetorically flat as Updike passes on the exoticizing and racist myths common in European writing about Islam. Updike spends twenty chapters composing a catalogue of Algerine characteristics. This narrative retreat demonstrates the depths of his trauma. If it is dull, it is because Updike has been forced into a rhetorical withdrawal more drastic than any before. The dullness emphasizes the safety of the genre of the travelog, which allows Updike the safety of distanced observation. Nonetheless, he practices the same type of Orientalism that Edward Said, Mary Louise Pratt, and David Spurr have recognized as typical of the Western view of the East.[22] His gaze exoticizes, appropriates, and negates North Africa and Arabia. Updike allows himself to understand the non-Western world only as something other, closing his mind to any potential significance it might bear. Moreover, this gaze allows him to identify the United States as part of a unified European effort to marginalize and contain the non-Western world, arguing against its own exclusion from the "civilized" world of Europe by joining its program of textual and rhetorical colonization.

In chapter 25, Updike again seems to demonstrate an ability to recognize the beginnings of intelligent and articulate commentary. In this chapter, he excoriates "European States," which "instead of uniting to vindicate their insulted faith, join together the cross and the crescent in unholy alliance, and form degrading treaties with piratical powers" (2:149). However, when one considers that Humphreys, to whom the book is dedicated, created a similar "unholy alliance," Tyler's irony again subverts Updike's oversimplified polemic and Updike is soon off on another tangent. Rather than recognizing American foreign policy as antithetical to the ideology of the Revolution, Updike retreats, ignoring the profoundly contradictory nature of his actions.

Updike remains in a relatively derivative adventure mode until the thirty-seventh and final chapter to describe his escape. When Updike's freedom is finally assured, he races through the details of his trip back to the States and, upon reuniting with his parents, indulges in an orgy of republican virtue: "I purchased a horse, and hastened home to my parents, who received me as one risen from the dead. I shall not attempt to describe their emotions, or my own raptures. I had suffered hunger, sickness, fatigue, insult, stripes, wounds, and every other cruel injury; and was now under the roof of the kindest and tenderest of parents. I had been degraded to a slave, and was now advanced to a citizen of the freest country in the universe" (2:227). This last time Updike's retreat to rhetoric allows him to erase from his memory his earlier observations on American slavery, the abuse he received as a young man, and his own participation in "an unholy alliance." Conspicuously absent is his previous promise to liberate American slaves. Updike remains profoundly unaware that his country shares the sin of slavery equally with England and Algeria. By focusing exclusively on the Algerian slavery, Updike remains a colonial, unable to see beyond of the hierarchy of civilization implicit to imperial thought; by creating Updike as conflicted in these ways, however, Tyler engages the work of decolonization.

The final page again finds Updike switching genres. This final chapter mostly resembles a sermon in which the homily is republican, not Christian. Here Updike demonstrates Tyler's final disquietude with the early republic's forms of writing. After declaring himself a "worthy FEDERAL citizen," Updike recreates the preface's connection of political and literary activities and its patriotic, didactic intent: "Let us one and all endeavour to sustain the general government. Let no foreign emissaries inflame us against one nation, by raking up the ashes of long extinguished enmity; or delude us into extravagant schemes of another, by recurring to fancied gratitude. Our first object is union among ourselves. For no nation besides the United States can that ancient saying be more emphatically applied—By Uniting We Stand, By Dividing We Fall" (2:228). The awkward addition of this speech to the end of the book typifies Updike's method. He seeks quick, easy answers, and ends not creatively but imitatively, delivering a cliché as his final resolution. The reader is safely confirmed in the diction and ideas that could be found in any number of publications. Updike's statement concerning the utility of his life as a model of American behavior demonstrates the completion of Tyler's irony: Updike teaches imitation, not freedom.

Updike's lifeless ending can be starkly juxtaposed against the final lines of a letter of John Underhill's: "Salute brother Fish and others, who, havinge been disappointed of libertie in this wilderness, are earnestlie lookinge for a better countre" (1:19). This recalls the irregular language and uninhibited courage of characters in Tyler's play *The Contrast* (1787). These Americans represent a national language and way of thought less bound to some false standard of British cultural legitimacy. *The Algerine Captive*, then, observes a closing out of revolutionary freedoms and the gradual return of colonial thought in the 1790s. Between the publication dates of the two works, from 1787 to 1797, Tyler observed a narrowing of the national consciousness, a loss of revolutionary energy as colonial order was reinstalled.

By reverting to what Robert Lawson-Peebles calls "redcoatism," Updike and writers like him undo the progress away from British models started in the fading Revolution. By matching Updike's physical and authorial slaveries, Tyler offers an equally chilling prospect for the future of American writing. Updike fails as a writer: his text only inverts the didactic purpose he has in mind. Tyler's book, however, succeeds where Updike's fails. Updike has attempted to synthesize a plethora of conventional forms into a coherent whole, demonstrating his mastery of all and his accreditation as member of an Anglocentric elite in the early republic. In "A Cultural Paradigm for the Second World," Alan Lawson suggests that "synthesis is a totalising enterprise which seeks to silence polyphony and focus double-vision. The Second World, postcolonial text prefers disintegration" (72). Tyler uses *The Algerine Captive* to "disintegrate" the hollow image of social and political coherence republican recolonization sought to impose on the new nation.

The noisiness and unfocused nature of this book, like that of both *Modern Chivalry* and *The Gleaner*, reveals an embrace of those anarchic qualities, those freer voices threatened with silencing. Tyler continued to participate in the republic of letters he had critiqued. Morever, his poetry still obeyed Augustan stylistic conventions. Tyler never implied that there was not room in the American public sphere for inherited techniques. His objections were to the attempted republican monopolization of American textuality and its subsequent costs: the intellectually stillborn Updike. In the more inclusive textuality he implies but cannot practice, readers and writers would have to be more aware than Updike could imagine.

Tyler may not have known what the decolonized American individual or writer would become, but his attack on the colonial Updike suggests two things. First, Tyler felt American experience was *different*. Updike's inability to define it in the inherited forms demonstrates a deficiency not only in the narrator but in the forms themselves. Second, American difference will remain unexpressed so long as leftover social and cultural institutions from the colonial epoch remain. In sum, these recognitions compel American readers to understand that the Revolution rid the nation of only political colonization: Updike reveals that intellectual colonization is still pervasive and so a continued decolonizing sentiment must be perpetuated. *The Algerine Captive*, then, like *Modern Chivalry* and *The Gleaner*, describes a fiction of authorship in which a representative American proves unable to write a coherent book, unable to express his thoughts freely, and unable to conceptualize the political and social problems he sees around himself as he writes. Brackenridge, Murray, and Tyler thus share a rather complicated vision of the nation's future: all three create fictional authors unable to free themselves from the tyranny of derivative thought, despite genuinely sincere efforts. Each is thus benign, an unfortunate puppet of a misguided ideology.

Unlike Brackenridge's author-narrator and Murray's Vigillius, however, Tyler's Updike Underhill demonstrates another side of the precariousness of the republic of letters. The social position of Brackenridge's author-narrator remains static: he makes no reference to how authorship has advanced him personally, nor does Vigillius. Although he shares their inability to compose a coherent text, Updike, more like Brown's Arthur Mervyn or Watterston's Morcell, uses authorship for reasons of personal advancement rather than benevolent public interest, no matter how misguided. He understands how recreating and mouthing the unoriginal and standard rhetoric and language of the republic of letters can transform one from the marginality of the colonial to centrality of the colonizer. Revealing his mastery of the colonizing text secures the fictional Updike personal gain, even at the cost of intellectual integrity. Just as the government meant to show its credibility by negotiating along European lines, so does Updike hope to legitimize himself. This trend reveals the encroaching corruption of Revolutionary ideals as the 1790s wore on. Tyler's subversion of Updike's aspirations, then, raise the alarm that the new nation is ceasing to decolonize itself and that selfishness and cronyism have replaced public interest and democracy as national characteristics.[23]

FOUR

꒰ꕤ꒱

The Reputation of Literature and Opulence: Charles Brockden Brown's *Arthur Mervyn*

IN 1799, TWO YEARS after the publication of *The Algerine Captive* and Updike Underhill's request for admission to the professional class by reason of his authorship, Charles Brockden Brown, in an essay entitled "On the State of American Literature," commented on the lingering predominance of the colonial nature of early republic life: "The love of gain . . . in a very remarkable degree, pervades the United States. Before the Revolutionary War, this spirit was very prevalent, and much cultivated. . . . To acquire property became the supreme and governing object; and the sordid colonial character was easily traced in almost every class of our citizens" (16).[1] Mercantile gain, as configured in the comments of historians of colonialism from Herman Merivale and Edward Gibbon Wakefield to Edward Said and Stephen Greenblatt, was always and perpetually the initial motivation for colonialist enterprises around the world.[2] Brown's critique of capitalism aside—many scholars have already addressed it—this passage also describes Brown's recognition of an intensification of the worst of the colonial epoch in the early republic.[3] Brown's finding that the Revolution had not created a pattern of liberation and virtue but rather continued one of stratification and greed would be more intricately explored in the novel he began that same year, *Arthur Mervyn; or Memoirs of the Year 1793* (1799–1800).

"The sordid colonial character," then, had somehow survived until 1799, and its emphasis on materialism had stunted the growth of writing in the new nation. While Brown seemed aware that national acquisitiveness and its colonial origins could not be purged from American life, he proposed that writing be detached from republican and capitalist propaganda so that it could endeavor less-compromised national self-examination. That is, before what Michael Warner calls "a modern nationalist imaginary" could evolve, American readers and writers had to develop "a repertoire of self-perceptions that, though national, can be detached from any context of action understood as political" (149). So long as writers and readers politicized their activities in the colonial framework that survived the Revolution to be relabeled as "republicanism," such detachment and decolonization would be thwarted and the "evil" would continue to thrive. In *Arthur Mervyn* Brown employs a fiction of authorship to encourage an enlargement in the "repertoire" of readerly and writerly self-perceptions by dramatizing the dangers of too narrow a range of possible identities on either side of the literary exchange.

Nonetheless, in the early republic "Americans . . . understood their engagements with print as activities in the republican public sphere subject to its norms" (151), according to Warner. Conventional republican authors assumed a readership that shared a common interest in promoting republicanism in sincere and altruistic texts and accepted their authority to craft such consensual documents.[4] Brackenridge's anonymous author-narrator, Murray's Vigillius, and Tyler's Updike all write with such a benevolent reception in mind, merging personal, public, and economic interest into a fabricated republican whole. In turn, readers trusted authors as recognizable sources of instruction and information.[5] As stable transmitters of cultural authority inherited from British tradition, these authors represented and recalled the stable and safe institutions of authority leftover from the colonial regime, when individuals could be secure in their subjecthood and not fear the dangerous responsibilities of decolonized citizenship—a very limited "repertoire."

In Brown's *Arthur Mervyn* another potentially significant abuse of the republicans' trust in and reinscription of colonial textuality is exposed. In it, those same paradigmatic shortcomings are inverted when a very slippery character gradually becomes an author. Both fictional and real authors write fully aware of the gullible and pliant reading audience accustomed to the empty rhetoric of republican writers seemingly cursed with echolalia. Brown implies that an overabundance of readerly trust configured the public as an easy target for counterfeiters or dissemblers, threatening the cultivation of an informed public capable of participating in a democracy by reconverting active citizens to passive colonial subjects.

An accessory to murder, a thief, an amoral opportunist, and a half-educated egoist, Brown's Arthur Mervyn seems an unlikely transmitter of the public interest, yet he easily meets the requirements of the republican paradigm. The fiction of Arthur's authorship allows Brown to dramatize the dangerous potential inherent in the motions, voice, and public presence of the conventionally empowered and authorized texts in the new nation. Bill Christopherson has noted that Arthur both "depicts and deposes" (125) American virtues. Republicanism meant to inscribe a monocultural, monolithic "culture of morality" (243) in the terms of David Reynolds, on the protean new nation, ignoring the complexities of the heterogeneous community. Larzer Ziff has particularly shown how Arthur complicates the simplicity of republicanism: "Representing and misrepresenting were dangerously alike and the individual's capacity to become other than what he had been was not clearly distinguishable from his ability to deceive" (82).

In other words, Arthur Mervyn reveals that post-Revolutionary society is still protean and unfixed. Rather than fabricating a false stability, Brown asks the reader to understand the social and cultural chaos of the early republic. In that sense, Brown, like Brackenridge and Murray, disrupts the unity of the text to recreate the disrupted nature of the American community. But from that disruption comes the energy and edginess of Second World life. Alan Lawson suggests that "the customary project of Western thought has been to contain disorder and divergence, to see the resolution of dichotomy, polarity, binary in harmony and unity, to synthesize and re-unify. Second World texts are under no such cultural imperative" (70). Lawson certainly oversimplifies "Western thought" as a monolith; however, Europeans deliberately misrepresented its singularity in its colonies. As the mimic men of the postcolonial early republic, *republican* thought sustained just such a homogenizing effort.[6]

To apply Lawson further, then, in the Second World text "the states of interphase exist epistemologically without the boundaries of resolution of their self-and-otherness and take the multiple perspective, the polyphony, the diachronicity, that is their birthright" (70). The world of *Arthur Mervyn*, I will suggest, reflects a similarly unresolved and problematic perspective on the early republic. William Dunlap, Brown's friend and biographer, has noted that Brown "played with shadows, he dandled and caressed them with a sort of idolatry" (70). In the shadows surrounding Arthur, Brown suggests that the naïveté of the republican paradigm created a willful ignorance of the complexities and ambiguities of human experience. Kenneth Dauber has said in his study of Franklin, early republic authorship "does not admit the possibility of alienation" (18). Throughout Brown's writing, however, citizens of the early republic are alienated from themselves, each other, and their communities.

In *Arthur Mervyn,* the alienation of author from reader, of text from truth, of language from meaning is explored in a complex story of how Arthur becomes an author. Brown encloses Arthur's authorship in two framing narratives, each of which casts authorship in an inherited mode. In a book Brown publicly announces as a novel, a Dr. Stevens is introduced as the first fictional author. Contextualizing both his own and Stevens's authorships within the boundaries of early republic print discourse, Brown sets the stage for exposing their potential corruptibility when an unreliable individual such as Arthur recreates their superficial motions of textual authority.

Modern scholarship is divided over how to read *Arthur Mervyn.* One group trusts Arthur's sincerity and so reads the book, to varying degrees, as a handbook to navigating the early republic's chaos: a path to virtue through overcoming temptation. This reading rephrases the novel as an American *Pilgrim's Progress* and so easily traced to eighteenth-century rhetoric.[7] Another, however, perceives an irony that resonates through Arthur's twisted narrative to emerge ultimately as an articulation of the ambiguous and romantic capacities of Brown's final vision.[8] To place him among American writers of the nineteenth century, this latter group often ignores Brown's explicit hope that his writings have a genuine public utility in the early republic.[9]

When Arthur is reconsidered as a fictional author, his moral standing is complicated by the immediacy of his text to the actual context of its publication. I am not as much concerned with Arthur the American individual—and whether or not he represents a typical American—as with Arthur the *author*—and how he reflects the increasing space between the assumptions of the republic of letters and the needs of its decolonizing readers. By reframing *Arthur Mervyn* as a fiction of authorship, I suggest that Arthur cannot be easily identified as either good or bad and that Brown's fiction, participating in both centuries, like the publication dates of the book itself, reflects a transitional view of the role of writing in the new nation.[10] Likewise, it straddles the colonial and postcolonial periods of American writing: rejecting the colonial, it anxiously ponders the "peculiar circumstances" of what happened since the end of the Revolution.

Caught between these, Brown's subject is the profound tension between the remnants of colonial dominion and the emergent national character. His awareness of the complications this condition places on the reader and the writer distinguishes him from other writers in the republican public sphere and demonstrates the exploratory and destabilizing nature of the novel. By restaging Arthur's act of presumably reliable authorship as morally and politically indeterminate, Brown critiques the oversimplification of the new nation by the elite in their effort to create a national community based on British ideals of benevolence and paternal public interest and demands a more honest examination of the complexities of decolonization.

Implicitly, Brown suggests that participating in a decolonized democracy requires a complex attitude toward language and authority. *Arthur Mervyn* points to serious flaws in the ways Americans were reading and writing by creating an ironic countertext: the fictional author mimics the language and format of authority for purposes that can be interpreted in many ways. In this very act of obfuscation, Brown rehearses and indicts colonial modes of reading in his broader critique of the early republic: thrusting the act of interpretation upon the reader compels the readers to explore the ramifications of their own interpretive authority.

This complex activity begins with the book's front matter which present it as the production of an author known and trusted by the readers. These construct the author in the standard eighteenth-century guise as craftsman, as the retransmitter of established truths, and not as a source of imaginative creativity or social disruption.[11] This occurs explicitly within the republican paradigm by taking into consideration the entire reading experience, starting well before the narrative's beginning and including both the author's reputation, the prefatory materials, and the framing narrative.

The title page establishes the novel's deliberate entry into the republic of letters, albeit reflecting a latent peculiarity.[12] The first thing Brown's readers saw in 1799 when volume 1 of *Arthur Mervyn* appeared was an anonymous title page that attributed authorship to "The Author of Wieland; and Ormond or the Secret Witness" (2).[13] Brown, although known as the author of these earlier novels, thus did not fully admit to the authorship of his text. In 1799, most fictions were not claimed by their authors, but Brown's reference to works known to be his suggests this book's difference from the motley assortment of Gothic, seduction, and adventure novels for which the American reading audience had a growing appetite. His subtle ownership of the text refers implicitly to both his own need for the reader to be aware of the context of the career of the author and a nascent reconfiguration of the author from craftsman to creator. Unlike the author of the preface of *The Algerine Captive*, Brown implicitly welcomes Jonathan and Dolly—nonelite readers—in the republican public sphere.

In 1799 Charles Brockden Brown was a recognized member of the middle states' literary establishment.[14] He had been publishing throughout the 1790s, and although his early fiction was not a financial success, it was never critically attacked or officially censured, as were a great number of other novels of the period. Unlike the works of many of the other writers of the early republic, Brown's writings were not the literary component of a political career; their discursive motivations cannot be traced to more public activities, as can those of Brackenridge or Tyler. Without direct reference to the parallel political activity, the book must look to itself and its own fictionality for authority. Brown's appeal to the growing middle-class readership, while at the same time claiming a place in the elite's republic of letters, reveals a calculated placelessness, a desire to be all things to all readers, just as Arthur himself would aspire to be. Moreover, the subtitle claims the volume contains "Memoirs," deliberately blurring the distinction between the author's fictions and *Arthur Mervyn*'s potential veracity. Perhaps Brown here reveals the duplicitous claim of British fiction to base itself in truth by showing how easily interchangeable the two are.[15]

The two novels themselves to which the title page refers had been well received upon initial publication, as was *Edgar Huntly*, which was published between the two volumes of *Arthur Mervyn* and so joined the others named on the otherwise identical title page of volume 2. Norman Grabo, however, notes that much of *Arthur Mervyn* was drafted before *Wieland* and *Ormond*; Henry Warfel has suggested that their moderate success encouraged Brown to complete *Arthur Mervyn*, the last of his publicly significant fictions (141). These compositional facts suggest that Brown knew that his long-concealed project would not be well received from an unknown writer. Therefore, he promotes himself as a trusted author and seemingly veiled his own uneasiness about this long-standing project, still only half-written but already older than the two novels he had published.

Brown, it seems, recognized that the shifting narrative voices and the absence of a total villain, such as *Wieland*'s Carwin or the title character of *Ormond*, represented a departure from the novelistic conventions of the earlier books, to the extent that its publication risked the public rejection he had previously avoided. However, the early republic reader started reading *Arthur Mervyn* unaware that this book was unlike Brown's prior novels. The title page hints at none of the complications to follow, so assuring the book a conventional reception.

Immediately following is a preface, signed by "C.B.B."—initials that William Hedges in his "Charles Brockden Brown and the Culture of Contradiction," suggests represent a mask that conceals the author (114)—which begins the process by which the reader questions the text. Steven Watts, in *The Romance of Real Life*, links Brown's prefaces to the disruption of the colonial reading experience "that began to overturn many traditional expectations and assumptions" about the interrelations of readers, writers, and texts (185). Aware of this change, Brown taps into the creeping decolonization of the reader to create an alliance in which reader and writer will work together to challenge tradition.

While the preface purports to participate in the inherited mode of didactic fiction, it is oddly ambiguous and stands out both from Brown's prefaces to his earlier novels and from the standard use of such a device. When prefacing *Wieland* and *Ormond*, "C.B.B." explicitly set forth how he wanted his book to be read, noting the specific improvement the reader was meant to gain from the narrative.[16] In the manner of the day, the presumably reliable author foreclosed alternative readings of his text, asserting his own authority not only as author but also as instructor in the act of interpreting authoritative texts. "C.B.B." understands that the preface was a device meant to assure the reader that the subsequent reading experience can be trusted. For example, William Hill Brown's *The Power of Sympathy* (1789) opens with an extensive preface that expatiates at length on the specific moral lessons the young female reader was to glean from her reading. This convention establishes a master discourse that monopolizes interpretive options, colonizing the reader to the writer's interest.

The preface to *Arthur Mervyn* alludes primarily to the yellow fever plague that struck Philadelphia in the summer of 1793 and acts as a backdrop to the narrative's early sequences. Yet it never mentions the main events of the book and contains only very vague and nonspecific instructions. Instead, "C.B.B." forces the act of interpretation upon the reader: "The schemes for reformation and improvement to which [the events of the book] will give birth, or, if no efforts of human wisdom can avail to avert the periodic visitation of this calamity, the change in manners and population which they will produce will be memorable" (3). In Brown's fiction of the book's authorship, "C.B.B." makes a promise that the book itself does not keep: unlike Franklin's *Autobiography* or Enos Hitch-cock's didactic *Memoirs of the Bloomsgrove Family* (1793), *Arthur Mervyn* con-tains no "schemes for reformation and improvement." In those texts, the paternal narrative presence continues once the texts begin. In *Arthur Mervyn*, "C.B.B." dis-appears after the preface. Without guidance, the reader is later forced to distrust the preface and compelled to improvise an interpretation that may or may not serve republican interests. Brown's abnegation of that authority openly tempts the reader to revise normal textual expectations.

"C.B.B." suggests that the "change in manners" shown in the novel might be regarded as a means of avoiding future plagues. Because the book mentions no specific behavioral modification to improve the city's physical hygiene, Brown can only be inserting a veiled reference to a need for change based on moral, not medical, means. In addition, "C.B.B." neglects to give specific instructions: "He that depicts, in lively colours, the evils of disease and poverty, performs an emi-nent service to the sufferers, by calling forth benevolence in those who are able to afford relief, and he who pourtrays examples of disinterestedness and intre-pidity, confers on virtue the notoriety and homage that are due to it, and rouses in the spectators, the spirit of salutory emulation" (3). Again, when this tone is abandoned when the text begins, the reader is left stranded. Further, this com-mentary on American writing, specifically in its defense of fiction as a vehicle for republican indoctrination, would appear to complement the attack on the ma-terialism in "On the State of American Literature." This is how writing and lan-guage that conforms to republican standards is supposed to produce virtue and public good. However, the centrality of the author—"He"—in this process is sub-tly called into question: as I discuss below, the issue of Arthur's purported "dis-interestedness" is perpetually smudged. Perhaps "C.B.B." is not as in control of the text as he thinks. Such a warning, however, anticipates that the reader might be tempted to see things another way. Even before the narrative begins, Brown has laid the groundwork for interpreting the book either ironically or conven-tionally. In this indeterminacy lies its decolonizing potential: Brown internalizes and forwards the "double-consciousness" of post-Revolutionary experience as a split between the authoritarian authorial voice and his empowerment of the reader's ability to challenge that voice, between the colonizer and the colonized.

Brown's use of a framing narrator is the third technique that makes *Arthur Mervyn* appear to be a healthy contributor to the republican paradigm. The nom-inal narrative voice that opens *Arthur Mervyn* belongs to Dr. Stevens, a Philadel-phia doctor battling the epidemic (5). He begins by describing how he found

Arthur near death on the street outside his house and nursed him back to health. When questions arise as to Arthur's character, Stevens asks him to explain himself, and the rest of the text is increasingly Arthur's. Such a framing device is fairly common to early fictions, both European and American: the safe domesticity of a physician's voice that shields the reader from the more dangerous narrative of the mysterious stranger.

Like Murray's Vigillius, Stevens's authority thus is that of the professional whose education has exposed him to the reading materials and the intellectual traditions needed for proper authorship. His voice itself is moderate and self-possessed and therefore represents the model by which the republican reader might be guided. However, Stevens's thoughts and actions are consistently undermined, suggesting that, despite his daily exposure to misery and disease, Stevens remains in the safe realm of conventional thinking, unable to account for inevitable vicissitudes in human behavior and so is often a victim of his own limited interpretive and conceptual skills.

Stevens's opening narrative features a debate over the reliability of a certain kind of authority and its relation to acts of authorship. Stevens, his wife, and Wortley debate Arthur's trustworthiness. In each case, the debate centers around the issue of how authority can be recognized and whether or not any given source will, in fact, contribute to the improvement of the characters' situation. Wortley holds that seemingly innocent texts or sources, in the past, have proved deceptive and so argues caution. This debate casts a shadow on inherited authorship, disrupting orthodox ways of recognizing and authorizing received sources of authority. Moreover, its place in the text alerts the reader that this is a book about stories and how they are told and created and heard, and not just about the storyteller himself as the title belies. Why create such a presence if not to involve the reader in the debate?

In any case, the presumably virtuous narrative is allowed to enter the public sphere, and Stevens and friends agree to hear Arthur's story. Before he speaks, Stevens credits his "modesty" and "deportment by a gravity very unusual at his age" (10). Because he recognizes in Arthur the orthodox signifiers of innocence and honesty, Stevens even advises him on the production of an acceptable text: "Sincerity is always safest" (13). Wortley, however, recognizes Arthur from his association with a known con man, Welbeck, who has disappeared from Philadelphia. Between these, the reader must have approached Arthur with a degree of caution.

Like Franklin's, Arthur's claims to literacy validate his hope to be trusted.

Among the first things Arthur tells Stevens is that, although he has no formal education, he is not only literate but intends to write: "Yet, he confessed, a mode of life which entirely forbade him to read, was by no means to his taste" (11), and that although he did not want to be a "copyist," "the pen . . . had always been a favourite tool with me" (21). If it was not copying the works of others, his pen must have been recording his own texts. These claims duly impress Stevens, as they should have the reader. Brown's biographers agree that he had seen the manuscripts of Franklin's *Autobiography* before writing *Arthur Mervyn*. The shared autodidacticism of Arthur and Franklin transcends coincidence: Brown implicates Franklin in the simplistic assumption that literacy represents integrity.[17]

Before Arthur's narrative begins, then, the early republic reader had to choose between feeling safely couched in layers of authority, which assures a reading experience within the confines of the republican paradigm, or feeling puzzled or tentative. Two elements compel the reader to make crucial decisions. First, the very weight of the number of claims to authorization creates doubt: why must there be such defensiveness if clarity is not manifest? Second, Wortley's and Stevens's opposing interpretations of Arthur reveal that the republican public sphere was rife with internal dissent. The reader is finally left at the mercy of the text itself. If the reader does not decolonize his or her own interpretive skills, Arthur will gain control, for better or worse.

By undercutting the singularity and stability of all these authorial voices, Brown reveals the corruptibility of republican ideology in general, if not identifying that corruption itself. J. G. A. Pocock discusses "corruption"—the implausability and untenability of the idea of a virtuous and disinterested ruling class—as a post-Revolutionary *given* at the Constitutional Convention in the wake of the abject failure of the proposed "natural aristocracy" during confederation. Instead, he argues politicians conceded "the movement from virtue to interest" (531) and constructed a government that assumed inherent human corruption and selfishness. Yet claims to virtue and disinterestedness still saturated the public literature of republicanism, often in texts explicitly endorsed by the same politicians (Adams, Madison, etc.) who privately dismissed "virtue" as a political unreality, in the hope of a "renovation of virtue" among a more pliant public (548), a troubling moral double standard.

This deliberate self-misrepresentation of the republic to the public, I would suggest, resembles a metaphorical recolonization of the demos. Nicholas Dirks refers to colonialism's effort "to freeze the wolf in sheep's clothing" (177); that is, to erase the existing identity of the colonial subject and to replace it with one more suited to the needs of the colonizer. The resultant misrepresentations and contradictions contribute to the confusion, then, of post-Independence societies as well. In the example of the preface, republican writers like "C.B.B." assumed three things: first, that his own text cannot be misinterpreted; second, that he has the ability to discern the sources of the "evils of disease and poverty"; and, third, that the "spectators"—the readers—will respond properly. In the novel itself, narrative almost always creates misinterpretation, the sources and remedies of "evil" are consistently misdiagnosed, and spectators act in unpredictable ways. On this level, the framing narrative of *Arthur Mervyn* evokes of the double-speak of the founders on the issue of the corruption of the ruling and writing class to destabilize its social and textual authority.

Nonetheless, the republican author, the "natural aristocrat" of the reading exchange, still attempts to rule the process unilaterally, erasing and disregarding the reader's needs and identity, as did all colonizers. Oblivious to local or specific conditions, the colonizer of either land or people carries on with his plans and imposes his vision on those subject to his will. Mark Patterson and Thomas Gustafson have discussed the "crisis" of misrepresentation in the early republic along lines of class; when we reconsider the colonial origins of the republican elite's notions of social hierarchy, we can also identify this effort as colonizing.

However, *Arthur Mervyn* also reveals the fictional nature of republicanism's plans for reshaping the national personality: Brown catalyzes a readerly skepticism of the hollow textual signifiers of authority and contributes to their deflation and discrediting by wildly diverging from their stated intent and, importantly, assuming his reader will follow. Recognizing that American readers were dubious of such impositions as the 1790s wore on, Brown works in the shadows of this paradox and asks the reader to query further the consistency of republican rhetoric.

When introducing Arthur himself, Brown deliberately identifies his "hero" with both villainy and virtue, never allowing the definitive placement of Arthur in relation to any inherited standard of legitimacy. In brief, he does not fit, suggesting that the paradigm offers a severely limited "repertoire" of options. In volume 1 of *Arthur Mervyn*, he is only a speaker. Nonetheless, his narration in volume 1 prepares the ground for his later ascent to author—a deliberate quest undertaken to gain public authority, wealth, and power—the seeds of which are planted in Brown's punning selection of his name, "Arthur." As an oral narration, his story in volume 1 enacts the same inherited motions of self-authorization as a written text, although Stevens is still nominally the transcriber and makes occasional interruption. Despite Stevens's asides, which compel the reader to share his growing trust, the signs of his unreliability are introduced throughout volume 1, and are fully displayed in volume 2.

They begin before Arthur's narrative itself starts. In Stevens's opening chapter, when confronted by Wortley's accusations, Arthur displays a "trembling consciousness" (11) and then retreats to consider how to tell his story. The next night, when Stevens gathers his wife and other members of Philadelphia's merchant class, Arthur prefaces his story by suggesting that it is "simple" and "tedious" (16) and suggests that "I can keep hold of your good position only by a candid deportment" (15). His false modesty—the story is by no means simple—and his stumbling deference to Stevens and his friends denote an ambition that transcends merely their acceptance of his story: he means for his story alone to allow him to join their group, but this is no dunderheaded Updike Underhill whose absurdity is relatively benign—darker shadings follow Arthur.

The members of this group are financially secure, publicly respected, and trusted as leaders in the community. Arthur's tale is purportedly the perfect vehicle for gaining their trust. However, he specifically requests that Wortley be excluded from his auditors (16). Arthur's exclusion of the one person who could challenge him before the group suggests that he feels compelled, like the typical author of the day, to control by discouraging conflicting interpretation or information. It would have been simple enough for Brown to permit Wortley to hear Arthur: the careful removal of the dissident voice, however, demonstrates that Brown intends Arthur's actions to seem mysterious and unclear, perhaps even spurious, even though his actual text bears all the signifiers of legitimacy.

Arthur buttresses his tale by reminding his new auditors—who now overtly include the early republic reader—of the fact of his literacy and his ambition to become a genuine author (21, 47, 53, 81). In the tradition of Caleb Williams, Tom Jones, and other figures from eighteenth-century English fiction, Arthur informs us that he is a youth from the country forced to migrate to the city when personal tragedy struck his family. After arriving in Philadelphia, Arthur embarks on an elaborate series of adventures, all of which he relates using terms borrowed from the Gothic novel. The excesses of coincidence, darkness, obfuscations, and passionate speeches—the properties that scholars have traditionally used to demonstrate Brown's artistic weaknesses—compose Arthur's story. By contrast, Brown's story is of Arthur *telling* his experiences to Stevens and his friends. Arthur consistently dwells on morbid and sensational details and his own adolescent and emotionally overwrought responses to the various events. For example, after changing clothes, Arthur meditates: "My senses are the sport of dreams. Some magic that disdains the cumbrousness of nature's progress, has wrought this change" (51). This manner of fantastic speculation characterizes much of his complex narrative. Furthermore, the many twists and turns of Arthur's story add to the narrative's excesses.[18]

While most critics have dismissed the occasional contradictions and repetitions as the result of Brown's haste in composition, I would suggest that they are rather *Arthur's* means of distracting his listeners and readers. He disguises a Gothic tale as a reliable personal narrative, smuggling a merely popular form into an approved text—this is a story about stories, and Arthur's life moves as much from genre to genre as it does from event to event. In the preface to *Edgar Huntly*, Brown attacked Gothic writing as a technique of "puerile superstition and exploded manners" (3)—the very devices used at length by Arthur. When *Arthur Mervyn*'s Gothic devices are reconsidered as Arthur's deliberate tools for the manipulation of his auditors' hypocritical taste for the salacious, his deeper motivations are suggested. This careful strategy of misrepresentation and possible misdirection gives him cover while he joins the group.

Arthur seems fully aware that while his audience is fascinated by his adventures, he can explain away the dubiousness of his actions and motivations. Concealed in his ornate language are confessions that he failed to pay tolls, that he abetted a murderer, and that he stole an important document from a private house. Even in an age of complex narratives, *Arthur Mervyn*'s convolutions are remarkable. In a sense, then, Arthur has tapped into the master discourse of sensationalism to subjugate his auditors, erasing their willingness to consider his actions or his texts critically. Contrariwise, Brown observes the willingness of early republic listeners to be erased in this manner: both colonizing performer and colonized audience are necessary to complete this equation.

Brown thus also accuses the early republic of complacency, of self-subjugation. His perception of this gap between the elite and the public shares Tyler's and Brackenridge's recognition that the growing distance between the reading and writing habits of the new nation threatened the integrity of the democratic process by contributing to the development of a stratified and hierarchical national community. Brown calls for fiction to combat the domination of the public's reading habits by such deceptive texts and authors through its blurring of received relations and its empowerment of the reader's imagination. Fiction might then be a force of decolonization and democratization by compelling the reader to question his relationship with the author, the text, and any other orbiting ideas.[19]

Significantly included in Arthur's twisted tale is a consistent recurrent commentary on the acts of reading and writing. By alluding to his mastery of the motions of authorized literary activity, Arthur repeatedly asserts that his activities as a literate person are those of a reliable figure. What Robert Ferguson has said of the founders in his essay "'We Hold These Truths,'" might also be said of Arthur: "The truth may be self-evident, but the people must be humored, duped, coaxed, and provoked into accepting it" (7). Likewise, Arthur manipulates his audience. These statements further complicate Brown's reflection of the chaotic nature of American reading and writing in the early republic, a development best illustrated in regard to Arthur's work as a translator of the text of "Lodi's manuscript," the book he steals from Welbeck.

Arthur translates this text after he has retreated from plague-ridden Philadelphia to the rural setting of the Hadwin farm in Malverton. By way of prefacing his return to the country he had fled only days before, Brown has him recall his reading of a nameless text that obviously reflects Jeffersonian agrarianism: "My books had taught me the dignity and safety of the middle road, and my darling writer abounded with encomiums on rural life" (47). Brown further alludes to Jefferson, as David M. Larson and Lawson-Peebles have noted, by borrowing agrarian imagery: "The land by which the dwelling was surrounded, its pure airs, romantic walks, and exhaustless fertility, constituted a powerful contrast to the scenes which I had left behind" (123).[20] Arthur cleverly uses such commentary to return his narrative to the standard phraseology of inherited texts—this is hardly the nightmarish American countryside of *Wieland* or *Edgar Huntly*. This bucolic imagery is compounded by his initiation of a presumably virtuous love affair with Eliza Hadwin.

Welbeck, the noted con man who had involved Arthur in his plots, recognizes the social power of a literary reputation. He claims that he means to translate the Lodi's manuscript and publish it as his own: "My ambition has panted, with equal avidity, after the reputation of literature and opulence" (100). Since this comes from a man who has just shot another, one might wonder about the narrow space

Brown observed between criminal behavior and public authorship. The seeming viability of this enterprise reinforces the notion available in Arthur's own story that conventional writing are easily faked.

When Arthur flees Philadelphia after what he thinks is Welbeck's suicide, he steals the manuscript and takes it with him. On the Hadwin farm, he translates the text. Near the end, however, he discovers twenty-thousand dollars in bank-notes glued between the pages (126). After this, he never finishes the translation, an action that suggests that, for him, literature is merely a means to wealth—not an activity worthwhile on its own, just as it had not been for Welbeck. Arthur later destroys the bills when Welbeck tells him they are counterfeit, but he never attempts to explain his actions to Clemenza Lodi, their rightful owner. But Wel-beck had lied to him; the bills were, in fact, real. While this episode demonstrates the virtues of careful reading—Arthur's monetary reward—it also undermines the legitimacy of Arthur's role as a presumably reliable reader: he fails to dis-criminate properly between the legitimate banknotes and Welbeck's deceptions. His inability to distinguish undermines his claim to reliable interpretive skills, and thus casts doubt on his entire narrative.

Lodi's text also allows Brown to enter the text in a way that comments further upon Arthur's possible corruption. The narrative, as Arthur tells it, champions "the Condotierre Sforza, a leader of out-laws against the popular enthusiasm of the Milanese." Trapped by his pursuers in a Roman tomb, he "found in it a trea-sure, by which he would be enabled to secure the wavering and venal faith of that crew of ruffians that followed his standard" (126). Arthur's hero is antidemoc-ratic, uncharismatic, and fully aware that power and support can be bought, all characteristics he finds attractive. But because Sforza is labeled a hero in print, he is welcomed by Arthur and his auditors. Brown again suggests that overin-flated language can easily disguise dangerous rhetoric, especially when put into print.

Soon thereafter, Arthur reenters Philadelphia in search of Wallace, the fiancée of the elder Hadwin daughter, and returns to his Gothic narrative. There he has further misadventures with Welbeck and finally is infected with the plague, be-fore being found by Stevens at the start of the framing narrative, bringing his lis-teners into the present of his narration. In this section Arthur frames a narrative of Welbeck, who had not, as it turned out, died. Welbeck introduces his own text with terms that obliquely recreate those used by Arthur at the start of the vol-ume: "You must not imagine that my stratagem was deep-laid or deliberately ex-ecuted. . . . I meant not to injure but to serve you" (175). Like Arthur, Welbeck assumes that "sincerity is always safest," and trusts that his use of the proper language will ensure his reliability. Unlike Carwin or Ormond, Welbeck the conventional villain is easily defeated by the purported hero, a fact that demonstrates less about the shortcomings of Welbeck than about Arthur's ability to outcon the con man. These devices allow Brown to cloud any clear interpretation of Arthur's narrative: while his crimes might not be clear, neither are his virtues.

Arthur concludes his tale in volume 1 with statements that allude to his ambition to create a text that will assure him entry into the republic of letters: "I have promised to relate the momentous incidents of my life and have hitherto been faithful in my enumeration. There is nothing which I more detest, than equivocation and mystery" (212–13). Again, this act of self-defense, for a genuinely sincere author, would be redundant and excessive. Next, he suggests that his narrative not only confirms his past but also his future: "It is only in one way that I am able to heighten the gratification which must flow from your [Stevens's] conduct—by shewing that the being whose life you have prolonged, though uneducated, ignorant, and poor, is not profligate and worthless, and will not dedicate that life which your bounty has given, to mischievous or contemptible purposes" (214–15). Arthur assumes the success of his narrative and requests a place among Philadelphia's professional class, even though his claims to being "uneducated" and "ignorant" appear spurious, coming as they do from an efficient translator of Italian.

At the end of volume 1, the issues of Arthur's innocence or guilt, or rather of his authorial or speakerly reliability or treachery, cannot be resolved. Nonetheless, in refusing to create a didactic or direct resolution, Brown can be seen muddying the waters of his own act of authorship: this fiction seems to look like a component of the republican paradigm, and the author's reputation and stated intent seem to affirm its public utility. But it does not finish the job: even in the final sentence, the purported hero's motivations seem unclear. The reader can only put down volume 1 confused, questioning the reading just as Brown's hesitation to publish had suggested. But this questioning, implicitly, should arouse critical thought.

The beginning of volume 2 (1800), instead of clarifying the final passages of volume 1, only complements its perplexities. *Edgar Huntly* was published in the interval between the two parts of *Arthur Mervyn* and sold rather poorly. Recent scholars have suggested that, like Brackenridge, Brown responded to the public's rejection of his work by paying less and less attention to pleasing public taste he found too slow to adjust to his demanding productions.[21] Therefore, Brown's comments on the dubious nature of printed communication in the early republic become firmer in volume 2, as Arthur evolves from speaker to writer. This transformation represents a growth in the sphere of his influence: in volume 1 he spoke to Stevens's group; in volume 2, by seizing the authorship of the text, he reaches the public at large.

In this, Brown suggests that so long as a complacent colonial public continues to privilege the corruptible forms and diction of standard discourse, colonizing forces of corruption insinuate themselves into the fabric of American life—"the sordid colonial character." Soon after the opening of volume 2, a "mystery" concerning Arthur's story arises, and he must immediately do the very things he claims to despise: he is compelled to "equivocate" at length to defend himself. These continuities suggest a narrative unity between the two volumes through the vehicle of the fiction of Arthur's ascent to authorship. Volume 2 was also published with volume 1's preface, which also suggests that Brown conceived of it not as a sequel to volume 1, but as a continuation of a single text.

Stevens's voice opens volume 2 with the testimony that Arthur's story had been successful and that his circle of friends had accepted him, simply on the basis of his tale, as one of their own: "They served no end, but as vouchers for the truth of his tale" (219). Arthur's power over language has translated into actual social power without the mediating proof of hard evidence: all we have is his story. His acceptance has been accomplished to such a degree that Stevens begins to train him in the profession of medicine: "By residing with me, partaking my instructions, and reading my books, he would, in a few years, be fitted for the practice of physic. A science whose truths are so conducive to the welfare of mankind, and which comprehends the whole system of nature, could not but gratify a mind so beneficent as his. This scheme occurred to me as soon as the conclusion of his tale allowed me to think" (220). This statement demonstrates Stevens's role as a typical member of the republic of letteres and Arthur's success in acquiring the degree of eloquence necessary for social advancement. It would seem that the system has worked: the reliable signifiers of authority have produced a healthy, new member of the new nation's leading class. In the meantime, darkly, the telling of the story had prevented Stevens from thinking about its paradoxes, blinding him to any view but Arthur's. Were Brown's story simply a tale of "virtue," it could be completed at this point. But, its continuation, and the introduction of even more evidence to hint at Arthur's unreliability, suggest that Brown has a more complicated text in mind.

The testimony of someone not in this group immediately complicates the matter. Before starting his training, Arthur sets out again for the Hadwin farm, to bring the now-orphaned Eliza to the city. In his absence, Mrs. Althorpe, a woman from Chester county, where Arthur grew up, offers a very different view of his character. Her view contradicts his story with such precision that Brown's intent to undercut Arthur's reliability is manifest. Using "the unanimous reports of Mervyn's neighbors" (232), she says he is selfish, lazy, licentious, effeminate, unfaithful, and morally repugnant—stating even that he had slept with his step-mother. She accuses him of being "not in his right mind," "very perverse and sin-gular," "averse to school," "inhuman," and "despised for his idleness and folly" (232–35). Her story is anchored by her willingness to call in male contemporaries to corroborate, a sign that she is able to support her observations using a source acceptable to people like Stevens or the reader whose implicit sexism further demonstrates the republic's divisive nature.

After hearing Mrs. Althorpe, Stevens and Wortley investigate Arthur's story and fail to find more than circumstantial evidence to support his claims. Stevens frets that "if Mervyn has deceived me, there is an end to my confidence in human nature. All limits to dissimulation, and all distinctions between vice and virtue will be effaced. No man's word, no force of collateral evidence shall weigh with me a hair" (248–49). Wortley replies: "It was time . . . that your confidence in smooth features and fluent accents should have ended long ago. Till I gained from my present profession, some knowledge of the world, . . . I was equally un-wise in my own conceit; and, in order to decide upon the truth of any one's pre-tensions, needed only a clear view of his face, and a distinct hearing of his words. My folly, in that respect, was only to be cured, however, by my own experience, and I suppose your credulity will yield to no other remedy" (249). Wortley un-derstands that the uncritical acceptance of the signifiers of authority are not enough: active participation in listening, reading, and interpreting alone can de-fend against deception. Stevens responds by suspending his judgment: "I want time to revolve [these contradictions] slowly, to weigh them accurately, and to estimate their consequences fully" (251). Stevens's act of reconsideration and doubt is also thrust upon the reader by Brown, implying that a more careful ex-amination of appearances is the hallmark of a truly informed citizen.

After further challenges are made to Arthur's veracity, Stevens finally is called to a debtor's prison by an anonymous note. There he finds Arthur, ministering to a dying Welbeck. When Stevens takes him back to his house, Arthur resumes his complicated narration. This time, having gained the trust of his listeners, he reveals more of himself by explaining his actions in a self-referential authorial voice, secure that he will be trusted by his listeners again. Before he begins, however, he mentions that he had sent letters to Stevens since leaving for the country—letters that never arrived. Given Mrs. Althorpe's recent allegations, one must wonder if the letters ever existed.

While relating the chaotic nature of his return to Malverton, Arthur describes his own activity as someone authorized to make decisions on behalf of others. In particular, he makes dubious choices concerning Eliza Hadwin that reveal his unreliability as a source of paternal responsibility: he buries the older sister in a shallow grave without consulting Eliza (271), offends the Hadwins' neighbors and relations (277), and leaves Eliza with strangers (293). While his actions are defensible, they are by no means clearly righteous. Again, Brown compels the reader to make decisions regarding his protagonist. Along the way, Arthur establishes himself to strangers by using the same technique he had used on Stevens: he tells them his story. His growing authority thus becomes decreasingly connected to actual evidence and increasingly to the creation of his mastery of the forms and language of inherited linguistic conventions.

Having completed the narrative that eventually led him back to Welbeck, Arthur reminds Stevens of his ambition to be an acceptable member of the professional class: "My path was already chalked out, and my fancy now pursued it with uncommon pleasure" (310). When he has finished this story, he seems aware that Stevens and friends may have found it less likely than his earlier narrative. Stevens observes "an air of inquietude about him, which I had never observed in an equal degree before" (339). At this point, Arthur has imposed his own authority over the lives of Welbeck, Eliza, and Clemenza, benevolently colonizing their interests. Welbeck, an expert at reading and manipulating human nature, despises him; Arthur has broken Eliza's heart; and Clemenza has been left bankrupt by Arthur's precipitous destruction of her fortune. Again, while his motives seem pure, the results of his actions are highly questionable.

With these suspicions in mind, Stevens confronts Arthur with Mrs. Althorpe's accusations. He defends himself rather glibly: "It is true they mistake me, but that arises from the circumstances of our mutual situation. They examined what was exposed to their view: they grasped at what was placed within their reach. To decide contrary to appearances; to judge from what they know not, would prove them to be brutish and not rational, would make their decision of no worth, and render them, in their turn, objects of neglect and contempt" (341). Rather than actually defending himself against their charges, he accuses his accusers of being deceived by his own manipulation of their small-minded opinions. In fact, he never directly refutes the charges. Moreover, he openly admits to presenting a false picture of himself to others in the past, an action that, in addition, he does not regret. Having established this pattern, Brown silently implicates Arthur's present actions in a larger scheme of dissimulation.

Just as he had in volume 1, Arthur obscures the true nature of his actions behind the formulaic invocation of generic imagery. Throughout this equivocation, he alludes to the Jeffersonian and Franklinian images available to any reader of the 1790s. Nonetheless, the seriousness of Mrs. Althorpe's accusations, along with some lingering doubts as to Arthur's role in the events of volume 1, suggests Brown nodding to the reader that Arthur may not be what he seems; that he is simply the wasteful boy Mrs. Althorpe suggests, now armed with a rhetoric and a vocabulary more authorized than her own. Stevens's, and the reader's, suspicions are left unresolved: "I shall pass over the reflections which a story like this would naturally suggest" (348).

At this point Stevens leaves to attend his business in New Jersey, and Arthur begins to transcribe his own narrative, evolving from speaker to author. With this, the process whereby a conventional authority is removed from *Arthur Mervyn* is complete: neither a *real* author nor a conventional framing voice stands between Arthur and his intended reader. The almost seamless transition between the two dramatizes the precariousness of republican textual authority. Demonstrating that his "credulity" is still intact, Stevens continues to believe Arthur and advises him that "an honest face and a straight story will be sufficient" (349) even while writing, just as it had been when speaking. On the contrary, Brown suggests such signifiers rely on tremendous superficiality and artifice: the face that is "honest" may not be straight, and the story that is "straight" may not be honest.

The final quarter of the novel, then, is all Arthur's. He writes in two sequences. The first, chapters 16 through 22, is composed upon the completion of what he considers his mission to right the wrongs of Welbeck. Particularly absent from this final section of the novel are accusations such as those of Mrs. Althorpe. So long as Stevens dictates the text, dissonant voices such as Mrs. Althorpe's impede

Arthur's quest for validation. As such, Stevens, like Murray's Vigillius, was willing to allow otherwise marginalized voices a presence in the printed text. Brown, whose feminism was established by *Alcuin* (1797), on the other hand, has Arthur meticulously silence the dissonance that precludes his creation of consensus. By becoming an author, Arthur, like all republican writers, can assure his readers of a monolithic representation of his qualifications for receiving their unqualified trust.

The first of the two sequences describes a fictional authorship that, like his spoken text, employs a variety of Gothic and Franklinian techniques. As before, the fiction describes his ambition to join the new nation's elite. The second, chapters 23 through 25, is written on the eve of his departure for Europe with his new wife, Acsha Fielding, a wealthy widow, and employs the private language of the Richardsonian sentimental novel. The second fictional authorship describes Arthur's final ambition not only for public authorization but also for attaining an even more insidious means of colonization: the internal authority of emotional manipulation. If Warner's "national imaginary" is to develop, the citizen/reader needs an uncorrupted "private" intellectual space to develop the appropriate "repertoire of self-perceptions" needed to defend against the interested sophistry of corrupt or biased texts. Arthur enters that space to assure that that "national imaginary" welcomes someone as slippery as himself.

The first sequence depicts Arthur's self-assigned quest, through both his actions and his composing of an acceptable text to repair the damage done by Mrs. Althorpe's accusations. To reestablish his place among his immediate friends and, now, his readers, he graciously thanks Stevens for writing the text to this point: "I am glad, my friend, thy noble pen has got so far upon its journey. What remains of my story may be dispatched in a trice. I have just now some vacant hours, which might be more usefully employed, but not in an easier manner or more pleasant. So, let me carry on the thread" (354). In this passage, like any writer of the republic of letters, Arthur suggests that literature is a leisurely activity to be undertaken by gentlemen. Brown's refusal to approach his craft in this manner clearly reveals his distrust in leaving literature to the politicians. Moreover, though he bears none of the doctor's traditional signs of authority besides language, Arthur silently inherits the textual authority established by Stevens.

The chapters immediately following mostly describe Arthur's supposedly valiant righting of Welbeck's wrongs. At many points, Arthur is in the position of being able to abscond with large sums of money, but he does not. Based strictly on actions, Arthur's virtue seems established—but it is only Arthur's story that tells the reader about these actions. One character ponders, "I can scarcely tell whether this simplicity be real or affected" (359). Neither can the reader. When similar questions are raised, Arthur retreats to his previously successful conventional text. To preface his self-referential explanations, he uses phrases such as "perhaps my narrative" (360), "my proper task is to relate the truth" (371), and "I related what had just passed" (385) to assure his listeners and readers that any more recent action is based on his version of the truth—a version worthy of trust since it is conveyed in such a literate style.

Having completed his purported atonement for the sins of Welbeck, Arthur again retreats to his plan to join Philadelphia's professional class: "I now set about carrying my plan of life into effect. I began with ardent zeal and unwearied diligence the career of medical study. . . . My curiosity grew more eager, in proportion as it was supplied with food, and every day added strength to the assurance that I was no insignificant and worthless being; that I was destined to be *something* in this scene of existence, and might sometime lay claim to the gratitude and homage of my fellow-men" (396). Having assured this group that Mrs. Althorpe's statements were without foundation, he rejoins it with a candid declaration of his willingness to dedicate himself to the career of enlightened public interest that was the early republic's ideal. However, the brevity of his pursuit of such a noble career darkens this statement. It is possible that Arthur had planned from the start that his entry into the professional class was only a stepping-stone on his path to broader social prestige.

The first section of Arthur's authorship concludes with his explanation of why he seized the text himself. Using the self-congratulatory tone of Franklin's explanations for his own authorship of the *Autobiography*, Arthur nods to conventional techniques: "Mrs. Wentworth has put me upon a strange task—not disagreeable, however. . . . I have, oftener than once, and far more circumstantially than now, told her my adventures, but she is not satisfied. She wants a written narrative, for some purpose which she tells me she will disclose to me hereafter" (412). Again, he thanks Stevens for starting the narrative and suggests that Stevens had done so for "the safety of my reputation and my life, from the consequences of my connection with Welbeck." He concludes that "time has annihilated that danger" (412). While time may have been annihilated, a plethora of evidence that the reader must consider has not.

This first sequence, then, describes the consolidation of Arthur's place among the nation's privileged. He purportedly means for his text to be useful as an educational instrument for other aspirants to respectability. In many ways, he is successful: Stevens has obviously encouraged him, so the reader might feel inclined to do so as well, and the persistent doubts in Stevens's narrative may have been foreclosed by Arthur's assumption of authorship. In this way Arthur dramatizes the means by which language was employed in the early republic as a means of legitimizing the elite's colonization and containment of the lower classes by dominating the terms of social mobility.

However, starting in chapter 23, Arthur's second act of authorship raises doubts again. In this text, he borrows the emotive and romantic language of the sentimental novel to describe his relationship with, courtship of, and ultimate betrothal to Acsha Fielding.[22] In brief, upon returning to Philadelphia, Arthur professes that he feels obligated to marry Eliza Hadwin at some undetermined point in the future. Soon he becomes distracted by Mrs. Fielding, a Jewish widow whose appearance is not conventionally attractive. Arthur introduces this section in a language quite different from any he had used before: "Move on my quill! Wait not for my guidance. Reanimated with thy master's spirit, all airylight! An hey-day rapture! A mounting impulse sways him: lifts him from the earth. I must, cost what it will, rein in this upward pulling, forward urging—what shall I call it? But there are times, and now is one of them, when words are poor" (413). Like his earlier use of the didactic, Arthur's use of sentimental language in a text seeking authority might seem problematic. But this text never announces itself as fiction and so its excesses seem to demand tolerance. Again, Arthur smudges genres to distract his readers from the questionable aspects of his behavior. For example, his "zeal" for both the medical profession and Eliza are silently forsaken as he moves with his wife to Europe. Just as Lodi's manuscript was deserted when Arthur chose wealth over literary activity, he quickly abandons Enlightenment virtues when a greater glamour becomes available.

Moreover, Arthur's move to Europe fulfills the colonial's goal: to return to the metropolis and its centrality. Arthur had never accepted not being the center of attention, being on the margins. As an American, he recognizes that part of his identity will always be decentralized and colonial—that the important place of commerce and society is abroad, not local. His marriage to a Jewish woman consolidates his cosmopolitan aspirations; simultaneously, Ascha's marriage to a gentile, like those of most Jews in the new nation, contributed to the erasure of ethnic distinctions, another component of republican monoculturalism.[23] At once

Arthur seeks to shed his American marginality and serve the need for homogeneity implicit in European concepts of national identity. Remaking himself this time as a First World metropolitan, Arthur pays his final tribute to the departed colonizer by joining him, and by leaving America. However, while Arthur leaves in body, in the text he leaves behind his American legacy remains.

The sentimental text appeals to his audience's emotions. Not content merely with planting himself physically in their midst, he now attempts to enter their hearts and their minds. When he claims that "the pen is a pacifyer. It checks the mind's career" (414), he compels the reader to identify with his rapture, not with the socially irresponsible nature of his actions. Arthur himself makes sure that his reader favors his distracting text. In regard to the reading that Stevens prescribes as part of his training as a doctor, Arthur responds: "Books are cold, jejune, vexatious in their sparingness of information at one time, and their impertinent loquacity at another. Besides, all they chuse to give, they give at once. ... They talk to us behind a screen. Their tone is lifeless and monotonous" (411). Given that Arthur himself is writing a book, he can only be referring to other books whose authority he may be usurping. In either case, Brown is depicting a treacherous literary environment: readers can choose either the slippery but attractive Arthur or the sincere but boring sources of convention and responsibility.

Arthur Mervyn ends with a passage that suggests that the fiction of authorship was a part of his text that Brown felt was essential to the work's final impression. In reference to his pen, Arthur concludes, "Lie there, snug in thy leathern case, till I call for thee, and that will not be very soon. I believe I will abjure thy company till all is settled with my love. Yes, I *will* abjure thee, so let *this* be thy last office, til Mervyn has been made the happiest of men" (446). Again, personal aims supersede the purported public service of his authorship. The suggestion of future authorships insinuates that Arthur may again call upon his mastery of verbal communication to reach yet a higher level of cultural colonization, repeating the pattern this first book of his fictional career as an author has established, this time writing from the European center, not the American margin.

But neither the modern nor the early republic reader can be entirely sure. On one level, Arthur's virtues seem clear: he patiently sorts through the chaos of 1793 Philadelphia to find wealth, true love, and an articulate voice to contribute to the new nation. On another, he commits crimes, misrepresents himself, and carefully counterfeits conventional ways of writing to gain a position from which he can impose his selfish will on others. In the context of his age, he could be either the valorized Benjamin Franklin or the notorious Stephen Burroughs, an admitted con man whose *Memoirs* (1797) sold widely in the new nation. Or he could be both.

❧

Brown's ambiguous text, while significant for its meditation on the compromised nature of American individuality, also must be understood as an important document in the history of the decolonization of reading and writing in America. Brown's presentation of a text in which only the reader can decide whom to trust takes place in the specific cultural conditions of the early republic. *Arthur Mervyn* allows Brown to demonstrate how the inherited linguistic and generic textual base upon which the early republic placed so much trust for the identification and consolidation of a safe and honest society are susceptible to corruption and depravity. However, by no means did Brown favor an even harsher limitation of the available modes of expression.

Because Brown wrote primarily to the novel-reading public, not the elite who distrusted fiction, his emphasis is on the cultivation of a national readership as well as on a national literature. Those who question Arthur's duplicitous pose and prose are thus better equipped to reconsider other forms of authorized discourse. Brown tacitly suggests that the actual institutions of reading and writing are much more complicated than those inherited from England. Needed was an alternative textuality and method of reading that balanced power between the reader and the writer so as to prevent the new society from becoming as diseased socially as Philadelphia was physically in the summer of 1793.

Having finished *Arthur Mervyn*, Brown wrote only two more novels, *Clara Howard* (1801) and *Jane Talbot* (1801). Both are in the rather commercial didactic mode, a transition Brown's biographers contribute to his growing financial straits. What little creative writing Brown did before his death in 1810 went mostly unpublished during his lifetime.[24] The pieces are difficult to place in the context of the republican paradigm, reflecting the discontent with the forms and voices disputed in *Arthur Mervyn*. Two in particular, "Sketches of a History of Carsol" and "Sketches of a History of Carrils and Ormes," offer an especially experimental style, anticipating in some ways the dark and challenging worlds of George Lippard and Robert Montgomery Bird.[25]

In "Carsol," Brown describes the ascension of an Arthur-like figure, Praya,

to regal status in a distant land. Instead of outright seizures of power, Praya relies on "invisible and insuperable hedges" to construct a personal authority that
transforms into "a sacred kind of awe" to the point that his "mandates came to
be obeyed like those of a physical necessity" (208–9). This more abstracted version of Arthur Mervyn reveals the excesses of authority Brown recognized and
feared not only in individuals but in texts and language, the powerful "hedges"
of Praya's and Arthur's power. Ultimately, Brown suggests that social and discursive power in the early republic had become vehicles for the suppression of
free thought and the exchange of ideas.

Decolonizing both readers and writers by creating a demand for mutual participation in the construction of meaning, Brown asks more of American readers than a colonial writer could ask of his subjects. To identify the lingering
"sordid colonial character" in the early republic, Brown chose authorship as a
contested site for contesting the perpetuation of colonial values that threatened
the integrity of the revolutionary enterprise. By compelling the reader to work
harder at reading, he implies the application of similarly rigorous and privately
determined standards to other public arenas. By demanding that the reader investigate the diversity and conflicted "double-consciousness" of the American
personality in the wake of Revolution, Brown demands a Second World reading
strategy which challenges received representations and attempts to incorporate the
nearly silenced plurality and dichotomy of early republic life. Like the other writers addressed in this study, having exposed the contradictions of conventional
writing in a fiction of authorship, Brown was unwilling to participate creatively
in the community of writers and readers he considered duplicitous, although his
work as an editor and pamphleteer continued.

In that light, Brown's *Arthur Mervyn* must be added to that part of American
literature in which writers intervene in day-to-day use of language as a medium
of power: he would take readers aside and alert them to the precariousness of certain public assumptions, warning them not to be fooled by duplicitous men and
their dangerous language. Like Herman Melville in *The Confidence-Man*, William
Dean Howells in *A Modern Instance*, and Sinclair Lewis in *Elmer Gantry*, Brown
understood America as a protean land of charlatans whose use of language empowered them in the national logocracy. More immediately, *Arthur Mervyn*, pre-
dating Irving's creation of the term in *Salmagundi* by seven years, embodies the
logocracy: it demonstrates how much the early republic trusted textual models
as a basis for reordering the post-Revolutionary community and reveals just how
dubious a venture this was.

Instead Brown dramatizes how the nation was duped by the imposition of a false language and literature on an otherwise exuberant and intelligent populace and instead asks the readers to reject that subject position and authorize themselves to think independently, to decolonize themselves. By thrusting upon the reader the onus of interpretive responsibility, Brown suggests that the chaos in which Arthur thrives cannot be remedied from above through the republican reinscription of colonial monovocality and European tradition. On the contrary, Brown asks for solutions to come from the lower end of the social hierarchy, the American reader. By inviting heteroglossic interpretations of Arthur, Brown brings to the readership the need for rigorous critical thought and self-examination, asking them to see in themselves what Stephen Slemon calls "the ambivalent, the mediated, the conditional, and the radically compromised" nature of Second World experience (110) instead of the stable but false world and text of the republic.

❦

FIVE

The Peculiar Birthright of Every American: George Watterston's *The Lawyer*

IF CHARLES BROCKDEN BROWN suggested that the republic of letters engendered an unreliable and counterproductive basis for American reading and writing, George Watterston went one step further: in his novel *The Lawyer, or Man as He Ought Not To Be* (1808), he identifies his fictional author with crime and deceit. With the possible exception of Brown's *Arthur Mervyn*, the other books in this study dramatize republican authorship as misguided acts of a benevolent, almost Kiplingesque colonization of the reader in which malfeasance is incidental; Watterston is more concerned with the more covertly invasive aspects of the reintroduction of social hierarchies leftover from the post-1763 colonial period. Save for Arthur Mervyn and the occasional selfish motivation of Royall Tyler's Updike Underhill, the other fictional authors for the most part have innocently mistaken recolonization and republicanism for a much-needed source of stability after the Revolution, a means of creating a better version of the parent country.[1]

However, as republicanism promoted imperialism in the West and tolerated slavery in the South, again and again suppressed local rebellions (Shays's, Whiskey, etc.), and continued to "mechanize" the nation's society and geography, in John Seelye's terms, or to "redcoat," in those of Robert Lawson-Peebles, to remake the new nation along English lines, its claim to virtuous public interest had worn thin. Jack N. Rakove has observed that the new government was only acting "here as elsewhere" (18)—doing what all governments do. Given that the republic was supposed to be different from other places, its acquiesence in European methods of coercion seemed to violate revolutionary principles. The Revolution had been over for an entire generation, and its ideals long since appropriated and redirected by the battles between the two political parties. In the meantime, republicanism had created an environment wherein the selfish, the immoral, and the exploitative could thrive by becoming eloquent enough to gain the respect of their neighbors.

Michael Kramer and Christopher Looby have separately observed and documented how republicanism created a dangerous opening through which tyranny reentered American life. In regard to language Looby writes: "Americans, who had been schooled in monarchical forms, certainly continued to use the cognitive schemas inherited from the monarchical past even when monarchy had been repudiated" (43). Watterston's fictional author simply means to exploit for personal reasons the received "cognitive schemas" that encouraged a passive citizenry. Watterston's depiction of the fictional authorship of a purportedly didactic text reveals and subverts the most insidious means by which inherited textuality intervened in the individual's decision-making process: moral choice.

By identifying the appropriation of this presumably private and personal arena as a site of political and public indoctrination, Watterston observes the processes of imperium on an individual level and demands that decolonization involve abrogation of the private as well as the public sphere. Received, "monarchical" authorial forms discouraged active readership, and the moral text certainly monopolized the reader's options. If, as Slemon and Lawson have argued, Second World postcolonialism is essentially a position of "double-consciousness," in the terms of Gary Richardson, conformist, passive readership reinscribed a single-consciousness and ignored local difference or its potential.[2]

Many scholars have identified the consistent presence of moral texts in the early republic: Murray's and Brown's overt manipulation and subversion of the genre's methodology reveals the reader's familiarity with them. In fact, David S. Reynolds claims that during the 1820s and 1830s, "dark reform" novels by George Thompson and George Lippard inverted purportedly moral texts to help "transform a culture of morality into a culture of ambiguity" (59). By this reasoning, a singular "culture of morality" dominated the early republic, emanating from a unified literary establishment. Such a culture served republican interests by creating a subject audience and by containing sources of social deviation and difference. This was purportedly yet another manifestation of the monovocal early republic.

Such a culture was presumably characterized by conservative values of Calvinism and conformity communicated by reliable and legitimate authors.[3] Emory Elliott has recognized that "those of superior intelligence and training had the power and duty to lead the less enlightened toward truth and improvement" (31). Lawyers, in particular, were posited as arbiters of and spokesmen for the public good, a remarkable linkage of authority and authorship.[4] In regard to fiction, this system privileged the didactic novel as the sole mode of fiction acceptable for publication and distribution.[5] While the law may have been a middle-class profession in England, in the new United States, lawyers transcended their assigned role as intermediaries to claim the center of their country's ideological debates, becoming a de facto aristocracy through their special access to the arcana of law. In *Law and Letters in American Culture*, Robert A. Ferguson writes in reference to 1803 that "thirty years before Alexis de Tocqueville's famous equation of the legal profession to an intellectual aristocracy, American lawyers had already arrogated that status to themselves" (12). R. A. Burchell has also recognized both the existence of an upper class of lawyers in the early republic but further traces its parallels to the English gentry of the colonial period.

The unwritten equation of moral and legal law in the early republic is an especially revelatory instance of Elliott's concept of associationism. Presumably, citizens in control of themselves morally would enact a parallel self-control legally. Therefore, lawyers often wrote moral texts in an effort to contribute to the establishment of a knowable and contained voting (and non-voting) public. Even more important than the politically colonizing effects of this action are the personal ones. Since these texts were particularly aimed at the politically disenfranchised—women and the working class—they represent, in a sense, moral taxation without representation. Reading such figures as Fisher Ames, John Adams, and Samuel Miller, all lawyers, then, historians have assumed that such a culture existed in more than theory and, in fact actually dictated acts of readership during this period: American books and readers presumably interacted with an explicit trust in the author's reliability and in the incorruptibility of the language and forms to convey messages of order and reason. David Paul Nord has most recently traced the history of republican reading and writing habits, concluding it "was not a popular, democratic literature produced by or even for the lower classes" (131).

Dr. Benjamin Rush was central to establishing the educational policies that promised the creation of both readers and writers suited to this model: "I consider it as possible to convert men into republican machines. This must be done if we expect them to perform their parts properly in the great machine of the government" (11), wrote Rush in 1786. Mechanizing experience confines it within knowable and measurable limits: questions of corruptibility would become irrelevant if all new Americans—including women—were properly educated and indoctrinated in republican ideology. Rush's statement reveals two important distinctions: first, the need to "convert" implies that the post-Revolutionary public was far from this ideal; and, second, the distinction between "we" and "they" implies a hierarchical arrangement in which "they" become the passive receptacles of republican conversion. Each demonstrates the retrogression of the early republic away from its revolutionary origins.

But republicanism was always a fiction in American life, an ideal of national homogeneity and universality, never genuinely achieved. Let me reiterate here that it was primarily the republicans who imagined and attempted to inscribe a stable British model of social order on the new nation: in fact, British culture of this period was fluid and similarly antagonistic toward older eighteenth-century institutions and traditions. Nonetheless, as a pervasive presence in the national print media, republicanism tried to sell itself and its notions of textual and social order as fact, not theory. Especially by 1808, American readers were buying it less and less: the processes of decolonization had resisted recolonization and other, less conformist, texts were selling better.[6]

That is, the public's own tastes were increasingly heterogeneous during this period. In the enormously popular *Memoirs of Stephen Burroughs*, Burroughs, passing as a professional, uses elevated language to seduce and dupe gullible New Englanders. Moreover, his book had a broad and diverse list of subscribers, suggesting unusual popularity.[7] The public, evidently, had retained a degree of its revolutionary sense of antiauthoritarian resistance. This suggests that a "culture of ambiguity" always cohabited in the American public sphere.[8] Therefore, the early republic's literary atmosphere can be more accurately viewed as more heterogeneous than previously assumed. The fictions of authorship addressed in the present study were only a fragment of the process of social decolonization; nonetheless, in a logocracy like the early republic, their resistance to recolonizing textuality represents an important demonstration of the national mutability and heteroglossia republicanism tried to prevent and, failing that, conceal.

While moral textuality indeed predominated in the new nation, its control was never total, and acts of reading and writing thus occurred within and be-tween the moral center's hope for a malleable public and the less pliant tastes of the actual public. Nonetheless, the pervasive and coercive presence of moral texts—co-opting and colonizing the reader's ability and willingness to make in-dividual choices based on personal, not received, authority—even in 1808—required the generic displacement of received forms in a way typical of the Second World to preserve the democratic readership. Watterston constructed his fiction of authorship toward that end. The identification of "dark reform" texts from the early republic would further expand our understanding of how fiction originated in the United States.

Watterston's *The Lawyer* is a metanarrative pretending to be a conventional didactic novel.[9] It is presumably the autobiographical account and confession of a thoroughly corrupt lawyer, Morcell, written at the conclusion of a life of se-duction, gambling, violence, and, most importantly, altruistic penance. When Morcell, posing as a conventional author, exploits conventional signifiers of au-thority for personal gain, Watterston creates a "dark reform" text in an effort to reveal how conventional texts discouraged creative authorship and critical read-ership. In an internal narrative of the book's composition, Watterston ironically crafts Morcell as an author aware of how his book was supposed to be written, read, and empowered by a passive audience—a definition cleverly and implicitly embedded in Morcell's gestures of sincerity toward his readers. Morcell deploys standard homiletic rhetoric from republican genres—sermons, polemics, and di-dactic novels—to declare that "charity and benevolence" (234) guide his author-ship. Ultimately, then, Morcell exploits the authority of his professional status and its accompanying access to authorship to reestablish himself as an authority in the protean society.

Unlike Burroughs, who openly indulges the rebellious nature of his readers, Watterston uses Morcell to make his readers understand that this text suppos-edly takes place within the republic of letters. That way, he can convince them that the activist reading methods that informed their love of Burroughs were also a valuable public skill unfairly condemned as trivial and dangerous. When Bur-roughs's sincere narrative of deception is paired with Morcell's deceptive narra-tive of sincerity, the reader is compelled to accept the former: an acknowledged con man becomes preferable to a fawning reformer. With this in mind, Watter-ston successfully undermines the recolonizing pretensions of both the didactic text and the lawyer figure in the early republic.

Any reading of *The Lawyer* depends on whether one trusts Morcell's sincerity. While Cathy N. Davidson (236) and Henri Petter (324) read him as sincere, others read his penitence as a lie, demonstrating Watterston's deeper skepticism. Julia E. Kennedy reiterates Lillie Deeming Loshe's suggestion that he was "the only contemporary of Charles Brockden Brown 'who showed any disposition to follow in his footsteps'" (vii). Reynolds briefly recognizes "cries of nihilistic despair . . . the kinds of torrential passions and anguished speculations that were rechanneled and more firmly managed in the major writing [of Poe, Hawthorne, and Melville]" (193).[10]

Unlike these later figures, Watterston lived and wrote in a society for which "anguished speculations" were not romantic indulgences but rather discouraged vices presumably beneath the contempt of authors. Instead, they were meant to be hidden away, and thus became the forbidden fruit for the disenfranchised novel readers. By marginalizing novels, novel readers, and emotional participation, the republic of letters monopolized the public sphere in an effort to recolonize and stabilize the unruly, pre-Jacksonian demos. Thus, these readers were instructed not to take themselves or their feelings seriously, to act objectively, like Rush's "republican machines." Similarly, a lawyer was intended, then, to become the mechanic, to follow the metaphor, assuring the smooth operation of the machine. By placing these emotions in the control of a corrupt lawyer, Watterston asks his readers to decenter the dictates of the republican elite and reexamine the possible worth of both themselves and the emotional, imaginative experiences otherwise suppressed.

Biographical and bibliographical information on Watterston (1783–1854) reveals his problematic relationship with the authorities of his day. Watterston reluctantly trained as a lawyer in Hagerstown, Maryland, while writing amateur fiction, drama, and poetry, before abandoning the law in 1815 to become Librarian of Congress, a post he held until 1829. Aside from *The Lawyer*, Watterston published four other novels, poems, a dramatic comedy, and a series of histories and travel books. The most interesting, the play *The Child of Feeling* (1809), hints at the author's views on freedom and colonialism: "My language is the language of independence, and the language of my country. I feel a spirit within me, that teaches me to resist oppression, though exercised by one who ought to be my parent and to assert that freedom both of mind and body which is the peculiar birthright of every American" (94). In the 1830s he wrote criticism informed by similarly revolutionary principles, including reviews for Poe's *Southern*

Literary Messenger. In reviewing Byron, for example, Watterston praised "the violent energies of passion; . . . the wild and eccentric wanderings of a diseased imagination, and the deep and intense feeling of a broken or tender heart" (qtd. in Kennedy, 46).

By validating these feelings, as Lawrence Buell has observed, the postcolonial American writer of the 1830s participated in a larger democratization of the reading process taking place in the mid-nineteenth century (422). I would argue that the creation of the devious Morcell in 1808 revealed Watterston's own ability to portray a "diseased imagination" as a fascinating and dangerous presence in the early republic. The cultivation of a responsible member of the republican elite was meant to create a stable leading (if not ruling) class that could be trusted with social, moral, and political authority. The abject failure of this process in the case of Morcell reveals Watterston's resistance to this part of republicanism's reinscription of colonial hierarchies.

The fictional author Morcell pretends to have composed *The Lawyer* as a conventional didactic text. However, a consistent irony, running from the preface to the conclusion, reveals that Morcell's repentance is never true and his sins too salaciously described to support his stated moral intent. He is thus not only a duplicitous lawyer but also a corrupt author. The ending's irony resonates out into the public sphere by implicating the act of reading as it was predicated by those who championed the culture of morality as an act of dispossession and seizure. Watterston postulates a more complex formulation of human personality than the simplistic republican faith in associationism and altruism, compelling the reader to take a more active role in the processes of reading and writing, urging the autonomy of thought central to decolonization. When patterns of manipulative repetition, exploitative description, and an inverted resolution smudge the genre's norms, Watterston disrupts the complacency of orthodox reading by omitting the easy resolution of standard texts to decenter and disrupt complacent reading habits.

From the beginning, the book appears to be the legitimate creation of Morcell, presumably a real person. Like many novels published in this period, *The Lawyer* opens with extensive and carefully constructed front matter, a hint that Morcell is well aware of the signifiers of authority expected by his readers. However, Watterston has Morcell master and manipulate them to show how easily a con man can meet those same standards. By doing so, Watterston demonstrates that the early republic's blind trust in the reliability of British-based literary forms has opened the door for unreliable texts and authors, threatening the viability of print media as legitimate transmitters of information and public debate.

The subtitle, *Man as He Ought Not To Be*, could refer either to the lawyer Morcell, who seduces and steals, or the author Morcell composing the narrative. In either case, unlike most subtitles for didactic novels, Watterston's betrays a potential irony. While most subtitles clarified a book's title, Watterston's shrouds constructive meaning: if this is what man ought not to be, it never claims to teach what he should be.[11] Furthermore, the volume was published as "A TALE," anonymously, and in Pittsburgh, where Watterston was unknown, all facts that suggest a more complex motive for Watterston than the run-of-the-mill moral instruction so ubiquitous in the early republic.[12]

The word *tale*, as opposed to *romance* which was often used to introduce didactic sentimental fiction, also reveals an ambition to attract males as well as females, the normal audience for early American fiction. When *tale* announces the subsequent narrative as fiction, Watterston, like Brown, internalizes the close relation of fiction to fact in the tradition of the eighteenth-century British novel. According to that tradition, while Morcell might not be real, the events and the character could be situated in a continuum of real history: his personal narrative resembles "news stripped of its reference to immediate events," in the terms of Lennard J. Davis (145). Watterston's story of Morcell writing the book emerges as a comment on the tradition of Fielding and Smollett, breaking the "one discourse" of British writing Davis observes.

By dividing and rearranging the standard discourses, Watterston complicates his text in ways suited to decolonizing his reader. Moreover, the word *ought* foreshadows a didactic intent, as opposed to the more indulgent subtitles of the time. The reader might then recognize the text in the similarly blurred genre of allegory or some other form of instruction. In both cases, it does not matter if the tale is true or not: the reader is supposed to trust his or her betters, as denizens of a higher level in the social hierarchy. By positioning himself high on that ladder by virtue of language and profession, Morcell is also granted license to conceal and rearrange both materials and morals.

The dedication and the preface set the stage for Morcell's duplicitous manipulation of the social rhetoric of didactic novels. Morcell dedicates the book to the "Hon. John Buchanan, Esq. Chief Judge of the Fifth Judicial District of the

State of Maryland" (iii). The historical Buchanan (1772–1844) was an accomplished jurist who could be said to personify the ideal republican lawyer.[13] The tone of the dedication suggests that Morcell might have more in mind: "Sir, the Expectation that the following production, the offspring of occasional paroxysms of labour and momentary interludes of solitude, will tend to beguile the *tedium* of an hour, is the only motive which induces the author to dedicate it to you" (iii). Given Morcell's many digressions on various topics in the text, this dismissal seems hasty. Morcell wants Buchanan to assume that the text is intended for those in need of its lessons—those less likely to detect his deceptions. Morcell continues to establish himself as a professional man of authority: "Knowing you, sir, to be a man whom the profession, which is too often attended with pernicious consequences to those who adopt it, but which you have practiced for a series of years, with honour and reputation, has not been able to coerce from the broad line of undeviating rectitude, he feels a gratification in having an opportunity thus to evince the respect he entertains for your character, and thus point you out as an example worthy of the most studious imitation" (iii–iv). Asking more than the passage of the tedium of an hour, this obsequious sentence smacks of pretense and cronyism in regard to the fictional author's social advancement.

The preface next celebrates the early republic's promotion of professional education as a means to social authority. In this section Morcell intends to sound like Rush or any other tract writer who fit the culture of morality's norm: "The following sheets were written, chiefly with a view to exhibit the pernicious effects which result from a vitious education, and thus show the propriety of early instilling into the youthful mind principles of justice, of truth, and of honesty. . . . Man is an imitative being. In a state of infancy, when his faculties are yet plastic and unformed, he readily adopts those motives of action, and pursues that mode of conduct he sees followed by those he deems his superiors" (v). This statement demonstrates Morcell's mastery of the colonizing methods of conventional authorship: that the human mind is a tabula rasa on which indelible principles can be easily traced and patterns of behavior so inscribed that they remain consistent throughout life. That etching, of course, precludes the formation of autonomous individual identity and thus resembles an act of colonization. Not surprisingly, this idea is based in the same Enlightenment notion that taught all of Europe that the rest of the world was in fact empty, for all practical purposes.

Graham Huggan and Peter Mancall have extended this notion to European cartography of the "Age of Exploration" that preceded and prepared the ground, literally, for European imperialism.[14] By this reckoning, both young people and the various *terrae nullii* around the world were knowable and controllable. But just as the globe was not, in fact, empty but rather quite full and complex, the young mind, according to Watterston, anticipating Freud and Jung, was similarly predisposed in rather complicated and unknowable ways. That is, just as Brackenridge rejected the way the early republic treated the West as empty, Watterston observes a parallel miscalculation of the human psyche.

The preface continues to address the legal profession. Before relating an unstinting record of his abuses as a lawyer, Morcell hints that he means to reestablish a bond with his brother jurists: "Though some gentlemen of the law may feel disposed to censure the author for his observations on the general tendency of the legal profession; yet he presumes the more candid and intelligent part of them will not hesitate to acknowledge, on a strict and impartial examination of the subject, the justness of his remarks. . . . It is from the liberal and prejudiced, he expects that candour and indulgence to which he conceives himself entitled, and from none but such" (iv–v). Morcell is aware that some readers might not be taken in by his ruse and forestalls their objections by reiterating the standard republican faith in the association of social status and eloquence with virtue. Nonetheless, he exposes the tenuousness of this connection: his appeal to the "liberal and prejudiced" observes a basic paradox—one or the other must be false—one cannot be both free-thinking and closed-minded. Even before the beginning of the narrative, Watterston has deftly established Morcell as a complex character capable, like Melville's Confidence-Man, of using the language of public trust to achieve strictly personal ends.

More importantly, Morcell reveals his mastery of a plurality of voices. His awareness of the multivocality and polyphony of American language, as he weaves his way through classes and genders of readers, presupposes a heteroglossic and heterogeneous readership. Nonetheless, within that, to position himself as a worthy republican he seeks to "silence polyphony" by homogenizing his readers through the inscription of a universal moral code, as does every colonialist author.[15] His ability to move so quickly from one voice to the other, from virtue to villainy and back again is his strength. Only a public that uncritically accepts these oppositions, however, can be victimized by this republican trickster. Implicitly, Watterston encourages a reading strategy which recognizes the fictional nature of any totalizing authority and instructs readers in the need to be aware of the complexities of their polyphonic community.

Before establishing a pattern of ironic repetition in which the book becomes enmeshed, Watterston has his fictional author describe his education. The text itself opens with a voice aware of reliable imagery: "My name is Morcell. I was born in Maryland of a family neither illustrious for its antiquity nor conspicuous for its virtue." On the death of his mother he remarks that, had she lived, he could have moved "through the varied scenes and vicissitudes of human life, unmoved and undisturbed by the fascinating temptations of sophisticated vice" (9). Citing the image of Franklin, Morcell promotes himself as the average American without history or sophistication. This deceptive pose erases the inevitable contradictions of settlement.[16] That is, Franklin (and Morcell) could announce themselves strictly as colonials in the Enlightenment tradition, as blank slates fit for the inscription of the best of the colonial culture. Republicanism by no means retransmitted the entirety of British culture; instead, it filtered and distilled it to those more traditional aspects relevant to the transformation of the American public from revolutionary crowd to controllable, knowable citizenry.

However, following Slemon's notion of the bifurcation of Second World experience, this reckoning ignores two facts: first that white Americans were displaced Europeans, often economic, religious, or political refugees; second, especially after 1763, American colonists were gradually stripped of their rights as British citizens and treated increasingly like second-class subjects of the empire. In brief, the blank-slate version of American identity, so central to the educational policy of Rush, ignored this part of the nation's past, that of being colonized, of being rejected and repudiated by the English whose traditions they so aspired to fulfill. At heart, this kind of erasure of American identity erased the Revolution and allowed a realliance with colonial social institutions. Nonetheless, it serves the republican need to ignore the complicated past before reinscribing their simplistic hierarchies.

The first section describes Morcell's "vitious education." Here, Watterston immediately breaks with republican optimism: Morcell is born mean and selfish. His father recognizes in him an opportunity to exploit the simplistic system that automatically trusted professional men to oversee the public good. If such a bad person were made a lawyer, he would have an especially effective opportunity to employ his skills. Watterston is not necessarily critical of all lawyers but rather of the social structure that granted them cultural authority: "The fame of my exploits at length reached the ears of my father, who, being highly delighted with this early demonstration of superior sagacity as cunning as he supposed it, resolved to make me a lawyer; justly concluding, that I should, at the bar, have abundant opportunity of bringing into public view those powers, for which I was so early and so greatly distinguished" (12). To teach Morcell, his father hires Dorsey, a traveling lawyer "acquainted with the *arcana* of legal villainy, the juridical cunning by which gentlemen of the long robe arrive at celebrity" (13). Dorsey's lesson is that law is a means to wealth, "the opus magnum of human life" (14). Dorsey does not invent the system that rewards villainy; rather, he merely recognizes a corrupt status quo and turns it to his own advantage. That is, the profession charged with the transmission of righteousness can be manipulated by deception and selfishness: although not all lawyers are corrupt, the fact of their being lawyers does not guarantee their righteousness. Watterston here deftly inverts the usual expectations of orthodox authorship: if lawyers cannot be trusted in their professional pursuits, should they be trusted in their avocations as authors?

Moreover, Watterston's break with convention is fraught with ideological implications. Instead of starting with a tabula rasa, Morcell's education presupposes his innate corruption and only hones his amorality to create a monster. Watterston is aware that individual personality choices are not always imposed from without and that education does not necessarily produce responsible authority. The naive assumptions of associationism are thus challenged and revealed as specious. Watterston recognizes the incompatibility of these ideals and articulates the dangerous opening they create through which a man like Morcell can gain access to public discourse. Watterston concedes that bad men will attempt to gain power in any society; to remedy and check this pattern, he looks not to authors but to readers, who must be empowered to resist the charms of men like Morcell.

The more explicit charms of Morcell are made apparent soon thereafter. His education complete, Morcell conducts a life of crime, repentance, and relapse, in which a careful pattern of repetition reveals Watterston's hand. All of Morcell's sins begin as the righteous rectifications of some harm done to him: he feels he has been wronged and means to act, as every lawyer was told to, not for personal advancement but rather in the spirit of impersonal public interest, or so he claims. By this, Watterston neatly has Morcell pre-empt any accusation of genuine evil: Morcell the author means to assert that his crimes had to do with his judgment, not with his character. Whether Morcell is lying to himself or his readers matters little: the legal profession encourages such deception in the name of sophistry. His first "correction" allows him to justify seduction.

This episode inverts the seduction plot of most sentimental fiction by recording it from the seducer's male point of view. One day, when walking with Dorsey, Morcell attempts to rape a woman on the road "to convince my amazed tutor that his moral precepts had not been uselessly thrown away" (16). Morcell is attacked from behind and knocked unconscious. When told that the woman he attacked was Matilda Ansley and his own assailant her brother Edward, Morcell plans to avenge his wounded dignity: "I resolved (the reader will forgive me, I mean 'naught to extenuate') to seduce the sister, and chastise the brother" (18). But of course Morcell does "extenuate," and proceeds to describe in lascivious terms, his carnal and vindictive wants. As both author and seducer, Morcell has no problem finding the words and the arguments to justify any action.

Significantly, Morcell's actions as a seducer are analogous to his actions as a lawyer: in both, he uses a twisted sense of self-righteousness and his mastery over the language of his training to force his will upon others—a process that will be completed by his ascension to author. Moreover, Morcell's attitude toward women especially demonstrates his attitudes toward his gullible audience: like Murray's Sinisterius Courtland, his targets are those excluded from the public sphere, those who are presumably powerless and in need of the guidance of trustworthy figures such as lawyers. Unfortunately, no Margaretta emerges to defeat and expose him, as she had *The Gleaner*. Just as Morcell acted privately as a seducer of the unsuspicious when a lawyer, as an author he acts publicly as a deceiver. The mind of the colonizer and the mind of the sexist are thus one and the same. Watterston's feminist inclinations, like Brown's in *Alcuin*, had been established elsewhere.[17] Watterston therefore communicates a more general antiauthoritarian texual and social alternative that welcomed traditional Others, such as women, into a more self-consciously decolonizing and heterogeneous national scene.

Claiming to have been drunk, Morcell succeeds "with my senses clear, my mind free from the damning influence of illegitimate lust" (23) and earns the brother's forgiveness. He seduces Matilda with promises of marriage and, when she gets pregnant, immediately abandons her, going so far as to blame her for tempting him. This allows Watterston to place a conventional hero against his ironic hero. Edward Ansley fits the superficial model of the republican culture's ideal: "Ansley was a youth of singular excellence; his soul possessed an elevation scarcely human; from the loftiest pinnacle of virtue he never, for a moment, descended; nor from the line of eternal and immutable truth did he ever, even in moments of jocularity, diverge. His conduct was governed by the strictest and most rigid principles of unsophisticated justice, morality, and universal good. . . . He possessed a mind of the very first order, grave, sublime, and energetic" (20–21). As an author, the retrospective Morcell means to valorize Ansley's heroism and condemn his own depravity. But Watterston recognizes the dangerous gullibility of a man so easily fooled by the proper diction of Morcell. The narrator notes that Ansley "was human; . . . he had his faults. . . . Subject, by nature, to the influence of ungovernable passion, his education and philosophy were frequently unable to resist its violence" (21). This is soon demonstrated; when he learns of Matilda's seduction, Ansley challenges Morcell to a duel, wounds him, and is forced to flee. Watterston here points up the inability of an education in rationality, such as Ansley's, to deliver on its promises to check the excessive passions of the individuals to whom the nation's future was trusted.

Watterston has Morcell (writing after the fact) borrow the language and plot of conventional didacticism, just as he had the figure of Ansley, to show its embedded contradictions and implicit threats to individual thought. In reference to himself, Morcell writes: "The reader will perhaps, be shocked at this instance of human depravity; he will say, it is not in the nature of man to be so wantonly, so deliberately wicked: would to heaven it were not so!" (34). While this passage seems sincere, a subsequent statement hints at Morcell's private purpose: "But suspicion is the property of a mind grovelling and disenguous [*sic*]; of a mind incapable of being enlarged by knowledge, or expanded by philanthropy" (38), a clue that Morcell may have been aware of his reader's growing skepticism. Just as he had convinced Matilda to forgive his initial assault, he asks the reader to do the same. For the careful reader, suspicion is thus championed not just in the characters who suspect Morcell, but implicitly also in the readers who suspect their author.

This pattern is redoubled in Morcell's frequent moments of repentance. After Matilda's death in childbirth, Morcell experiences his first repentance: "My heart sunk within me, and I felt for the first time, the throb of sorrow and compunction: alas! (cried I mentally) is that all that remains of my beauteous Matilda? . . . Every desire of revenge was that moment banished from my breast, and I inwardly cursed myself for being the unworthy cause of such calamity" (41–42).

Nearly identical passages often appear (63, 88, 174) and the same promises are made, most importantly at the end (233). Their repetition demonstrates the meaninglessness of Morcell's promises of reform and Watterston's manipulation of the simplistic didactic formula and its slippery language. Given Morcell's ultimate inconsistency, what is to prevent him from once again dissembling, now as an author, stained as he is by a "vitious education"?

After each reform, Morcell attaches a long speech that borrows freely from didactic novelists such as Susanna Rowson and Enos Hitchcock.[18] Morcell uses empowered clichés to convince himself of the error of his ways, but they always fail. Each apology ends with the sentence "but to return" (51, 68, 183). While Morcell the supposedly reformed and altruistic author means to return to the chronicle of his life, the return is thematically significant for Watterston's characterization of Morcell as a man incapable of self-reinvention: once a con man, always a con man. Afterwards, Morcell returns to a life of deception and greed.

Much of the next one hundred pages consists of similar misadventures after the fashion of *Stephen Burroughs*, which include Morcell's becoming a gambler; being chased out of Monmouth, Maryland; getting rich; "advocating the cause of the oppressor against the oppressed" (57); settling in Baltimore; living as a country gentleman on his dead father's legacy; and being stalked by a mysterious figure overheard plotting his murder. Despite his diverse activities as lawyer, Morcell is consistently successful. As it had been for Burroughs, it is easy for him to make the legal system suit his selfish ends. However, unlike his real-life compatriot, when he becomes an author, Morcell claims to express regret.[19] These lengthy episodes allow Watterston to make a variety of observations about certain corruptible points of law.

Most importantly, he expatiates on the divergence of legality from morality. As a lawyer, Morcell can act immorally without violating the law. Hence, his public behavior is merely an extension of his private character. Moreover, Morcell's public behavior as a lawyer so closely resembles his private behavior as a scoundrel that it reveals no new information about his character. In fact, his authorial silence on the immorality of his legal actions while simultaneously confessing private sins reveals Watterston challenging the enormous public trust held by capable members of the professional class. Contrariwise, Morcell the author would do nothing to alter or challenge the profession he means to reenter—he wants the same opportunities to exploit awaiting him when he returns.

In the primary narrative, Morcell's critique is limited to himself; nevertheless, in the secondary narrative, Watterston addresses the values and assumptions that produced Morcell the lawyer and empowers Morcell the author. For instance, aware that he will be a better lawyer equipped with "literary accomplishments," Morcell "prosecuted [his] studies, supposing that the acquisition of learning would contribute to the more speedy acquisition of wealth, the great object of [his] pursuit" (54)—which, of course, it does. Here Watterston directly confronts the associationism at the heart of orthodox writing in the early republic. While he recognizes that lawyers are necessary and often virtuous, he questions the legitimacy of allowing lawyers and other professionals to control the nation's literary and moral character.

Watterston found law and letters incompatible, and perhaps even mutually corrupting: access to authorship granted lawyers an excess of power that compounded existing temptations for corruption; in turn, literary authorship was soiled by the occasional misuse of the written word for selfish ends. In sum, both were diminished by their association, and the nation was the worse for it. Moreover, eloquence here is equated exclusively with self-interest, which works in every case to defeat public interest, the supposed necessary contingency of eloquence. Most significantly, when championing the cause "of the oppressor against the oppressed," Morcell inverts republican ideology and reveals its theoretical impracticality and corruptibility.

Watterston has been accused of exploiting conventional and derivative Gothic devices in the middle of the book.[20] However, Watterston's fiction is that he is not writing the book: it is Morcell who wields these conventions to ingratiate himself to a presumably slavish and passive readership. While the readers are supposedly thrilled, Morcell means to convince them that their compliance to his textual authority will assure their moral improvement. However, if the reader has noticed Watterston's embedded ironies, these devices will be revalued by the reader as exploitative and deceptive. I would suggest that Watterston was cognizant of his readers' familiarity with both Stephen Burroughs *and* Enos Hitchcock: by making Morcell sound simultaneously like both the con man and the Calvinist, he smudges the distinctions between the two and asks them to rely more on themselves and less on the authors.

Starting around chapter 16, the narrative begins moving toward what appears to be a conventional resolution. To extend his critique to other forms of authority in the early republic, Watterston allows Morcell's identity as a lawyer to fade from the narrative. From this point he is merely an educated man, representative of no profession in particular. At a party Morcell witnesses a struggle between Ansley and Dixon, a fop whose literary allusions grant him social prestige. Ansley begins by quoting his version of Robert Burns's "Cotter's Saturday Night":

> Is there in human form, that bears a heart
> A *wretch*, a *villain*, lost to love and truth!
> That can with studied, sly ensnaring art,
> Betray sweet Jenny's unsuspecting youth? (150)

Ansley means these lines for Morcell, who had seduced his sister. Instead, Rattle, an already-reformed character who had seduced Morcell's sister, feels remorse, while Morcell reads the recitation as a challenge. In larger terms, Ansley, a teacher, presents a didactic text to a sinner who responds by contemplating further sin.

In microcosm this episode establishes Watterston's view of the necessity of reading and thinking critically about all language—no matter how impressive. Missing from this process of textual interpretation is the interdictory authority of early republic textual or social institutions. Watterston disrupts the conventional early republic reading experience by forcing interpretation on the reader, abdicating authorial power and compelling the reader to participate in the transactions of literacy, just as Watterston would activate the reader in a broader cultural sense.

After this, Morcell mistakenly stabs Rattle while trying to kill Ansley, gambles away all his money, and again promises to reform (174). This acceleration of the pattern of sin, repentance, and relapse so soon before what Morcell claims to be his final transformation from sinner to author compounds the irony of the conclusion. Moreover, Morcell, in an authorial aside, makes a statement that reflects negatively on his reformation: "He who possesses wealth, possesses everything desirable in life, his power to gratify the propensities of his nature is unlimited; he may be either eminently serviceable or utterly useless, he may either rear the fragrant germs of virtue, or cultivate the nauseous weeds of pestiferous vice: the power of his wealth gives him a dignity which nothing can destroy" (186). This statement, which is not introduced by a "(cried I mentally)," is clearly spoken by the putatively reformed author, not the sinning lawyer. Davidson has noted that this passage compromises the subversiveness of Morcell, who "hardly refutes the world of getting and spending that he so recently, profitably, and selfishly inhabited" (236).

To "refute" this world would go against Morcell's main purpose in writing his memoirs: reentry into that very world. Indeed, Watterston does not refute the processes of "getting and spending": he alerts his readers that an honest recognition of the selfish aspects of these enterprises is preferable to the hypocritical promise that the republican elite's only goal is public betterment. By suggesting a reformulation of the means to authority, Watterston pleads for a dissociation of power from wealth. Decolonization, then, has to do with a more honest representation of normal human activity. To disrobe republican rhetoric of its pretensions to virtue, Watterston places its words in Morcell's mouth.

As the conclusion nears, Watterston further undermines Morcell's legitimacy, refusing to find the conventional resolution his readers may have expected after such a disruptive text. For almost fifty pages, the text consists of narratives by Ansley and Edwards, the "mysterious stranger" heard plotting Morcell's murder. Each relates a slightly different version of the events of Morcell's life; none is established as the truth. As a result, the reader is again left to decipher the evidence and come to his own conclusions, an activity normally undertaken by the author. Like Brown, Watterston refuses this luxury to his own readers.

Moreover, by suggesting that there might be more than one version of the truth, Watterston critiques the objectivity claimed by so many early republic texts. By internalizing a plurality of narratives, Watterston disrupts his readers yet again. Like Brackenridge and Murray, Watterston textually recreates the polyphony of American voices that republicanism sought to monovocalize. Watterston destabilizes the narrative by introducing variant versions of events, suggesting a plurality of perspectives from which any event might be understood. This challenges what Ferguson has labeled the rhetoric of "consensus" in the founders' political writings as it carried over into other public texts such as didactic fiction. Implicitly, then, there is no moral or, subsequently, political consensus and the nation has become increasingly decolonized despite republican efforts to the contrary.

However, unlike Brown, Watterston never appended his own homiletic comments, an omission further suggesting that Watterston is conducting an even more radical subversion of the norms of the early republic.[21] Without even this shallow layer of authorial guidance, Watterston's reader was left more alone with Morcell than Brown's was with Arthur Mervyn. When the lone authorial voice is that of a corrupt character, the reader is more isolated than before. Ansley's concluding statement on Morcell exemplifies his depraved nature: "All his pleasures are momentary and all his gratifications insipid. From the first damn of life, until the last expiring gasp of nature, he pursues a delusive phantom which constantly eludes his grasp, and at last, tired of the ineffectual pursuit, he sinks into the cold grave, which terminates at once his cares, his griefs, and his disappointments" (205). This betrays Ansley's inconsistency and thus the unreliability of conventional heroism as a practical guide to human behavior: earlier, Ansley, the perfect didactic hero, believed in reform and growth. Ansley seems the conventional republican authority capable of combating Morcell's villainy, but he fails: despite a life of being corrected by the pedant Ansley, Morcell is still corrupt. Furthermore, Ansley is boring. Watterston and Morcell both know that early republic readers would be more interested in Morcell than Ansley. In fact, his sanctimonious self-importance seems included to make the fictional author even more attractive. Given a choice between a republican pedant and an admitted con man, Watterston and, implicitly, his reader would choose the latter.

A significant reference to Morcell's grave recurs in the final passages. After hearing the other versions of his life, Morcell claims he will retire from the world and close his days in "merited obscurity . . . endeavouring by charity and benevolence to expiate, in some degree the crimes of which I had been guilty" (234). Like so many other dubious heroes in American literature, Morcell retreats to the wilderness to redefine himself. However, Morcell means to reenter the civilized regions as a new man. Kennedy rightly observes that "the reader harbors a suspicion that in his sylvan retreat of repentance Morcell is tormenting the birds for want of something meaner to do" (20). The last paragraph, however, suggests that not only the birds need fear Morcell's "unconvincing" apologia:

> If any should ask the motive which induced me to put my character in so unfavourable a point of view, I briefly answer that I conceived it to be an act of justice I owed to the world, and a sort of expiation of the offenses I have committed in my journey through life. . . . It ought, therefore, be the peculiar care of those to whose protection nature has intrusted him, to impress upon his youthful mind a strong sense of truth, of justice, and of humanity; and when death has put a final close to his existence, he will sink into the silent mansions of the dead, pitied, lamented, and honoured. (236)

Given Morcell's pattern of temporary atonements, this "sort of expiation" is nothing but a final attempt at reinstatement through citing conventional phraseology. Like any good colonizer, he recognizes that language, more than violence or economics, is the ultimate means of control.[22] Hidden is his basic ruse: if "man is a creature of education," how could he have changed to the degree that his text can be trusted? Morcell answers this by raising the umbrella of the clichéd master discourse of republicanism—if it sounds right, it must be right. Or so he would have his readers think.

⁂

If nothing else, Morcell is aware that the simplistic anticolonial individualism by which he had once prospered had out-lived its revolutionary origins. In the early republic, the real means of gaining the public trust is not individuality but pretended conformity. Rephrased, the anticolonial impulse of the 1770s had been displaced by the recolonizing image of republican passivity in the 1790s. His power derives from the fact that he is a colonizer let loose in a community of colonial subjects. By realizing the centrality of his own self, Morcell gains the upper hand. Watterston's book is carefully crafted to tell a story about how certain types of men—both lawyers *and* authors—might very possibly counterfeit genuine literary expression and social activity for selfish ends.

Morcell is an intriguing and complex character in early American fiction, a voice that, like Burroughs's, reveals republicanism's effort to transform the American public from revolutionary crowd to complacent audience—a dissident role embraced more overtly by Thoreau and Whitman—through the reintroduction of modes of writing likely to reverse the subject-to-citizen growth initiated in the Revolution. In regard to the practice of this same technique in later American fiction, *The Lawyer* foreshadows the more expansive exploration of the literature of con artistry later in the nineteenth century. Like Melville in *The Confidence-Man* (1852) and Twain in "The Mysterious Stranger" (1900), Watterston identifies and arms his readers to resist those who attempt to dupe, control, and finally colonize the American public.

One incident from Burroughs's *Memoirs* particularly illuminates *The Lawyer* and its immediacy to the textual politics of the early republic. Working as a schoolteacher in Bridghampton, New York, Burroughs proposes the collection of a library. He polls the citizens: they want histories and "books on secular subjects." The local "first-man" responds with a list composed entirely of didactic "ethics" and religious works which he then imposes on the public because "he understood what books would suit *his* people" (284). When Burroughs confronts this local authority figure, the populace is "surprised" but eventually bows to his whims. Morcell would be one of these first-men: he wants passive readers whom he can colonize and call his and so writes his autobiography as a homiletic text in the ethical tradition.

Nonetheless, Watterston's and Burroughs's observation of the divergence of the elites from the people underlies both this anecdote and Watterston's book: the reading public of the aging early republic had retained the antiauthoritarian habit of Revolution, even if it was submerged: republicanism had failed to recreate them as its machines. Watterston, then, like all the writers addressed in this study, wanted to write for that audience, but to do so he first had to convince those readers that they could no longer allow others to select which books "suited" them.

Watterston hoped that the American reader both deserved and expected a less pedantic and more liberating literature. Later, as he celebrated Byron, under the editorship of Poe, Watterston felt no compunction to protect the American readers from the "violent passions" of romanticism: the man of letters has no right or ability to protect the readers from such books, or more importantly, themselves. His abjuration of that authority, implied in 1808 and enacted in 1838, represents his final deconstruction of the republic of letters. Like his character in *The Child of Feeling*, Watterston understands that only a "language of independence" can teach Americans to "resist oppression." Fictionalizing the questionable nature of conventional texts allowed Watterston to suggest that they compromised the integrity of the experiment in democracy by encouraging the public's exploitation by easily counterfeited authority figures—the easy targets of Morcell.

In one way Watterston concludes the process began by Brackenridge. We have traveled from Brackenridge's confused and deluded author-narrator to the wily and cunning Morcell, from identifying conventional writing as being merely absurd to linking it irretrievably to deception and corruption. Seemingly all the avenues permitted for the expression of republican values could easily be shown as ridiculous or corruptible or both, forever contrary to the enlightened public interest for which they were presumably the foundation. The growing distance between the writers—and their readers—and the politicians mirrors the growth of the republic away from its revolutionary origins as the politicians resisted and the writers encouraged decolonized modes of self-expression.

More importantly, as first Burroughs and then Watterston and finally Washington Irving's work reveal, as I will explore in the next chapter, the readers followed the writers (or perhaps vice-versa). Without a readership, the conventional and colonial modes of writing championed by the republicans, manipulated by men like Morcell, and abrogated by the figures addressed thus far in this study, became irrelevant and anachronistic as the processes of decolonization continued amongst the populace. It was then up to Irving to conclude the process by collapsing and, finally, burying the aspiring early republic author in the person of Diedrich Knickerbocker.

꙳꙳

SIX

The Syllogistically Fatal World of
Washington Irving's Diedrich Knickerbocker

WILLIAM CULLEN BRYANT, eulogizing Washington Irving in 1860, misidenti-
fied Irving's early work as predominantly derivative: "I find in this work more
manifest tracings than in his other writings of what Irving owed to the earlier authors in our language. The quaint poetic coloring, and often the phraseology, betray the disciple of Chaucer and Spenser" (11). Bryant's celebration of Irving is
based in his notion that a mastery of the best of "the language" was necessary before a young writer could create, an idea he had more fully explored in his *Lectures on Poetry*, in which he compared poetry to mathematics, the next genius
taking up the work where his predecessor had left it.[1] The accusation of mere
mimicry has haunted criticism of Irving's early career into the present. For example, Martin Roth claims that Irving's first book, *Diedrich Knickerbocker's A
History of New York* (1809) essentially reflects the literary perspective of a colonial European whose constant reference to European literary conventions suggest that the *History* celebrates inherited modes of representation.

However, Irving's extensive and careful creation and promotion of Diedrich
Knickerbocker as the book's author reveals a more complex literary negotiation:
this is the text and textuality of a fictional creation, Knickerbocker, in the midst
of a public performance in the republic of letters. Irving constructs Knickerbocker as a colonial specifically to challenge ways of thinking about the new nation born of derivative European influences.[2] In fact, Irving's appropriation of
received forms and language for his own purposes describes the *History*'s dichotomous place at the end of the early republic: it annihilates and makes un-

usable all narrowly British or European forms for describing the new nation but never transcends this annihilation to propose an alternative textuality. Its importance lies in its thoroughness: completing the process begun by Brackenridge in the first part of *Modern Chivalry*, the *History* comprehensively deconstructs Enlightenment textuality and clears the way for exploring local alternatives and a more sober means of reckoning the ongoing relevance of British culture in the United States; that is to say, for decolonization.

Nonetheless, Bryant's and Roth's recognitions that the *History* is based in "literature, not life" (Roth, 115) bear consideration: Irving is primarily concerned with the act of representation as a politically involved entry into early republic society.[3] In particular, in the *History* Irving addressed how certain versions of history were employed as a means of social coercion: historians who borrow inherited modes of historiography to establish an official version of the national past subvert Revolutionary ideals by perpetuating the language and theories of retrogressive, colonial ideologies. Foreshadowing Ashcroft's, Griffiths's, and Tiffen's notion that Second World writers "explore, in their figures, themes, and forms, the conceptual dimensions of the act of writing itself, and the tensions and anxieties traversing the institution of literature in marginalized societies" (137), Irving identifies how colonial thinking has reduced American experience to meaninglessness and diverted Americans from understanding local conditions in more informative and appropriate ways.

Rephrased, the prioritization of a Eurocentric past represents an effort to retain social and cultural conditions leftover from the colonial period. Irving seems to have recognized that the practice and promotion of Enlightenment modes of history in America were an effort to recolonize versions of history that validated a stable, republican, "natural aristocracy" as the only possible means of legitimizing the new nation. By subverting this historiography, Irving invites the exploration of alternative historiographies to serve anticolonial and protean national ends. To decolonize national identity, Irving understood that a new historiography was necessary. Knickerbocker's *History* is Irving's fiction of the authorship of history that challenges its readers to resist the logocracy imposed upon them by the fading literary aristocracy Knickerbocker aspires to join.[4]

The *History* is more than an attempt to hunt down or annihilate American history as a meaningless slough of absurdity and accident, as some critics have suggested.[5] If the book targets anything to annihilate, it is American *historiography*, not the history itself. Irving is not claiming that the settlement history is meaningless; rather, the privileged modes for understanding it risk converting

American experience to a marginal outgrowth of European civilization, precluding the construction of a less restricted alternative identity. European versions will always make the pre-Independence past unusable to the decolonized nation. Given this context, Irving's fiction of the authorship of historiography demonstrates a rhetorical stratagy for decolonization, for searching for a more usable past.

❧

By implementing an eighteenth-century combination of empirical and classical methods, American historians of the early republic for the most part perpetuated the colonial methodologies for justifying social injustice and inequality through the construction of pasts predestined to serve the present's political needs. In particular, early republic social institutions were validated by conventional histories that defined an American past made meaningful by its realization of the Enlightenment theories of history held by Gibbon, Hume, and others.[6]

Arthur Shaffer observes that in the early republic "the writing of American historians became the intellectual counterpart of the political concept that the nation's success depended on a sense of personal loyalty with the nation-state. . . . We recognize here the use of scholarship to support the social and political order. From a foundation of scholarly nationalism American historians constructed a national past" (28–29). "Constructing" thus enters "life" as a vital force of social representation: "American historians, then, regarded themselves as insiders, spokesmen for a society to which they felt both personally and ideologically committed" (41). The mere existence of an insider status reveals an aristocratic republican elevation of author above audience, reinscribing the hierarchical nature of the colonial period.

Shaffer and other students of this period's historiography recognize David Ramsay's *The History of the American Revolution* (1789) as typical.[7] In 1794 Ramsay expounded his technique: "The discovery of America is the first link of a chain of causes, which bids fair to enlarge the happiness of mankind by regenerating the principles of government in every corner of the world" (qtd. in Shaffer, 50). Thus, the republic culminates a rationally discernible system of causation divinely ordained to fulfill human potential: colonization was the ultimate vehicle for this development. Moreover, by monopolizing empirical truth, Ramsay pre-empts terms of discussion and dissent.

Similarly, the government he champions resists rational challenge: his method is scientific and objective, refuting alternative versions of the past that are not so flattering to the republic. In his book, William Hedges identifies the disguised subjectivity of the empirical method: "As the imagination of the historian contrives significant relations among facts assumed to be more or less known, it imposes a useful order upon the past" (71).[8] While Ramsay relies upon subjective reconstruction, his claims to rational authority overwhelm accusations of subjectivity or bias. He and others such as William Gordan, Ebenezar Hazard, and Jedediah Morse implemented the history-as-science method of Scottish historians Kames, Blair, and Macaulay.[9] Referring to the objective textuality of Newton's, Reynal's, and Buffon's scientific prose forecloses interpretive challenges, colonizing the reader, as it were, in a subject condition to their version of the past and the truth.

Republican technique also referred to classical models. Lester Cohen observes that classical historiography presented the past "as models which ought to be followed, or as examples to be censured and avoided" (189). A principle of selectivity thus further compromised the objectivist ideal: within the "contrived relation" of empirical facts imagined by the historian, subjective evaluation undermines its own advertised basis in objective truth. Early republic historians painted the pre-Revolutionary past as a uniform climb toward republicanism. Benjamin Trumbull in *A General History of the United States of America* (1810) claimed that if England had been Catholic "the colonists would have been . . . so enslaved and broken, that they never would have enterprised the late revolution, nor have risen to their present importance and glory" (177–78). This contrivance, given revolutions in Catholic France in 1789 and Ireland in 1798, demonstrates the limitations of the republic's search for affirmation in the colonial past.

A reverence for the classical past is also evident in the historians' glorification of ancient Rome and Greece. Ramsay's reference to "regeneration" recalls a desire to revive classical models of society.[10] By clothing a figure such as George Washington in terms borrowed from Plutarch or Tacitus, historians established the authority of his government by portraying him and it as reincarnations of ancient glories. Inherent in this method is an obeisance to authority and texts that confirm political representations of truth. For these insiders, as Cohen notes, "writing history was a present- and future-oriented instrument of political and moral values and national mission" (22).

Implicit in the methodology of the historians were values contrary to the revolutionary ideals of freedom and individuality: their license to contrive a past based on empirical information and classical models similarly empowered their government to impose like-minded a priori models for reshaping American society developed in aristocratic communities. The needs of the nation-state are thus granted virtually unlimited license to supersede those of the individual, the public, or, ultimately, the truth itself. The historian was granted enormous powers to define the shape of reality in the name of republican ideals.

Moreover, it is important to note that Irving's targets were the American practitioners of Enlightenment historiography. While British writers, particularly Carlyle in *Sartor Resartus* (1834), may have similarly challenged eighteenth-century textuality, the context of their attacks differed. For Carlyle, older histories were absurd and inaccurate, evidence that England had been deceiving itself; for Irving and other Americans, the risk was greater: Enlightenment history could not account for the newness of the country or its difference from European models. While Carlyle undercut a stable British legacy, Irving was trying to prevent the stillbirth of *any*, as yet unformed and undetermined, American self-knowledge. Irving thus demands a local historiography as diverse as its subject and rejects the notion of the Enlightenment author as monovocal polymath and prophet.

In *Salmagundi* (1807), Irving had already mocked writers who granted themselves such license: "So soon as a writer has accomplished a volume, he forthwith becomes wonderfully increased in altitude—he steps upon his book as upon a pedestal" (6:245). The interested nature of this form of history writing limits interpretive possibilities to both inherited models and partisan political needs. Irving knew something else was needed. By creating Knickerbocker as the absurd epitome of the derivative and unoriginal school of Trumbull, Ramsay, and all other American writers unwilling or unable to overcome the colonial legacy, Irving refuted conventional historiography and the Eurocentric ideology it sought to perpetuate.

The story of Knickerbocker is that of a man—specifically an author—made absurd by his effort to transpose eighteenth-century fictions of order on the colonial Dutch past for a decolonizing American readership. Two points emerge from Irving's attack on colonial textuality. First, Irving devalues the discursive authority of empirical and classical models as a part of a broader critique of inherited social institutions. Second, Irving's subversion of conventional authorship disputes the right of representation in ways that would redirect nineteenth-century American historiography by foreshadowing a more openly imaginative, postcolonial method.

More immediately, Irving's implicit demand in 1809 for a more expansive American historiography reflects the early republic's complex and protean public sphere as a site for a national struggle over identity. Richard McLamore has recently observed postcolonial qualities in Irving's later writings, recognizing Irving's profound and career-long fascination with understanding the complex positions of the new nation, somewhere between London and the frontier, a phenomenon Peter Anteyles has also observed.[11] The tension between the colonized Knickerbocker and his American subject, however, suggests that even in 1809, Irving was aware of the necessity of decolonizing American genres.

Such an activist text might seem unlikely from a writer best known for the romantic "Rip Van Winkle" and "The Legend of Sleepy Hollow," a figure Hedges recognized "as romantic escapist, lover of the picturesque, genial humorist" (1). However, Lloyd M. Daigrepont observes "Rip" as an attack on "those assumptions about reality which make men incapable of distinguishing between earthly and spiritual goals" (56). How we make "assumptions about reality" is also the subject of the *History*. There, an official assumption about the past is subverted: the early republic's inflation of history to gospel-like public indoctrination is enacted as a burlesque of self-absorbed and inflated rhetoric. Knickerbocker is cast as the tragicomic clown who personifies the assumptions that allowed the historian to aspire to republican prophet.

From the opening pages Knickerbocker employs a web of allusion and reference to establish his credentials for creating a text eager to meet the colonizing standards of British conventions; as such, the "overtly derivative" nature of the *History* must be considered Knickerbocker's, not Irving's.[12] Knickerbocker freely wields allusion to establish his authenticity as a reliable historian writing in an established tradition. In Knickerbocker, Irving magnifies convention to expose its doctrinal fallacies. Irving eventually reveals the tragic nature of the inevitable failure and self-destruction of such a mission on both personal and national levels: Americans cannot be merely the inheritors of the colonial past— they must risk becoming something new, as Knickerbocker cannot.

As he writes, Knickerbocker slowly realizes that the Enlightenment theories of history he valorized has nothing to do with the facts of his study and that no amount of authorized imaginative reconstruction will grant meaning to his text.

Irving shows that Knickerbocker's initial uncritical embrace of the prophetic license of conventional history, when revealed as false, leaves him defeated, tragically unequipped to reconstruct a more meaningful world. When he has finished, Knickerbocker retreats to welcome his own destruction: unable to decolonize himself, he commits intellectual suicide. With the burial of Knickerbocker, Irving ends—more than he ever knew—the republic of letters.

After Knickerbocker, no writer could aspire to the comprehensive authority embraced by the Enlightenment and its republican adherents. Graham Huggan has connected such efforts to postcolonial Second World textual self-identification: "Many of these fictions testify to the perceived need to challenge previous accounts of imperial/colonial history whose Eurocentric biases have repeatedly supported fallacious notions of cultural superiority" (110). Knickerbocker tries to write such a "colonial/imperial" account and fails. Yet, in the process of recognizing his failure, Knickerbocker earns the reader's respect for his honesty and self-effacing humor. He fails because he cannot reconcile factual contradiction to the ideological agenda whose duplicity and hollowness Irving would identify. This fiction is planted in three places: the prefatory materials, book 1, and the periodic interruptions conducted by Knickerbocker throughout his narrative.[13]

The prefatory materials, including the prepublication "Notices," the title page, dedication, the "Account of the Author," and Knickerbocker's own "To the Public," introduce the fiction of Knickerbocker's authorship. Republican histories employed such materials to validate their narratives by attesting to the text's authenticity and articulating the values the author means to promote. Irving recognizes the basic insecurity and egotism that made such materials necessary and parodies them through Knickerbocker's comedic misuse of their language and function.

Six weeks before the publication of the *History* on December 6, 1809, four prepublication "Notices" in the *New York Evening Post* introduced Knickerbocker to the public. The first, appearing October 26, establishes Irving's irony. Knickerbocker has disappeared from the Columbian Hotel, and the landlord places a missing-persons ad. Knickerbocker is described as being "not entirely in his right mind," but the paper notes that "printers of newspapers would be aiding the cause of humanity in giving insertion to the above" (xv).[14] In the third notice, dated November 16, a fictional landlord, Seth Handaside (whose name alone should suggest the author's irony), mentions that "a very curious kind of a written book" will be published to "satisfy" Knickerbocker's overdue rent. The second notice, however, tells a more significant event: having left New York, Knickerbocker is seen "very much fatigued and exhausted" near Albany.

A few weeks later in New York, a book was published with a title that demonstrates the fictional author's original intent: *A History of New York, From the Beginning of the World to the End of the Dutch Dynasty. Containing Among many Surprising and Curious Matters, the unutterable Ponderings of Walter the Doubter, the Disastrous Projects of William the Testy, and the Chivalric Achievements of Peter the Headstrong, the three Dutch Governors of New Amsterdam; being the only Authentic History of the Times that ever hath been, or ever will be Published* (363). Among other things, such a title satirizes the inflated self-possession of historians such as Ramsay who also favored such long titles, in Knickerbocker's claim that his text is more authentic than any other "ever will be."

The dedication (366) to the New-York Historical Society expands Irving's critique of the solipsism of early republic authorship. This group included many prominent politicians whose work in the society complemented their Jeffersonian political activity, an attack on whom is conducted more fully in book 3 in which Jefferson is mocked in the guise of Governor Kieft.[15] Like Tyler's Updike Underhill, Brown's Arthur Mervyn, and Watterston's Morcell, Knickerbocker seems astutely aware that the favor of the inner core of the republican elite mattered more than the integrity of his text, that the approval of this unofficial American aristocracy was a more likely means to success than any direct appeal to the public. Irving thus implicitly dramatizes the undemocratic way by which books gained publication and support in the early republic, revealing the embedded and stultifying reign of convention in the American public sphere.

Irving next has Handaside contribute an "Account of the Author," in which the character of Knickerbocker *while writing* is more fully drawn. Irving's use of voices has been extensively documented, but Handaside is not just another character taken from eighteenth-century England.[16] Like Brown's Dr. Stevens, he is an American Everyman leading a moderate and sane life, seemingly unaware of the cultural implications of the book. This distancing indicates two things: first, Irving uses the pragmatic Handaside to illustrate the growing gulf between ordinary American citizens and American writers—the writer has become irrelevant; second, unconcerned with content or convention, he sees the text as a commodity. Each of these reveals the decolonizing American public that exists outside of the confines of the self-referentiality of early republic textuality.

Handaside also notes the self-serving motivation behind Knickerbocker's work. When asked what he is doing, Knickerbocker replies that he is "seeking for immortality" (374). His commitment to the colonial Dutch is thus subsumed in selfish personal glorification, a quest for insider status in an authorized intellectual establishment. All the players, the reader, Handaside, and, most importantly, Knickerbocker, are just going through the motions. There is a set notion of what type of book is supposed to be written, what sort of book people are supposed to buy, and how it is supposed to be read, passively. Irving's dramatization of this process articulates the hollowness, in 1809, of the republic of letters.

In Knickerbocker's prefatory note, "To the Public," Irving reveals his fictional author's motives and methods for seeking immortality. Knickerbocker appropriates conventional methodological and textual techniques, allowing Irving to reveal his targets. Like Ramsay and others, he emphasizes the necessity of empirical method: without his work, he fears that "the origin of our city . . . will be enveloped in doubt and fiction," linking his mission to republican condemnors of fiction Samuel Miller and Benjamin Rush. Citing seven classical historians in four pages, Knickerbocker blindly applies their theories to American history: "like my revered prototype Herodotus, where no written records could be found, I have endeavoured to continue the chain of history by well authenticated tradition" (377). By aligning himself at once with both Herodotus, a speculative historian, *and* with a drive to eradicate "fiction," the fictional author only reveals his ignorance.

Knickerbocker's obliviousness represents that of all historians whose methods veil the precariousness of the truth and the disinterestedness of their texts: "For after all, gentle reader, cities *of themselves* and in fact empires *of themselves*, are nothing without an historian. It is the patient narrator who cheerfully records their prosperity as they rise—who blazons forth their splendour of their noontide meridian—who props up their feeble relics as they decay—who gathers together their scattered fragments—and who piously at length collects their ashes into the mausoleum of his work, and rears a triumphal monument to transmit their reknown to all succeeding time" (379–80). Despite this admittedly speculative activity, Knickerbocker comfortably complains that he has limited himself, like all "modern historians," to "dull matter of fact" (380). Here, Irving unveils the underlying role of imagination in Enlightenment historiography: imagination is nothing more than self-aggrandizement built upon the haphazard circumstances of individual needs, hardly a method likely to produce a text worthy of expressing useful versions of the past.

Therein lies Knickerbocker's embrace of colonial stratifications. He elevates his effort by repeatedly lauding New York through comparison with Rome, Nineveh, Persepolis, and other empires. He compels his reader to mimic his bowing to established authority, instilling a sense of public submission: "Thus the historian is the patron of mankind, the guardian priest, who keeps the perpetual lamp of ages unextinguished" (380). The historian assumes that what is shown in his lamplight contains something of genuine public utility; if it does not, he will make it do so. Moreover, it erases local identity by forcing it into pre-established models of legitimacy.

Aware that doing so has made earlier historians "immortal," Knickerbocker digresses, corrupting his text the same way Kieft's (and Jefferson's) "projects" will redefine later American communities with "disastrous" results. Most importantly, Knickerbocker demands that the only way the 1809 United States can invest itself with meaning is by stressing its lineal inheritance from its European past, Dutch, English, or otherwise. Knickerbocker is insistent that his New York is not a culturally independent entity but rather the product of an aristocratic tradition of colonizing, claiming, and transplanting. As was also the case for Ramsay, the discussion of alternatives is foreclosed: the messy ambiguities of the Revolution disappear in the more orderly history that reinforces America's colonial status, as merely a realization of European history and insignificant as a distinct and separate potentiality.

Having presented his fictional author and established his method, Irving sets Knickerbocker loose not only in the Dutch past but also on the American present, since the narratives of the seventeenth-century Dutch and the early republic historian become hopelessly intermingled. The creation of such a mixed internal narrative of the *History*'s origins reveals Irving's embrace of what Gary Lee Stonum has called "the obvious formal disunity of texts professing organic wholeness" (3) that serves as a vehicle for critiquing authorial claims to comprehensiveness and coherence. Given such a fractured beginning, the *History*'s claims to coherence are doubly undercut to reveal, in Stonum's words, "the subversive underside of dominant cultural traditions" of the early republic.

Book 1 of the *History* shows a blundering quest after "immortality" through historiography. Knickerbocker borrows the assumptions of empirical and classical methodology to convey a history of the world leading up to the settlement of

Dutch New York. However, as his author extends this method to its logical extremes, Irving exposes internal paradoxes that threaten to infect the reader with the same insanity that has disturbed the fictional author. Trusting in the method, Knickerbocker recognizes contradictions, understands them as standard operating procedure, and willingly enjoins his text to their meaninglessness for the sake of grafting himself on to their specious authority. Knickerbocker exuberantly flaunts republican standards that rewarded the sycophantic mouthing of colonial platitudes.

First, in regard to method, Irving exposes the duplicity of the methods his fictional author so wants to master. In the first chapter, Knickerbocker cites Smollett, Gibbon, Hutton, and Erasmus Darwin—historians known for their scientific method—each of whom began his book by rewriting the history of the earth with an eye toward making his subject part of a scientifically defined natural process, a coherence Irving finds highly unlikely. While this section relates more to European historical method, its American adaptations—such as Ramsay's eternal chain—are also implicated.[17]

Their openings demonstrate a fundamental belief that the world could be comprehended in a singular act of ratiocination. Knickerbocker pays homage to this ideal: "The world in which we dwell is a huge, opake, reflecting, inanimate mass, floating in a vast ethereal ocean of infinite space. It has the form of an orange, being an oblate spheroid, curiously flattened at opposite ends for the insertion of two imaginary poles, which are supposed to penetrate and unite at the center; thus forming an axis on which the mighty orange turns with a regular diurnal revolution" (385). This opening statement articulates his intention to write the history of the Dutch settlement within a far-fetched construct of order. He concedes that he has smudged truth and creatively rearranged occurrence to suit the theory's demands for coherence and unity. To defend the occasional inaccuracies of his otherwise theoretically correct predecessors, he suggests: "It is a mortifying circumstance that nature often refuses to second his most profound and elaborate efforts; so that often after having invested one of the most ingenious and natural theories imaginable, she will have the perverseness to act directly in the teeth of his system, and flatly contradict his most favourite positions" (389). These contradictions, however, are dismissed as distracting anomalies, nothing worth discrediting the theory at hand. Just as Ramsay dismissed Shays's Rebellion as a temporary aberration, Knickerbocker regards the disordered universe as a mere distraction. Irving implies that concepts of order exist only in convoluted minds like Knickerbocker's. Likewise, the ordering of human society in stable social hierarchies is also indicted.

Later, Irving demonstrates how empiricism engendered a paradoxical validation of fictionalized history. Knickerbocker acknowledges the fictionality of conventional explanations for inevitable disorder: "Should one of our modern sages, in his theoretical flights among the stars, ever find himself lost in the clouds, and in danger of tumbling into the abyss of nothingness and absurdity, he has but to seize a comet by the beard, mount astride its tail, and away he gallops off in triumph" (397). Because comets represent fictionalized means of exempting theory from factual disputation, Irving here identifies the self-interested nature of claims to empirical authorization. Such intervention was presumably safeguarded by the historian's public-spirited and disinterested objectivity. However, when historians's "comets" carry the nation away from its genuine condition and into a fantasy of wish-fulfillment, the unacknowledged fictionalizing of history becomes a biased act serving nonscientific interests.

Irving does not necessarily object to speculation; rather, he challenges the reliability of texts that do so while simultaneously celebrating their purely empirical and objective standards. This deliberate deception of the public by the republican elite represents a monopolization of the sources and perspectives available to the average citizen wishing to stay informed about the crucial issues that would inform his voting and political activity. By excluding the public from the narrative of its own past, Irving suggests, orthodox historiography participates in a broader coercion of the democratic public, betraying inclusive revolutionary ideals.

In regard to textual sources, Irving also subverts the reactionary veneration of antiquity in the early republic by allowing Knickerbocker to revere authority of inherited texts so slavishly that the absurdity of such behavior cannot be overlooked. In the second, third, and fourth chapters of book 1, Knickerbocker catalogues an encyclopedic list of authorized histories of "Cosmogony," the "Admiral Noah," and the "Peopling of America." His sources include Hesiod, Pythagoras, Plato, the Bible, and others deemed unquestionable for their intellectual authority. These sources constantly contradict and undermine each other. Knickerbocker, however, concludes by uncritically accepting their paradoxes: "And now, having adduced several of the most important theories that occur to my recollection, I leave my readers at full liberty to choose among them. . . . One thing however appears certain—from the unanimous authority of the above quoted philosophers, supported by the evidence of our own senses. . . that this globe really was created and that it is composed of land and water" (398). This retreat to fundamental common sense seems accidental: while Knickerbocker authorizes all texts and methods, Irving adheres to none. To this point, Knickerbocker is content with these contradictions, uncritical of his models and content to be the colonist of the past rather than dare to be something new.

Irving's repudiation of convention is expanded in the final chapter of book 1. Knickerbocker's fable of the colonization of Earth by Moon-men suggests a writer at odds not only with the political uses of history but more importantly with the most fundamental ideological underpinnings of Western thought. Even before this essay starts, Knickerbocker finds himself in need of a "comet": "For unless we prove that the Aborigines did absolutely come from somewhere, it will be immediately asserted in this age of skepticism, that they did not come at all, then was this country never populated—a conclusion perfectly agreeable to logic, but wholly irreconcilable to every feeling of humanity, inasmuch as it must prove syllogistically fatal to the innumerable Aborigines of this popular region" (405). That a world without theoretical sanction would be "syllogistically fatal" is Irving's hyperbolic satire of such hubristic solipsism. Of course, Knickerbocker welcomes this theoretical sanction to privilege ideology over reality, epitomizing the implosive nature of Enlightenment writing.

Furthermore, by challenging the right of Europeans to colonize the Americas, Irving questions the Eurocentric delineation of humanity into savage and civilized camps. Implicitly, the "Aborigines" are humanized and are, in fact, elevated to a sensibility above that of Knickerbocker. Irving thus satirizes how imperialist writing—such as Enlightenment historiography—simply erases what it cannot rationalize. In this case, Irving indicts the notion of lands held around the globe by indigenes as empty and thus ripe for colonization. Unlike many of his contemporaries, he understands the messiness of history, how neat binaries like savage and civilized fall short of accuracy.

Ultimately, because the Dutch similarly cannot be fit into his model, the Enlightenment threatens them with syllogistic fatality as well. Irving thus links the white settlers and the indigenes in a single process of marginalization from European meaning and implicitly ventures a heterogeneous community incomprehensible by any imported standards and so in need of a self-definition of more local origin. Separately, Jenny Sharpe and Dolores Janiewski have identified how the work of colonization continued after Independence in regard to native Americans. Janiewski traces the very act of erasure Irving mocks: "White or European, as defined by the first federal naturalization statute in the 1790s, corresponded to citizen; non-whites and non-Europeans could not aspire to equal citizenship" (133). In fact, such a statute was fatal in ways much more overt than syllogistically.

Along the same lines, chapter 5 begins with a question very current: "What right had the first discoverers of America to land, and take possession of a country without the consent of its inhabitants, or yielding them adequate compensation for their territory?" (412). Using the rational mode of the *Federalist Papers*, Knickerbocker answers that the legally defined rights of "Discovery" (412), "Cultivation" (414), and "Extermination" (419) made Dutch invasion and settlement legal. Both the laws Knickerbocker cites and his method of thinking are obviously biased by selfish interests, skewed by Irving's skepticism of his age's imperialist pretenses. Next, Knickerbocker writes of a hypothetical invasion of Earth by Moon-men who justify conquering and enslaving the entire planet with the same argument, an act whose legality forces Knickerbocker's approval. Irving thus satirizes the colonizing tendencies of the early republic, revealing the narrow proximity of the intellectual slavishness of writers like Knickerbocker to actual policy and violence.

While Knickerbocker claims that this argument makes the book "the most accurate of histories" (424), Irving articulates a very complex skepticism: he questions the mission of Euro-American civilization, the viability of legal reasoning, and the presumption that human achievement matters on a cosmic scale, revealing his sense of the complexity of Second World American experience. By disrupting the usual formulation of center and margin, Irving reminds the reader of the impurity of all human motives in general and of the questionable nature of the European presence in America in specific. One passage particularly reverses the usual power dynamic: "It is true they [the native Americans] neither stole nor defrauded, they were sober, continent, and faithful to their word; but though they acted right habitually, it was all in vain unless they did so from pretext. The newcomers therefore used every method, to induce them to embrace and practice the true religion" (418). Knickerbocker himself is set against the noble example of the Natives. He acts from nothing but "pretext"—theory—and emerges as a joke. Knickerbocker means to present this fable as an exemplar of republican reasoning. Irving also means to instruct, but his values are the reverse of Knickerbocker's. Instead, the reader must admire the natives and feel ashamed of the Europeans. While Irving oversimplifies his noble savages, American history could no longer be considered an unmitigated "constitutional" triumph. Perhaps Knickerbocker's inability to recognize the complexity of native American culture demonstrates the deeper failure of his language.

Book 1 ends with this reiteration of the problems raised throughout Irving's opening: the natural world as a whole and American history in particular cannot be discussed as orderly, exemplary, or ideologically righteous—the most central assumptions of the school of Ramsay—without reenacting Knickerbocker's absurdity. The establishment of Knickerbocker's allegiance to this language and method, despite the paradoxes he acknowledges, is nonetheless the primary function of book 1.

⁂

Through the remainder of the *History*, Irving unravels the implications of any reactionary adherence to the culture of the colonial epoch. When the Dutch colony is shown to lack the materials suited to the authorized theory in which he has promised to write, Knickerbocker becomes aware of the futility of his ambition. In this failure Irving begins to break from the other writers addressed in the present study. Far from the stable—if deluded or deceptive—fictional authorial voices that came before, Knickerbocker loses confidence in himself and his language. In a way approaching postmodern metafiction, Knickerbocker confronts his and his book's potential meaninglessness. The humor Irving employs in telling this story connects the self-deception and willful ignorance implicit in conventional history derived from European models to the absurd conditions Irving observed in 1809 America.

The remainder of Irving's book is only incidentally about the Dutch: its true fiction concerns Knickerbocker's aspiration to prophetic powers through a comprehensive act of controlling nature and history. As he moves from theory to practice, Knickerbocker becomes progressively disillusioned with the method valorized in book 1. He finds that the Dutch past falls outside both Enlightenment and classical theory. By the end, having lost all anchoring, Knickerbocker retreats from the very act of writing and abjures the authorial immortality he had earlier craved. Through the negative example of his fictional historian, Irving can be seen demanding a narrative form and language more expressive of a world in flux, a decolonizing society in which ambiguities and disorder make the elevation of a specific moment a futile exercise in small-minded self-congratulation. Irving dramatizes the progressive crumbling of Knickerbocker the historian in the fictional author's occasional interventions and asides. In a two-part pattern, the narrator first holds up a theory to reality and observes its failure; second, he meditates on the meaning of that failure to his text, his place in his community, and finally on his society itself.

In book 2, one significant passage reveals Knickerbocker's developing frustration over the incompatibility of his subject with Enlightenment theories of universality. Although unprovoked, Knickerbocker finds himself anxious to defend his method: "many of the inhabitants of this fair city . . . will unquestionably suppose that all the preliminary chapters . . . were totally irrelevant and superfluous—and that the main business, the history of New York, is not a jot more advanced than if I had never taken up my pen" (448). In the next paragraph, he admits that "I often have my doubts" as to whether he will "finish this history." On the next page, he directly harangues his "readers," an act that allows Irving, like Brown, to demand that the reader correct complacent reading habits: "I hear some of my captious readers questioning the correctness of my arrangement—but I have no patience with these continual interruptions—never was a historian so pestered with doubts and queries, and such a herd of discontented quidnuncs! if they continue to worry me in this manner, I shall never get to the end of my work" (449). Knickerbocker's internal dialogue illustrates the self-destructive nature of a reactionary trust in inherited thought. Through these asides, Irving's mock-hero slowly becomes aware of the hubris underlying his initial self-definition. The republican elevation of author above reader is thus challenged in favor of a more equal relationship.

This dissatisfaction next occurs in chapter 5 of book 3. It opens with Knickerbocker's narrating a walk he took around the shores of Manhattan in the autumn of 1804. As he observes that only traces of Dutch buildings remain, he recognizes the futility of conceiving of history as a progress toward righteousness, "contrasting, in sober sadness, the present day, with the hallowed years behind the mountain" (489). Momentarily freed from the burden of conventional authorship, Knickerbocker indulges in a picturesque description of the natural landscape that trivializes the Dutch history and Knickerbocker's theoretical mission in a way that importantly foreshadows Irving's later development: "Everything seemed to acquiesce in the profound repose of nature" (490). The worthwhile materials for this passage are not the musty records of the Dutch or the patterns of reason established by conventional authorship, but they nevertheless reveal beauty and insight. Their absence from other parts of the texts is thus attenuated.

The sky, the water, and the ruins act directly upon the imagination without being filtered through the pedantic sieve of eighteenth-century methodology.

The disappearance of the Dutch buildings also suggests a detachment of the colonial past from the early republic present. Frank Shuffleton has called such efforts one of the "various efforts to create a myth of ethnic homogeneity" (14). Ethnic homogeneity served republicanism through a process of deracination as a component of the nationalization of American identity. Here, Irving rescues the memory of the multiethnic American past by employing sources devalued in the eighteenth century. Imagination and nostalgia, to Irving, count as much as buildings and battle and so, both methodologically and historiographically, Irving reimagines an alternative American past more suited to the processes of decolonization. The change in language and the growth in perception that accompany his separation of the British and Dutch colonial pasts reveals the potential eloquence available to American writers when they are less preoccupied with inherited modes of expression and such limited versions of the past.

That Knickerbocker temporarily must lay aside his work implies further disquietude. He recognizes that the incompatibility of his original plan with his true materials has caused his text to collapse. Walking away from it, not only toward the river but also toward a romantic perspective in both subject and language, exhibits a character deeply troubled by the ways in which he had defined himself. Moreover, this interruption disrupts the text's self-proclaimed objective unity, a disruption absent from the masters he claimed in book 1. No longer able to limit himself unnaturally, Knickerbocker, like Murray's Vigillius and unlike Brown's Arthur Mervyn, begins to let other voices, including his own, open the text to the polyvocality of its American setting. Because he cannot abandon his single-minded assignment of writing about the colonial Dutch, he begins reshaping his text by subverting the methodology that has made his book virtually unwritable.

᠅

In book 4, not recognizing that any attack on orthodox technique implicates himself, Knickerbocker initiates his attack on the cultural traditions by which he feels cheated and deceived by venting his spleen on William the Testy, a figure generally recognized as an analog of Jefferson.[18] Having understood the folly of received methodology, Knickerbocker attempts to purge his text of its dangerous predilections. Instead of rejecting it altogether, however, he endeavors reform, to correct from within: he retains a trust in the ability of the conventional text to articulate unbiased truth. Chapter 1 begins with Knickerbocker's reconsideration of the duplicitous nature of recent texts:

> To let my readers into a great literary secret, your experienced writers, who wish to instil peculiar tenets, either in religion, politics or morals, do often resort to this expedient—illustrating their favourite doctrines by pleasing fictions on established facts—and so mingling historic truth, and subtle speculation together, that the unwary million never perceive the medley; but running with an open mouth, after an interesting story, are often made to swallow the most heterodox opinions, ridiculous theories, and abominable heresies. This is particularly the case with modern philosophers. (511–12)

Knickerbocker, unaware as he is, describes himself as he imagined himself in book 1. As he writes book 4, he doubts his earlier work and ambition. Afterwards, Knickerbocker reiterates his rejection of this method, "without claiming any of the privileges above recited" (512). However, still avoiding a language reflective of an alternative style, he demonstrates an intellect polarized by the oppositional method of his earlier thinking and, instead of openly casting aside convention, resorts to another part of Enlightenment tradition—the classical.

In book 4, Knickerbocker contrasts "modern" to "ancient" ideals—an act that only temporarily delays his recognition of the failure of all predetermined methods to describe American experience. Like Knickerbocker of book 1, Kieft demonstrates a reverence for Enlightenment method and classical textuality: "He was exceedingly fond of trying philosophical and political experiments; and having stuffed his head full of scraps and remnants of ancient republics, and oligarchies, and aristocracies, and monarchies" (515). But Kieft seems to be doing no more than the fictional author planned to do in "To the Public": "Where no written records could be found, I have endeavoured to continue the chain of history by well authenticated traditions" (377). Having now recognized that such continuation in the name of factional motivations constitutes an inconsistency in the text's claim to objectivity, Knickerbocker condemns the same practice he had championed without fundamentally changing his style. He contrasts doctrinaire republicanism with states and writings described in ancient books: "a species of government, neither laid down in Aristotle, nor Plato" (515). This observation allows Irving to reveal the emptiness of the founders' alleged claims to classical authenticity.

Through the remainder of book 4, Knickerbocker tries to avoid acknowledging the meaninglessness in his work and his subject by contrasting hollow modern ideas against classical sources. Irving, however, was not content with such superficial activity: his critique goes deeper than the topical republican-ism of Jeffersonian politics.[19] In the three final books, the same contradictions that had crippled modern thinking also reduce the *ancient* to folly and nonsense: the ambition, not just the failed attempt, to be like the ancients is parodied. Moreso than ever, Irving is here writing about writing, openly questioning and challenging eighteenth-century writing to "demand symbolic overhaul, a re-shaping of dominant images" (3), as Elleke Boehmer has said of all decoloniz-ing writers.

Knickerbocker means to depict the third Dutch governor, Peter Stuyvesant, as a hero for his text in the classical tradition. In his initial description, he com-pares Stuyvesant to Ajax, Hercules, Atlas, Coriolanus, and Achilles (565). Cloth ing his hero in such analogies, Knickerbocker would transfer the authority of classical reference to his work, having already realized the duplicity of modern method. As Knickerbocker begins his explication of Stuyvesant's reign, however, he perceives that classical texts are just as speculative as their modern counter-parts.

The incident that most convinces him of the unreliability of classical mod-els is the incident of the Dutchmen's battle against Swedish colonists near Fort Christina. He introduces the battle with Homeric allusion and imagery recast as satire familiar to the students of pedants: "the noted bully Mars" and "the ox-eyed Juno" (648–49) duly observe and participate in the combat. When the bat-tle is over, however, Knickerbocker finds that not "a single man was killed or even wounded" (659). As a response he "began to doubt the authenticity of many of Dan Homer's stories" (660). He, too, would like to rearrange the truth, as he promised to do in book 1, but now refuses: "I disclaim all such unprincipled lib-erties—let me have truth and the law on my side" (661). His differentiation of his truth from that of the Classics demonstrates his growth. By the end of book 4, he is a figure much changed from the man who began book 1.

From there, Knickerbocker further meditates on the meaning of his work. After identifying martial skill as the mark of a classical hero, Knickerbocker per-ceives all war as a quest for self-centered heroism—presenting Irving with an op-portunity to indict the strain of self-destruction and violence innate in the classical tradition. Knickerbocker concludes by ruminating on the dangerous ten-dency of such behavior: "Why are kings desolating empires and depopulating whole countries? in short, what induces all great men, of all ages to commit so many horrible victories and misdeeds, and inflict so many miseries upon mankind and on themselves? . . . So that the mighty object of all their toils, their hardships and privations is nothing but immortal fame—and what is immortal fame?— why, half a page of dirty paper!" (662). Irving here addresses the concepts of glory championed in texts from authorized antiquarian sources. In 1809 aging heroes of the Revolution populated the political and economic elite, justifying their ascendancy through their erstwhile violent bravery. Irving, a member of the next generation, however, seems to resent the continued presence of these outdated old men. He challenges them by suggesting that their emphasis on heroism and violence distracts from the more meaningful ideological potentials offered by the Revolution.

The rest of the *History* contains hardly a classical allusion, but Knickerbocker, without any model, is unequipped to conceive meanings unsanctioned by theoretical approbation. Thereafter, he reduces Dutch history to a meaningless degeneration toward nothingness, a process mirrored by the textual collapse of Knickerbocker's text. If the present is not a colony of the past and if Europe has bequeathed nothing applicable to America, originality and invention must be employed. Knickerbocker, ever the subject and never the citizen, is incapable of this transition.

❧

In book 7, Irving's narrator, like his subject, progresses toward self-destruction. After describing at length the downfall of New Amsterdam under the governance of Stuyvesant, Knickerbocker launches an extensive diatribe on the meaning of history. One section particularly applies to American subjects: "Behold the Roman eagle, fledged in her Ausonean aerie, but wheeling her victorious flight over the fertile plains of Asia . . . view the imperial Rome, the emporium of taste and science—the paragon of cities, the metropolis of the universe—ravaged, sacked, and overturned by successive hoards of fierce barbarians" (719). Here there is no attempt to assemble "scattered fragments" into a comprehensive whole. Knickerbocker has recognized that history has never confined itself to the strictures of Enlightenment theory: there is no reason, progress, or order.

In this case, the Roman eagle, a symbol borrowed by the United States, is shown to be as fragile as any of its imperial predecessors, thus denying special status to the republican state. Implicit is a recognition that all attempts at such order suggest self-delusion: "Behold—but why should we behold any more? Why should we rake among the ashes of extinguished greatness?—Kingdoms, Principalities, and Powers, have each had their rise, their progress and their fall—each in its turn has swayed a mighty sceptre—each has returned to its primeval nothingness!" (720). Knickerbocker proceeds to compare the Dutch colony to a "distended bladder" beaten about by "truant urchins." Behind his despairing fictional author, Irving can be seen here demonstrating how an insistence upon reason and order in history eventually produces despondence and hopelessness. Moreover, those things that had first attracted both author and reader to the quaint and humorous Dutch in the first place are lost in the grim humorlessness required by the eighteenth century.

In the next paragraph Knickerbocker articulates his only goal left in writing: "the direful spectre of my landlord's bill" (721), a phrase that restores the comedic absurdity of Knickerbocker's failure. He concedes the meaninglessness of his effort by reembracing the format he had earlier abjured. In a desperate attempt to salvage something—or at least sales—Knickerbocker returns to a rather obscure event in his text—the Swedish defeat of the Dutch at Fort Casimer—which he repositions as part of a Trumbull-like sequence that produced "the present convulsions of the globe!" (721). The narrator desperately repeats this sentiment three times in the final pages. He also invokes a heretofore absent patriotism in the manner of Tyler's Updike Underhill: "Let all the potentates of Europe, beware of how they meddle with our beloved country" (722). These pathetic grasps at the language and commonplaces of republican phraseology demonstrate the depth to which the historian will sink to gain insider textuality, or at least to pay the rent.

In a section detached from the final chapter, Knickerbocker attaches an epistle to his reader that testifies to the deflation of his ambition. He claims the events of the text are "not my fault" and that later historians will "spring up and surpass me in excellence"—a far cry from the inflation of the title. He also mourns that the world "does not prove itself worthy of the unbounded love I bear it" (728). Irving, of course, implies that poor Knickerbocker had been deluded by an impossible definition of what is worthy and so suggests that a new means of appreciation was necessary. No longer seeking insider status, Knickerbocker abandons all hope and seeks a romantic respite in death: "Already has withering age showered his sterile snows upon my brows; in a little while, and this genial warmth which still lingers around my heart, and throbs—worthy reader—throbs kindly towards thyself, shall be chilled forever. Haply this frail compound of dust, which while alive may have given birth to naught but unprofitable weeds, may form a humble sod of the valley, from whence shall spring many a sweet wild flower, to adorn my beloved isle of Manna-hata" (729).

Irving then buries Knickerbocker, who, to recall, is last seen "very much fatigued and exhausted" in the advertisements. The book concludes by collapsing in upon itself. In the *History* Irving dramatizes how writing about the nation in English ways disables the author from participating constructively in the fluid and organic American community. Irving's fiction of Knickerbocker's authorship thus recreates an uneven and disordered study in self-destruction drawn to reveal Irving's observation of the fallacies of his age.

⁂

The destruction of Knickerbocker had its own sobering relevance to his creator. Unlike the other fictional voices with which he had experimented in "The Oldstyle Papers" and *Salmagundi*, Knickerbocker must finally die, signifying Irving's deliberate break from the Addisonian and Swiftian technique so popular in colonial America.[20] Irving was not to write creatively for almost ten years when the *Sketch-Book of Geoffrey Crayon* (1819) marked the introduction of a remarkably changed American author, as I discuss in the epilogue.

What can be seen in the *History* is Irving's personal farewell to both the method and the political authority of English modes of authorship, a transition that marks a larger transition in American writing. Even the Knickerbocker who contributes "Rip Van Winkle" and "The Legend of Sleepy Hollow" to the *Sketch-Book* does not reflect the earlier satiric relationship to conventional authorship. Instead they show Knickerbocker considering a more ambiguous relationship between the past and the present, unresolved and exploratory. From this, his writing regains the strength it briefly grasped that evening on the pier. In the *History*, Irving is gradually reflecting the potential of decolonized textual alternatives, "setting out in one way or another to resist colonialist perspectives," in the terms of Boehmer (3); in *The Sketch-Book*, Irving is further along in the process of decolonization, exploring how Americans might "take their place. . . . as historical subjects" by exploring the differences, not the similarities of American and European meanings and histories.

In the *History* the insider becomes the insane: the only source of intellectual redemption therefore lies in moving outside authorized limits, such as the later experiments conducted throughout Irving's career. Gone, then, is the preoccupation with the colonial legacy and the marginal sense of inferiority of all new societies. Even in 1809, Irving's metafiction within the *History* sought a more organic form than Knickerbocker's authorized text, thus demonstrating a nascent textual alternative to inherited forms. This internal narrative, by centralizing an otherwise marginal topic, marks Irving's effort to decolonize the American subject by seeking a more balanced relation with European tradition than the secondary status offered to former colonials by eighteenth-century Eurocentrism.[21] Moreover, he transcends the reactionary anti-British rhetoric of Revolution by making Knickerbocker inherently likable and sympathetic. Acknowledging the British cultural legacy, however, is not the same as celebrating or centralizing it: Irving, as Gary A. Richardson said of Tyler, similarly exhibits the postcolonial "double-consciousness."

The next generation of historians abandoned the trappings of inherited order, whether they wrote fiction or nonfiction. Bancroft, Prescott, and the older Irving acknowledge the subjective presence in their texts of imaginative reconstruction. John P. McWilliams has noted how these writers freely adapted a mode of poetic discourse, the epic, to supersede the pseudoscientific nature of early republic historiography. In their books there is no effort to frame historical episodes in a super-structure of order that would simultaneously affirm contemporary institutions of social power.[22] Moreover, while these are "epics" there is no omniscient master narrative in the manner of Knickerbocker's model, "Don Homer."

Instead, these writers openly reveal the darker and idiosyncratic nature of the American past in texts resembling romantic fiction. Lingering republican reviewers "shudder᷈ ⸲ at its content, and kept silent about its implication" (185), according to McWilliams. These alternative histories are more likely to explore the difference of American and European experience and history and the contradictions of the settlement experience. Their blending of history and fiction breaks the rules of colonialist historiography by blending the objectivity of the colonizer with the subjectivity of the colonized, representing a problematic and postcolonial historiography of divergence and plurality suited to resisting republican Anglocentrism and demonstrating the irresolvable paradoxes of American life so long as received boundaries are exclusively employed.

Moreover, many of the important novels of the 1820s and 1830s sought a historiographic perspective from which to consider the meanings of American life suppressed in the early republic. Cooper's Leatherstocking series, James Kirke Paulding's *Koningsmarke* (1823), John Neal's *1776* (1825), and many other books attempt a reconstruction of the pre-Revolutionary and Revolutionary pasts that promotes the Revolution, not the early republic, as the source of meaningful transition from colony to country. In fact, their call to the Revolution, like Melville's revival of the revolutionary hero Isreal Potter who was an outcast in the early republic, or the citation of the Declaration of Independence by the women of the Seneca Falls convention of 1848, labels the early republic as in fact counterrevolutionary and antidemocratic. Only when remembering its revolutionary roots could later writers consider the ongoing need for decolonization and postcolonial self-exploration. Knickerbocker's hoped-for immortality, and the hubristic inflations of purpose stimulating that ambition, are not the concern of the next group.

Writing in the early republic, however, Irving thoroughly satirizes the first generation of American historians by revealing the solipsistic and derivative nature of their coercive subtexts. In the *History*, Irving initiates a process wherein the possessor of textual authority, such as the historian, shifts from being a methodologically Anglophilic insider, such as Ramsay, to being a visible outsider, like Prescott, Melville, or Cooper. Thereafter, American history had to be and could be reconsidered from the outside as well as from the inside, reflecting the necessary polyvocality of Second World experience. The resulting liberty of form and language represents and reflects the potential for a more fully decolonized national trope of self-definition.

Knickerbocker's death ends the period when the fiction of authorship was employed to challenge "thematically and formally the discourses which supported colonization" by "challenging the conceptual dimensions of the act of writing itself" to combine the definitions of how writing expresses decolonization, in the terms of first Boehmer (3) and then the authors of *The Empire Writes Back*. Paulding's *Koningsmarke* contains a similar interior metafiction, but, at the start, his narrator concedes "many learned persons are of opinion that all history is in itself little better than a romance" (4). This deconstructed view of history marked the disestablishment and discrediting of the colonizing modes of authorship used by the republicans to recolonize the post-Revolutionary nation. Once that manufactured authority fell away, a degree of decolonization had occurred and the technique was no longer relevant. Once the reader was alerted to the subjectivity of authorship, the older colonial hierarchies were transformed into a more leveled, liberal environment for communication and debate.

Larzer Ziff has suggested that, at the end of the early republic, for writing to remain relevant in the changing and liberalizing American public sphere, "the conventions of literature itself would have to be radicalized" (149). The work of the authors of the present study constitutes the first part of this process of liberalizing decolonization: disproving those conventions, or at least chronicling them as they passed from public esteem as the early republic gave way, in the terms of Steven Watts, to "liberal bourgeois capitalism" (179), which lacked any stable or stabilizing source of monolithic authority. Before radicalization could occur, the flaws of the established modes and their accompanying claims to monolithic authority had to be identified and purged, and postcolonial theory helps us view these transitions as they take place in the *History*. The poor deluded Knickerbocker, perhaps like the early republic itself, could only be buried as the country continued to grow away from its colonial origins.

The Vagrant Inclination

On September 26, 1810, John E. Hall, the publisher of the *American Law Journal,* asked Washington Irving, the nation's foremost literary celebrity after his popular *History of New York,* to edit a new "literary journal" that Hall would publish.[1] Irving declined, but his reasons for doing so reflect more than a personal disinclination: "In fact I do not wish to meddle with my pen for a long while— I would rather devote a year or two at least to study—as there are several branches of knowledge which I am but little acquainted at the present, which are indispensable to popular writing. Indeed I feel conscious that my mind wants much improvement, and it is impossible to give it the regular cultivation that is necessary unless I disengage myself from literary activities" (23:290). This confession rests on Irving's recognition that "literary activities," such as editing a journal, participated in the lingering textual paradigm of the early republic and so precluded the exploration of his true talents. In fact, his mind cannot be "improved" until he breaks away from such activities. In other words, a writer, established by satirizing and discrediting inherited modes of writing, understands that so long as his critique takes place within the paradigm, more original and accurate self-expression and self-representation cannot evolve on an individual level, nor can a genuinely decolonized literature ever develop on a national level.[2]

Furthermore, Irving wants his writing to be popular. Unlike Knickerbocker, Irving wants to find a readership and is willing to adjust his work to their tastes. This is a far cry from the minister in Bridgehampton, New York, described by Stephen Burroughs who dictated a narrow syllabus of sermons for "his" people.

To Irving in 1810, the literary aristocrat of the logocracy was a dinosaur, no longer the sole player in the American public sphere. At the very least, Irving's, like Brown's, attempts to live off his earnings as a writer forced a refiguration of the reader/writer relation—the old colonial hierarchies did not sell books to the increasingly decolonized American reading public as the last generation of former colonials passed from the scene.

Furthermore, Irving's writing after the *History* traces future patterns of literary decolonization in the United States that would characterize the next generation of writers and readers. Born in 1783, Irving had been exposed, as his career in *Salmagundi* and the *History* establish, seemingly to every branch of eighteenth-century writing on both sides of the Atlantic. Purportedly, these should have schooled him in all the prequisties of literary popularity and subsequent celebrity. But they had not. American readers, Irving seemed to feel, wanted something else, something unavailable so long as he remained within the British boundaries ascribed by republicanism. In 1812 he wrote, "We would rather hear our victories celebrated in the merest doggeral that sprang from native invention, than beg borrow, or steal from others, the thoughts and words in which to express our exaltation" (qtd. in Youmans, 150). But the materials of "native invention," the "thoughts and the words" were as yet undefined because American writers, as Irving attested in the *History*, were still struggling with the burden of the colonial past.

A more general North Atlantic transformation in the nature of authorship would open a new avenue for Irving. In *The Author, Art, and the Market*, Martha Woodmansee has recognized the transitions in the modes of authorship at the turn of the century: no longer was the artist to be merely an assembler—"always a vehicle or instrument" (36)—to live in words, not the world, to rephrase Martin Roth's comment about Irving, but, after 1800, the onus of creativity and imagination was shifted to the author in unprecedented ways: "The inspiration for a work came to be regarded as emanating not from outside or above, but from within the writer himself . . . distinctly the product—and the property—of the writer" (37).[3] By divorcing itself from traditional ecclestiastical or political alliances, this new mode of authorship, like revolutionary politics, could better express local experience free of received and imposed standards of legitimacy. In a sense, this development democratized authorship, or at the very least, made the author a free agent in the public sphere, able to experiment or criticize, bearing the risk of his venture alone, not as the representative of any coercive class structure or as the propagandistic component of a program of imperial hegemony.

The difficulty Irving had writing immediately after completing Knicker-bocker's *History* was typical of the writers addressed in this study and reflects the struggle of American writers first to complete the transition Woodmansee de-scribes and then to apply it to American subjects. What little writing most of them published after discrediting conventional authorship reflected a general in-ability and unwillingness to attach themselves to inherited modes of writing, even to criticize it: Brackenridge's "Mamachtega," Watterston's *A Child of Feeling*, and Brown's "Carsol" reveal each author in an experimental mood, exploring ways of writing and expression far less derived from British models and more willing to experiment with alternative strategies of authorship.[4] However, these experi-ments never flowered into completed or fully realized texts representative of a genuinely alternative postcolonial textuality.

In fact, most American writers of the period were less experimental and in-novative than their English contemporaries. While Wordsworth and Coleridge were publishing *Lyrical Ballads* (1798), American readers were still being assailed by the conservative neoclassical couplets of the Hartford Wits. Such fear of ex-perimentation, however, is typical of post-Independence communities. The lin-gering sense of marginality, and the fiction of metropolitan coherence imposed by the colonizers, make the literary tradition appear unassailable.[5] The writers born in the colonial period—Brackenridge, Murray, Tyler, and Brown—are more concerned with identifying the inapplicability and inadequacy of this mentality than with making something new.

Therefore, none of these writers is entirely successful or, at the very least, pro-ductive: their work still operates within the old paradigms, even as they appro-priate and subvert the textual foundations of their craft. These writers born in the colonial period—all of those addressed in this study with the exception of Watterston and Irving—seem unable to see through the process of decoloniza-tion to envision genuinely postcolonial modes of expression.[6] These writers ap-propriate, dismantle, reconfigure, and subvert colonial and republican reading and writing habits, establishing a need and a context for literary and linguistic decolonization by encouraging methods of American self-identification less shackled to imported preconceptions and more attuned to local conditions and complexities. By undermining republicanism and its reinscription of colonial hi-erarchies, the writers working before 1810 primarily ask for their nation to un-derstand its potential postcoloniality, its hybrid heterogeneity and finally to complete the process of Revolution by exploring the free polyphony of the Amer-ican community.

꽃

Irving, more than any other American author, was able to express Woodmansee's transition in the scope of his career. In the *Sketch-Book*, Irving's development reveals a mode of writing more radically divorced from the later compositions of the others, and more successful. Most importantly, the writing that appears there—on occasion—no longer defines itself merely in opposition to the colonial epoch but rather expresses what happens after the period of colonialism was just one part of the vast plurality of cultural presences that compose every community; only after that transition is a former colony postcolonial, in the cultural and social sense of the word.

In 1810 Irving was only twenty-seven years old, and the early republic was coming to an end. The movement toward republican consensus, as identified by Robert Ferguson and Albert P. Furtwangler, had disintegrated as party, regional, and class-based distinctions emerged to reveal a disharmonious and diverse nation.[7] In turn, the unified effort to meld American writing to overtly political causes for purposes of republican propaganda had begun to unravel, a development particularly revealed by the public reception of the *Sketch-Book* in 1819. The democratic culture, discouraged and hidden during the early republic but latent since the Revolution, had reasserted itself politically and now did so textually.

The fact of the *Sketch-Book*'s enormous popularity demonstrates the accuracy of Irving's prediction that such an experimental text could be both "profitable and reputable." As a result, Irving, who had found the fiction of authorship appropriate before 1810, realized that such an internal critique of official textuality was no longer sufficient. In 1811, in response to his brother William's question concerning his future, Irving's answer again hints at a profound disquietude with received modes of reading and writing. This time, however, he has begun the process of conceiving an alternative textuality:

I shall pursue a plan I had some time since contemplated, of studying for a while, and then travelling about the country for the purpose of observing the manners and characters of various parts of it, with a view of writing a work, which, if I have any acquaintance with my own talents, will be far more profitable and reputable than any thing I have yet written. . . . But whatever I may write in the future I am determined on one thing—to dismiss from my mind all party prejudice and feeling as much as possible, and to endeavor to contemplate every object with a candid and good natured eye. (23:305)

Now deliberately a political outsider, Irving has more in mind than merely another book: he hints at his ambition to work in entirely different literary modes. Instead of looking to the government and its official texts for a discursive environment, he now wants to observe and write for "the country" and its "manners and characters" to create a "profitable" book—one the public would want to buy, instead of one they would be coerced into buying. To do this, he aspires to a more democratic textuality that might better reflect his new intended audience: the "various parts" of the country. At the same time, younger writers like John Neal, James Kirke Paulding, and James Fenimore Cooper began their careers without having to undergo the purgation of the eighteenth century in the manner of Irving in the *History*.

Ironically, much of the *Sketch-Book* describes mostly English subjects. Nonetheless, unlike Knickerbocker, Geoffrey Crayon often seems a voice for Irving himself. As such, the constant authorial presence of the volume is American. Crayon constantly negotiates his own status as the expatriated ex-colonial, like some character from V. S. Naipaul or Christina Stead. At once Crayon recognizes England as *home*—just as would the American characters of Henry James—and its implication in his own displacement across the Atlantic; that is, he cannot go *home* again. Simultaneously, it is not *home* and it neither understands him entirely nor he it. The "Author's Account of Himself" introduces Crayon as the presumptive author of the *Sketch-Book*. Crucially absent from it are any aspirations to a social authority to be established by his authorship of an acceptable text. Moreover, Crayon and, through him Irving, recognize the otherness of British culture for an American. Unlike earlier figures, Crayon is free to explore the complexity of the two nations' mutual history but divided present.[8]

Before initiating his original authorship, Irving lets fly one barb concerning misguided European perceptions. In regard to European books about America, he sarcastically notes: "A great man of Europe, thought I, must therefore be as superior to a great man of America as a peak of the Alps is to a highland of the Hudson, and in this idea I was confirmed by observing the comparative importance and swelling magnitude of many English travellers among us, who, I was assured, were very little people in their own countries" (8:14–15). Such a remark silently articulates the failure of European ways of thinking about America, implying that Europe is not intellectually equipped to comprehend the new nation.[9] Reversing the imperial gaze of the European traveler, Irving, now exploring postcoloniality, affirms difference and incompatibility while acknowledging that colonial writing is simply no longer applicable to the former colony.

As such, acts of European-style authorship concerning the United States, like Knickerbocker's, are bound to fail. Crayon's preoccupation with the European gaze soon fades from the volume as he explicitly reverses it, appropriating the power of defining vision to rephrase British subjects, colonizing the colonizer, as it were. Richard McLamore has recently noted the specifically postcolonial aspects of this same strategy in Irving's later work: "Irving seems to have been disturbed by the use of literature as a tool of nationalist or colonialist interests" (28), and so argues that Irving sought a less corruptible form and language.

Unlike the fictional authors of the early republic, Crayon speaks of himself as a whimsical artist, not as a public man. Crayon's characterization seems without a central methodology in which the idea of impermanence is celebrated. Like his letters to Hall and his brother, Crayon reflects Irving's own search not only for other ways of writing but also for other means of thinking. Crayon concludes his account of himself by commenting on the necessarily fragmentary and inconsistent nature of his book: "When, however, I look over the hints and memorandums I have taken down for the purpose, my heart almost fails me at finding how my idle humor has led me aside from the great subjects studied by every regular traveler who would make a book. I fear I shall give equal disappointment with an unlucky landscape painter, who had travelled on the continent, but, following the bent of his vagrant inclination, had sketched in the nooks and corners and byplaces" (8:15). The "nooks and corners and byplaces" offered a more valuable source of "inspiration"—a word Woodmansee describes as integral to the new aristic conceptions of authorship (37)—for writing than the great public subjects of official history, polite manners, and political responsibility offered by the republican paradigm. The "vagrant inclination" is thus authorized as a source of decolonized observation that could appeal directly to the reader without demanding the reader's acceptance of the text on the basis of the social status of the author.

The decolonized, "vagrant inclination" is best expressed in the *Sketch-Book*'s two most famous pieces: "Rip Van Winkle" and "The Legend of Sleepy Hollow." Both of these tales have presumably been "Found Among the Papers of the Late Diedrich Knickerbocker" (8:37, 329). Significantly, Knickerbocker could not fit them into his *History*. Each relies on imaginative speculation, common subjects, and what Lloyd M. Daigrepont has called "the gnostic view of history" (56).[10] None of these could fit into the formulaic and inorganic text Knickerbocker was compelled to compose in the *History*. None matches the neatly rational and celebratory mode required by the republican mode of historiography.

But Crayon has no doubts about including them. In these stories Knicker-bocker's style is freer and more expressive, revealing an expansive mind whose potential had been suppressed by the formal requirements of his formalized text in the *History*. By exposing his readers to Rip Van Winkle and Ichabod Crane, two men whose experience would not be considered socially instructive in the early republic, Irving suggests that the most expressive narratives often have nothing to do with government or battle or anything as boring as public inter-est. Moreover, Irving leaves their stories unresolved and ambiguous as to what they reveal about the American character: there is no stable authorial voice telling the readers how to use the text, appropriating and colonizing their role in the reading. Instead, the writer's voice traces itself back to oral culture wherein the narrator's words alone signify his or her legitimacy.

While *The Sketch-Book* is by no means a fully decolonized text (if such a thing is ever possible) it has transcended the limited colonialist/anticolonialist binary that characterized early republic writing by initiating other possibilities. It em-braces the interconnectedness of English and American cultures but strives, par-ticularly in these two stories, for "indigeneity," the difficult signifier of local validity so much the goal of settler literatures, according of Carolyn Masel and Bill Ashcroft, Gareth Griffiths, and Helen Tiffin.[11] These stories express the idio-syncratic nature of local American scenes. In "Rip," the name of the pub changes from King George's to George Washington, continuing Irving's mockery of early republic pretensions, but Tarrytown itself has been transformed beyond any model provided in colonial history: it is noisy and chaotic but, for better or worse, itself.

In this sense Irving's writing reflects a postrepublican synthesis that both ac-knowledges and moves beyond its colonial past. The "vagrant inclination" is therefore a textuality of authorial experimentation, not of political compliance or imaginative constriction. Freed from adherence to the ominous national re-sponsibilities asked of the writer by republicanism, Irving and others can explore dissidence, counternarrative, and controversy in the multivocal American pub-lic sphere of the nineteenth century. Since American writing had engaged the process of decolonization, these new directions represent both postcolonial free-dom and anxiety: while the legacy of colonialism still lurks, it no longer pre-dominates.

Equally important, however, is the fact that the American reading public agreed. While the *History* had sold well, the *Sketch-Book* became a national trea-sure. In fact, by the end of the nineteenth century it had been reprinted more than any other American text.[12] David S. Reynolds and Michael T. Gilmore have noted, echoing William Charvat's recognition, that after 1820 the American literary environment changed from a company store to an open marketplace of texts and genres.[13] In this marketplace, a polyphony of republican, colonial, anticolonial, postcolonial, abolitionist, racist, antiracist, and many more voices competed for the American readership. Missing in this marketplace was any monopolizing presence: the decolonizing public had finally brought its revolutionary antiauthoritarianism to its reading habits. In fact, to recall Patrick Henry, there was not one "language of 'We, the people,'" but many.

Ralph Waldo Emerson's "The American Scholar" ushers in the next stage of decolonization: "We have listened too long to the courtly muses of Europe. The spirit of the American freeman is already suspected to be timid, imitative, tame. . . . What is the remedy?" (70–71). Rephrased, once we are no longer colonials, how do we become Americans? Like Emerson, the books in this study recognized Americans' tendency to live safely as colonials rather than explore American difference. The work of the six writers addressed here prefaced Emerson's question by helping to challenge colonialism in the early republic; however, writing in 1837, Emerson understood that the United States was still combating those same forces and he still awaited a more fully expressed postcolonial or national identity. In fact, at the 1996 Olympics, a British commentator noted that Australians, New Zealanders, and Americans were "colonials all." Decolonization, as Jenny Sharpe has argued, is never complete—anxieties about British culture linger in the 1990s—but, with the end of the early republic, the process was explored more openly and Americans began to stop thinking of themselves merely as colonials.[14]

However, as much as they involve themselves in the decolonizing nineteenth-century American public sphere, the texts examined in the present study also address the darker half of Second World identity. We have mostly explored the early republic's colonizing tendencies on the level of metaphor: colonization as a means of describing how republicanism's efforts at subjugation, stratification, and misrepresentation resembled colonization after the Revolution in its efforts to mechanize the nation using imported cultural, political, and economic models. Only Brackenridge and Irving overtly linked this process to the more genuine colonization undertaken by the early republic. The recent efforts of John Seelye and Dana D. Nelson address geographical colonization and racial colonization, respectively, throughout the Revolutionary and early republic periods.[15] Even though Americans had come to terms with their colonial past, the colonizing tendency had yet to be acknowledged and critiqued.

The quest for genuine self-knowledge and self-expression in the Second World predicates the acknowledgment of both sides of Slemon's bisection of the individual subject and Lawson's "dual inscription" (157)—that of colonizer. Furthermore, scholars of postcolonialism remove the United States from their discussions of settlement literatures at varying points in the nineteenth century. For instance, Lawson limits his use of the United States to its "pre-imperial" period. I would argue that the books I have addressed reveal this to be a false distinction: the United States was and is both postcolonial *and* colonizing simultaneously, dating back to the early republic. Moreover, the writers I have addressed internalized this dual identity from the start.

For example, Brackenridge both satirizes republican Anglocentrism as colonial mimicry and condemns its colonization of the transappalachian west. *Modern Chivalry*, *The Algerine Captive*, and the *History of New York* all deeply criticize American racial policy in regard to both slaves and indigenes; Murray engages the enclosure of women and the lower classes in the early republic and disparages racism. Just as these writers warned Americans against the dangers of their own experience of colonial subjecthood, they also sounded the alarm on creeping American imperialism and neocolonialism.

Only half of postcolonial self-description involves coming to terms with the colonial past; it also demands an internalization of the colonizing impulse that had created the colonies in the first place. Second World writers continue the work of decolonization by remaining always vigilant for any excesses that favor either side of the colonizer/colonized binary. Just as post-Federation Australian writers like Patrick White and Xavier Herbert critiqued Australian imperialism in the South Pacific, so too did the early republic writers I have addressed identify colonizing ambitions as ever and always parts of the postcolonial Second World personality.

Refusal or inability to acknowledge the bifurcated nature of Second World identity engenders destabilization, self-contradiction, occasional hypocrisy, and is underpinned by a seemingly pervasive desire for the right hand not to know what the left is doing. Perhaps its best expression is in John Adams's response to his wife's request for gender equity in the new nation: "We have been told that our Struggle has loosened the bands of Government every where. That children and Apprentices were disobediant—that Indians slighted their Guardians, and Negroes grew insolent to their Masters. But your letter was the first Intimation that another Tribe more numerous and powerfull than all the rest were grown discontented.—This is rather too coarse a Compliment but you are so saucy, I wont to blot it out. Depend upon it: We know better than to repeal our Masculine systems" (31). At once John Adams is anticolonialist and colonizer, both antiauthoritarian and authority, both liberator and racist. In addition, his conflation of race, class, and gender as equally disruptive sources brings to life the concept of symbolic colonization as a means of exclusion and exploitation. Simultaneously, Adams has straddled both sides of Memmi's binary without knowing the inconsistencies of his position.

⁂

The writers addressed in this study trace the self-ignorance of republicans like Adams as it produces, first, absurdity, then, deception, and finally annihilation, and always as it prevents and precludes more honest national self-examination. Two hundred years ago, these writers were doing what current postcolonial writers and theorists are still pursuing: their common narrative is that eighteenth-century European textuality merely "rediscover[ed] Europe" when it was applied in the early republic, as Helen Tiffin has recently said of poststructuralism. Instead, she suggests, postcolonial writers are impelled to explore not only local content and language but also decentered theories of reading, writing, and culture. The six books I have addressed thus function at both specific and theoretical levels to challenge the centrality of leftover colonial practices in American writing of the early republic, "narratives, that is, which, whatever their expressive or reflective purchase in the realities of colonial or postcolonial societies, also provide detailed counter-discursive 'readings' of the 'master works' of imperial culture" (xvii), in the words of Tiffin and her collaborator Steven Slemon. The fact of their being "counter" at once announces their importance and identifies their limitations: theirs is a literature of resistance, but not yet of reconstruction.

In Jacksonian America, the decolonization of American writing diminished the social authority of authorship by democratizing acts of self-representation. Furthermore, as the "master works" of British imperialism were increasingly replaced by masterworks of American writing with the rise of such figures as Cooper, Bryant, and the later Irving, other American writers now had more local writers to "counter." In the terms of Brown's Welbeck, "the reputation of literature" was no longer linked to "opulence" in the mid-nineteenth century, as it had been in the early republic.[16] While certain later fictions such as Hawthorne's *Blithedale Romance*, Poe's *Narrative of Arthur Gordon Pym*, and Melville's *Moby-Dick* employ fictional authors, they do so for reasons very different from those of the early republic writers.

Neither Miles Coverdale, nor Pym, nor Ishmael seeks the insider status hoped for by Brackenridge's narrator, Updike, Vigillius, Arthur, Morcell, or Knicker-bocker.[17] Instead, the fictional authors almost reverse republican authorship and seek resolution from the reader, as opposed to providing it themselves. Authorship, Steven Railton has noted, became dictated by the "empowered" (13) reader as much by the writer, inverting and replacing the hierarchical reading strategy associated with colonial dominion. No longer was American writing merely counterdiscourse—which is not to say that counterdiscursive writing did not exist, but just that it was one of many strategies employed to convey and communicate in the decolonized marketplace.

Emory Elliott has suggested that this first generation of post-Revolutionary writers "understood clearly only their disappointments and frustrations" (276). While disappointment and frustration have seemingly dogged every generation of American writers, this generation's work must have been particularly challenging: while they were living in the United States and wanted to be American—whatever that meant—in fact they were still colonials, still doing the work of Revolution, still dealing with the old business of decolonization and burdened by the legacy of the past. Only after they identified the need for continued and perpetual decolonization could future American readers and writers address and debate more specifically national and local subjects in more appropriate languages, forms, and fictions "sprang from native invention."

Notes

INTRODUCTION: The New Nation and the
Limits of Colonial Discourse

1. Main has discussed Antifederalism and anti-imperialism. Henry's view was representative of the majority of the Antifederalists, who doubted the ability of the federal government to police the limits of its power and feared a loss of democratic principles under the Constitution (136–39).

2. Said is speaking here in a way that is reflected generally in the field. Parallel terminologies are employed throughout by Bayly, Dirks, Anderson, and dozens of others. Virtually identical usages are employed in the work of Bhabha, Pratt, Spurr, and Spivak. While there is divergence among these scholars regarding the equation of empire and hegemony in fact, they share these distinctions on a theoretical level.

3. While Anderson is drawing postcolonial, post-Independence models primarily from Asian sources, in this passage he is speculating more generally about the regressive nature of postliberation governments in general. King (45–51), Arendt (179–217), Greene in *Negotiated Authorities* (25–42), and Thomas (102–16) have traced similar patterns of restabilization after revolutions.

4. Furtwangler (42–51) and Kramer (119–36) have discussed the rhetorical appropriation of "We" in the Constitution.

5. Boehmer—like Ashcroft, Griffiths, and Tiffin in *The Empire Writes Back* (6–11)—emphasizes how colonialism's power was often rooted in its ability to control systems of representation, how dominance of imagery and language made possible more overt forms of dominion. However, each stresses as well—breaking from Memmi, Spivak, and Bhabha—that colonial self-representation was in fact insecure and unstable. While that may or may not have been true in the colonized Third World, in places like eighteenth-century America, as Shields (1–32) and Greene in *Pursuits of Happiness* (170–206) have

noted, shifting representations of British imperialism created a divergence among the colonies, depending on imperial policy at the moment of colonization.

6. Ferguson notes in his "'We the People,'" that the founders conceded that "the truth may be self-evident, but people must be humored, duped, coaxed and provoked into accepting it" (7).

7. Thacher's call for a national literature foreshadows Emerson's far more than the usually cited calls for "American Literature" by, for example, Fisher Ames or Noah Webster. Perhaps more than they, and more like the writers addressed in the present study, Thacher understands that decolonization, checking British primacy, must come before the invention of more locally appropriate self-expression.

8. Wakefield discusses colonial relations in strictly economic terms, all but disregarding political independence (337–65). Like Tocqueville, Wakefield also comments on the colonial and anxious nature of American manners and self-esteem, suggesting that the American hunger to please the British is another sign of their colonial character (319–36). See Bhabha on postcolonial mimicry of the departed colonial parent.

9. I would emphasize that Boehmer limits her definition with the word *seek*. Boehmer, like many of the postcolonial theoreticians I will be employing, understands the incompleteness of the postcolonial condition. In fact, as I discuss below, it is the initiation of the process of seeking that Tiffin notes as most central to literary and cultural decolonization (95).

10. In "The Scramble for Postcolonialism," Slemon writes: "I remain suspicious of ahistorical and I think intolerant calls for homogeneity in a field of study which embraces radically different forms and functions of colonialist oppression and radically different notions of anticolonialist agency" (51). Slemon wants postcolonialism to have a "big tent" and the term itself rooted in its historical origins—a condition following colonialism—and not linked intolerantly to specific regional, racial, ethnic, or gendered interests.

11. This link has already been established in the work of Richardson, McLamore, Laura Murray, and, in a slightly later period, Buell. Moreover, scholars such as Lawson and Tiffin often include, in a rather marginal way, the United States in their studies of postcolonialism.

12. See Wood's *Radicalism* (43–56) and *Creation* (10–17), Bushman (135–75), Bailyn (94–143), Maier (27–50), and Greene's *Imperatives* (174–80). While there is slight variation in the assignment of a specific date, most observe the change somewhere between 1760 and 1765.

13. See Pocock (333–60), Bayly (75–99), Don L. Cook (70–87), and Knorr (130–40). Each dates the birth of the policies that would link nineteenth-century British imperialism to the Seven Years' War, known in the colonies as the French and Indian War. All share the conception that the vast amount of territory ceded to Great Britain at the end of that war made older, mercantile imperial policies untenable and that a more cen-

tralized and hierarchical imperial theory was needed to secure and stabilize the new lands.

14. I am particularly indebted to Knorr (135) and Bayly (95–99) for this analysis of changes in British imperial policy during the late eighteenth century. At the heart of the issue is the acquisition of India. Although the theories of Wakefield, Merivale, and other nineteenth-century thinkers were more directly implemented in Australia, New Zealand, and Canada in the nineteenth century and not in Africa or Asia, Spurr (75–83) and King (38–57) have noted a parallel rhetorical colonization in both settlement and administrative territories. The passages assigning white Americans subaltern status were not dissimilar from those later assigned indigenes in other parts of the Empire. See Bailyn (161–74), Maier (198–227), Wood's *Creation* (36–42), and Greene's *Imperatives* (268 –89) and *Negotiated Authorities* (429–60) for a more extensive discussion of how changes in British imperial policy were realized in the colonies as a series of taxations.

15. See Lawson's "Cultural Paradigm for the Second World," Slemon's "Unsettling the Empire," Tiffin's "Postcolonial Literature and Counter-Discourse," Huggan (42–61), and Janiewski. Lawson writes in "Comparative Studies and Post-Colonial 'Settler' Cultures" that the Second World has been expelled from the "First," but that "on the other hand, there has been a reluctance on the part of some so-called Third World critics to 'allow' these 'settler' cultures a place on the table of cultural repression, dispersal, and interpellation" (155).

16. Nelson applies Memmi's binary for understanding racial divisiveness in the early republic, particularly in the work of Jefferson (22–23). She identifies colonists/founders in Memmi's terms as "colonizers who resist" and resists the notion that white settlers or their descendants can, in fact, be colonized. Americans instead resemble Memmi himself, a Tunisian Jew: "They live in painful and constant ambiguity. Rejected by the colonizer, they share in part the physical conditions of the colonized and have a communion of interests with him; on the other hand, they reject the values of the colonized as belonging to a decayed world from which they eventually hope to escape" (81–82). Jefferson, like Memmi himself, becomes both colonizer who resists and colonized revolutionary when we understand the Second World as a means of imagining the colonial condition that transcends the oppositional ideology rooted in colonialism itself.

17. I am indebted to Nelson for bringing this source to my attention (147). While Ringer and Lawless (as well as Nelson) are more concerned with the racial aspects of colonization, their distinctions problematize the way most historians have used the word *colonial*—in a strictly chronological sense—to allow the use the the term in its more modern manifestations to discuss the early republic.

18. I refer specifically to Anderson (83–112), Geertz (234–54), and Arendt (111–38) because they remain the most intriguing and rigorous students of what happens "after the revolution."

19. See Pocock (401–22), Appleby's *Liberalism and Republicanism* (210–31), and Wood's

Creation (244–53) and *Radicalism* (195–200). Appleby comments: "Achieving stability by balancing the superior talents of the few against the numerical strength of the many meant, of course, that the few acted as statesmen, judges, and generals who ran government, whereas ordinary people acted solely to check any undue augmentation of elite power" (214–15).

20. See Warner (122–32), Looby (54–67), Jordan (51–57), Simpson (40–51), and Kramer (49–63) for a broader discussion of this subject.

21. See Warner (122–27), Elliott (30–35), and Davidson (83–109) for a more complete discussion of generic policing in the early republic.

22. Warner (1–33), Gustafson (137–72), Davidson (15–37), Ziff (134–40), Jordan (5–14), Looby (78–85), and others have informed my description of the politics of reading and writing within the republican paradigm. Gustafson writes: "Theories of language and fears about the power and duplicity of words influenced political thought and the form of American government; and how language came to be seen by Americans as a political instrument that possessed many of the advantages and disadvantages of government itself" (12).

23. See Dowling (54–65). He confirms Thacher's suspicion that British models predominated in regard to both sales and influence in the early republic.

24. See Kennedy (429–35), Meyer (49–60), and Commager (125–42). In all three, the emphasis is on how the United States culminated European historical progression. Such a view locks the new nation into a colonial pattern of local insignificance and perpetual deference to the metropolitan centers of Europe.

25. See Young (67). Furthermore, Beer writes: "defensive, secure, compacted, even paradisal—a safe place; a safe place too from which to set on predations and from which to launch the building of an empire" (269). Memmi (33–45) and Bhabha also discuss the misrepresentation of the metropolis in colonial discourse, suggesting that it is part of the colonizing strategy.

26. Young has most ably commented on this fear: "This was not a simple process of the production of a new mimesis, however. Analysis of colonial discourse has shown that no form of cultural dissemination is ever a one-way process, whatever the power relation involved. A culture never repeats itself perfectly away from home" (174).

27. See Spurr (21–25) and Brantlinger's *Rule of Darkness*. Brantlinger refers to a process that creates the colonial space as "an enabling space where the colonizers can be at least partially redeemed" (109) through a rigorous imposition of British values.

28. I refer specifically to Miller's *Retrospect of the Eighteenth Century* (1803), Dwight's Introduction to *Greenfield Hill* (1793), and Ames's "Mire of Democracy" (1804). Davidson provides an extensive history of the controversy over fiction in the early republic (151–70). The phrase "republican machine" was employed privately by Benjamin Rush to describe the goal of republican education.

29. See Daiches, *Free* (57–76), and Woodmansee (35–56). Dauber (39–77) traces similar patterns in the development of American authorship more specifically from Benjamin Franklin through Charles Brockden Brown.

30. In *Radicalism*, Wood demonstrates that while the Revolution was guided by democratic principles that favored the broad empowerment of the populace, the early republic was characterized by the elite's effort to find a safer middle ground between aristocratic hierarchy and what they considered democratic anarchy (271–86).

31. Ferguson in his "'We Hold these Truths'" and Nord have discussed this development. Ellis similarly recognizes this trend (83–84).

32. Thomas suggests that "colonial projects are construed, misconstrued, adapted, and enacted by actors whose subjectivities are fractured—half here, half there, sometimes disloyal, sometimes 'on the side' of the people they patronize and dominate, and against the interests of some metropolitan office. Between the Scylla of mindlessly particular conventional colonial history . . . and the Charybdis of colonial discourse theory, which totalizes a hegemonic global ideology . . . lies another path which amounts to an ethnography of colonial projects: that presupposes the effects of larger objective ideologies, yet notes their adaptation in practice" (60). Thomas, following Wole Solyinka's suggestion that most Third World postcolonial theory itself represents "a second epoch of colonisation" on account of its "universal-humanoid abstraction" (qtd. in Tiffin's "Transformative Imageries," 429), argues for a study of the entangled presences, the interactive and intercultural exchanges that overcome simplistic binaries in favor of a more open and inclusive methodology.

33. Richardson, along with McLamore, Buell, and Laura Murray—the most important writers to link postcolonial theory and early American writing—has a problematic relationship with postcolonial theory. Murray means to demonstrate "that to 'disqualify' settler colonialism from serious consideration would impede understanding of colonization of indigenous peoples, which took place in cultural, ideological, and economic relation with settler colonialism" (226). Second World theory offers a resolution to the double presence Murray problematizes by creating a framework for multivalent simultaneity.

34. See Richard D. Brown's *Knowledge Is Power*, in particular the essay "William Bentley and the Ideal of Universal Information in the Enlightened Republic" (197–217), whose title suggests his subject.

35. See in general Looby (86–96), Elliott (45–52), Kramer (125–30), and Warner (63–72). See particularly Gustafson: "Through verbal misrepresentation, a link in the process of free government becomes a manacle of slavery. In the American logocracy, consent by 'the People' to the words of the founding fathers authorized the United States, and consent to the words of orators authorized more compromises with slavery. Writers in the early republic were not unwilling to probe all that made consent to words less than voluntary and informed" (22).

36. My ideas about authority and representation in the early republic are informed by Patterson (3–33).

37. *The Empire Writes Back,* by Ashcroft, Griffiths, and Tiffin, provides more extensive discussion of the inversion of First World conventions in the Second (133–45). See also King (1–21).

38. See Fliegelman's *Declaring Independence* (28–34) and Ziff (100–106) for more extensive discussions of these techniques in early republic writing.

39. Elliott (19–23) in particular but also Gustafson (270–90), Warner (63–67), and Ziff (25–33) recreate the very self-conscious processes by which the republic of letters was crafted. Warner refers to it as "republican metadiscourse" (63). Their work, as well as mine, addresses a body of writing openly constructed to engage the relationship of writing to politics.

CHAPTER ONE. To Deceive the World:
Hugh Henry Brackenridge's *Modern Chivalry*

All page citations to *Modern Chivalry* employ Newlin's 1937 edition.

1. I refer specifically to Cowie (54), Petter (126–36), Wendy Martin's "The Rogue and the Rational Man," and Leary (36–53). This generation of scholars was less concerned with internal issues of the politics of linguistics, since looking too closely at Brackenridge's style would reveal his profound shortcomings by New Critical standards. Nonetheless, their work documenting the book's scope and range of representation foregrounds future scholarship by legitimizing Brackenridge's profound historical self-awareness.

2. See Elliott (171–218), and Hoffa.

3. The preponderance of scholarship on *Modern Chivalry* in the 1980s embraced either Elliott (171–217) or Hoffa. Followers of Elliott include Patterson (34–60), Kelleher, and Engell's "Brackenridge." Those of Hoffa include Davidson (173–78), Lawson-Peebles (62–65), and Jordan (58–77).

4. Hereafter, I shall refer to the fictional author as the "author-narrator." For the relation of postcoloniality and mimicry, see Bhabha and King (157–77).

5. See Elliott (202–13) and Lenz. Leary's 1965 edition of *Modern Chivalry* excludes part 2 altogether, recognizing that its connection to part one is, at best, tenuous. Rice has noted the degeneration of part 2 more extensively: Brackenridge's interest shifted away from the republic of letters after 1800 and focused more on the impact of the transappalachian frontier on the national imagination. As Seelye (151–53) has argued, Brackenridge's critique of the early republic then addressed the eastern seaboard's colonization of the Midwest, an extension of his earlier critique, but not directly relevant to my present argument.

6. Lawson-Peebles, as I discuss in the introduction, refers to this process as "red-coatism," a tendency by the elite to reembrace and reinstall the stable stratification and institutions of the colonial era. Historians of postcolonial independence from Arendt (217–30) to Anderson (47–66) to Said in *Culture and Imperialism* (191–208) have recognized this trend as typical, especially in Second World settings.

7. My summary of the history of language in 1790s America is drawn largely from four seminal studies: Simpson (101–17), Baron (7–40), Kramer (141–47), and Cmiel (51–80). Each contains extensive and invaluable commentaries on the explicit relationship of the debate over language to parallel political battles and controversies.

8. Comments in this paragraph are based in Thomas (60–65) and Barrell (201–13). Thomas suggests that the metropolis's stability in any given colonial situation is false, and Barrell particularly explores the changes in British culture in the late eighteenth century. The republicans constructed a false universality for British culture to stabilize their own version of Anglophilic American nationhood.

9. See Steven Watts's *Republic Reborn* (42–58), Nance, Hirsch (50–74), and Unrue. See also Engell, Davidson (75), and Jordan (63–68).

10. Marder's collection, *A Hugh Henry Brackenridge Reader*, collects a representative sampling of Brackenridge's writing from this period and provides invaluable commentary.

11. See Ellis (73–112). Ellis charts Brackenridge's alienation from both the East and republicanism as component parts of a single process of rejecting how the early republic had grown away from its Revolutionary origins. Seelye documents this process more completely (62–63).

12. For information on Brackenridge's complex and controversial political career, see Newlin and Marder. Both of these illustrate a man of many identities: immigrant, Princetonian, poet, minister, lawyer, westerner, novelist, mediator, etc. Like his book, Brackenridge himself embodies, fifty years before Emerson, the plurality and flexibility of the Second World American.

13. JanMohamed argues that "faced with an incomprehensible and multifaceted alterity, the [colonizer] . . . assumes that the Other is irredeemably different" [and so can] turn to the security of his own cultural perspective" (18). That is, colonizers of all stripes rely on simplistic oppositions to justify their dominance and monolithic arguments. Brackenridge's attack on these binaries is therefore also epistemological: his linguistic and cultural perspective is more diverse and paradoxical at a paradigmatic level. The republicans, that is, function within binary pairings, and encourage the citizenry to do so as well.

14. Such a claim characterized most texts of this period: Dwight's *Greenfield Hill* (1793), Jeremy Belknap's *Foresters* (1794), and William Hill Brown's *Power of Sympathy* (1789), all conventional and very popular texts, opened with statements concerning how

their contents would and should contribute to social stability and improvement. The republican author therefore was in fact assuming two roles at once: author and interpreter.

15. Brackenridge's own open-minded opinion of ethnic/racial difference can be seen in "The Trial of Mamachtaga" (*A Brackenridge Reader*, 355–63) and will be discussed below. Lawson-Peebles has suggested that several dubious references in *Modern Chivalry* suggest Brackenridge's rather benign racism (130–33). However, I would argue that those references are made by the author-narrator, not Brackenridge himself. Brackenridge's placement of racism in the mouth of such a conventional republican as the author-narrator, moreover, reinforces his indictment of the small-minded binarism of republican thought.

16. See Engell's "Brackenridge." Engell reads *Modern Chivalry* as a satire based on class differences. I would agree but add that class distinctions were colonial remnants revived by republicanism to reorder society after the Revolution. Suppressing the potential and nonrepublican contributions of the lower classes would have served that purpose.

17. "To the Dissenting Assemblymen by an Assenting Constituent" in *A Hugh Henry Brackenridge Reader* (129–31).

18. I refer here to the Scottish commonsense theory of rhetoric that was broadly imposed on American education during the early republic. See Terence Martin's *Instructed Vision* (13–27) and Daiches.

19. A good example is Fisher Ames's "Mire of Democracy" (51–54). Such tracts are discussed in the work of Kennedy (436–44), Commager (143–54), and Meyer (ix–xxvii), all of whom champion the imposition of classical models on the early republic.

20. Nelson reads similar passages in Jefferson quite extensively in the process of identifying men like Jefferson as "colonizers who resist" colonialism, following Memmi, who, ironically, only affirm and strengthen colonialism's racism (22). In this case, Farrago fits Nelson's critique; however, Brackenridge does not. The rhetorical victory of the Quaker and the conceit of the author-narrator place Brackenridge with abolitionism and anti-colonialism.

21. Brackenridge's own attraction to the linguistic freedom of phonetically unorthodox speech is available in the Scottish dialect poetry he wrote throughout his career, most of which has been reprinted by Marder.

22. Bush's "*Modern Chivalry* and 'Young's Magazine'" provides a useful discussion of the introduction to volume 3.

23. Brackenridge's own more moderate views are available in Marder's collection, *A Hugh Henry Brackenridge Reader*.

24. See Howard and Dowling (32–62) for a more extensive discussion of this subject. The author-narrator's parody of the Wits' neo-Augustan pretensions also mocks Brackenridge's own attempts at this type of poetry in the 1780s. While Brackenridge had

moved on to greater stylistic and linguistic experimentation, they, by implication, remained mired in colonial models.

25. See Slaughter for the most recent and complete discussion of the rebellion and Brackenridge's role in it (90–96).

26. Looby suggests that the two narratives, while running simultaneously, represented separate "temporal schemes" (246): Farrago's and the actual community's is linear, the author-narrator's is cyclical. As the closed, cyclical world of classical republicanism faded after 1800, the presence of the cyclical "chronicity" had become anachronistic.

27. See Ellis (93–95) for a catalog of antifiction tracts. However, neither volume 4 of part 1 or part 2 as a whole bears any resemblance to any of the fictional formats condemned by such conservative literati as Fisher Ames and Samuel Miller. Brackenridge's experimental fiction, as a whole, moreover, suggests that something other than the "novel" inspired the development of American fiction.

28. Both "Mamachtaga" (355–64) and the Conclusion (376–77) from *Gazette Publications* are available in Marder's collection.

CHAPTER TWO. The Mental Commonwealth of
Judith Sargent Murray's *The Gleaner*

1. Ketrak is one of a series of postcolonial feminist theoreticians whose observations could be applied here. Spivak (1–16) has also been consulted. While each is a Third World scholar, each generally includes European women in settler communities in her formulations of postcolonial feminist identity.

2. The work of the female writers of the early republic has been studied by Davidson (55–82), Emily Watts (29–62), and Kerber in *Women of the Republic* (137–56). All identify the enclosure of women in the years following the Revolution. Each also maintains, however, that this effort vitalized an energetic body of women's writing of which Murray was a part.

3. This chapter was completed before the publication of Wilkins's article on Murray. Our arguments share much about Murray's use of fictionalized authorship to subvert the masculine predominance of the early republic public sphere. Wilkins suggests that this complex book encourages the young female reader to "read herself out" of such subjection; I would call the same process decolonization.

4. Derounian-Stodola explores and explains the conscription of a narrow gender-based readership for fiction, both British and American. Along with Davidson (38–54), she argues that this generic enclosure paralleled a broader shrinkage of women's role in the post-Independence public sphere.

5. See Hatch (3–16). Hatch argues that the pulpit retained a degree of Revolutionary

rhetoric in the face of growing suspicion toward it. Samual Wales's "The Dangers of Our National Prosperity" might serve as a model for the dissident sermon.

6. See Davidson (38–54) and, for example, Jordan's comments on this subject (14–23). Here I employ Bhabha's term *master discourse* to link the notion that female enclosure and post-Revolutionary stabilization were described as parts of the same story of re-colonization.

7. Field offers an extensive discussion of *The Gleaner*'s publication history. More recently, Harris's "Judith Sargent Murray" and her Introduction to *Selected Writings* provides a more general background, as does Baym's Introduction to the recent republication of *The Gleaner*. Like her neighbors and friends, Abigail Adams and Mercy Otis Warren, Murray was a sophisticated participant in the cultural debates of her day even outside her work as an author. The gender politics of the early republic's publishing industry are also discussed in Warner (48–49).

8. Looby has discussed the prominence and prestige of Addisonian technique in the early republic (117–19). Newton has also engaged this discussion, with particular attention to its relationship to fiction and women's readership.

9. See Warner (73–96), Elliott (30–35), and Gustafson (19–36). This model of both social and literary leadership possessed the portable intellectual acumen to shift between and among both literary forms and more public leadership needs. It was dependent on leisure, education, and access to the press, thereby favoring wealthy white males of the eastern seaboard.

10. My discussion of the history of American authorship is indebted to Simpson (56–62) and Dauber (3–38). Furtwangler (1–14) has provided the most succinct discussion of the relation of style to persuasion in the early republic.

11. Terence Martin's *Instructed Vision* (57–76) remains the most important study of the predominance of inherited textuality in the early republic. More recently, Daiches has echoed the enforced generic constriction of the period.

12. I use the term *republicanism* as it has been employed by recent historians of the early republic. Appleby's *Liberalism and Republicanism* (230–40) and Wood's *Radicalism* (101–9) represent the most recent studies of this political philosophy. In his article, Taylor has called this trend "the political cult of gentility" (140), which was meant to fabricate a stable leadership class after the Revolution.

13. Kerber's *Women of the Republic* is still the most important study of this pattern. Her more recent article, "'I have Don . . . much to Carrey on the Warr': Women and the Shaping of Republican Ideology" rephrases her earlier work in the context of observations such as Wood's and Appleby's. Subsequent quotations are from her article.

14. See King (51–57) and Anderson (37–46) for discussions of the dissolution of Revolutionary coalitions in postcolonial communities. Said likewise identifies the emergence of a postrevolutionary ruling class that silences or erases its former partners in revolution (303–25) in *Culture and Imperialism*.

15. See Spivak for a more extensive observation of the role of gender in the formation of postcolonial nationalities (50–58). While Spivak's concern is primarily with contemporary Third World colonialisms and feminisms, her ideas transfer well to the early republic.

16. See Kerber (119–48) and Davidson (55–62). Their arguments describe a virtually segregated society as forming with astonishing rapidity after the Revolution. The volatile reception in the early republic of Mary Wollstonecraft's *Vindication of the Rights of Women* especially illustrates this, equating the enclosure of women with other forms of social restabilization.

17. Harris and Kritzer have recently edited volumes that republish a plethora of other materials that employ similar devices.

18. Landes writes, "Worse yet, women risked disrupting the gendered organization of nature, truth and opinion that assigned them to a place in the private, domestic, but not the public realm" (98).

19. The most important commentators on *The Gleaner*, Harris in her article and Introduction, Kerber in her article, and Baym in her Introduction, as well as Wilkins, disagree as to the degree and nature of Murray's feminism. While Kerber and Harris argue for a feminist undercurrent, Baym suggests that the theme is secondary to Murray's ultimate attachment to egalitarian ideology. By linking the book's democratic and decolonizing patterns, I mean to argue that these perspectives coexist.

20. See Baym and Wilkins for a more detailed history of Murray's publication history and use of masks. While virtually every eighteenth-century writer on both sides of the Atlantic employed masks, it is the point of these scholars, and my own, that Murray has appropriated this convention for her own purposes and uses it to disrupt conventional reading practices.

21. Biographical information relating to Murray is available in Harris, Field, and Baym's Introduction.

22. Writing as Davila, Adams questioned the stability of the republican form as a political theory. However, in his practice as a politician, Adams's notion of the day-to-day republic was marked by control and restraint. See Furtwangler (32–46).

23. See Fliegelman's *Declaring Independence* for a discussion of the trend of male early republic authors to relinquish the responsibility of formal experimentation to seek refuge in inherited models (169–80). As he observes of the Gleaner, this pattern in politics bore an analogous concealment in the development of authorship.

24. Newton has informed my placement of the story of Margaretta in both *The Gleaner* and the early republic.

25. Histories of didactic fiction in the early republic include Davidson (110–50) and Radway (194–96). Didactic fiction was one of the few nominally creative genres permitted within the republic of letters. However, it was constantly bracketed by patriarchal sermonizing.

26. The second of these has recently been reprinted in Kritzer (97–135). She also discusses the scathing reviews they received. Harris reproduces "The Traveller Returned" in *Selected Writings*.

27. Schofield's article is the only scholarship on Murray's drama.

28. In "A Cultural Paradigm for the Second World," Lawson refers to "Second World" consciousness as primarily a "reading strategy" (72). By that, Lawson suggests that the Second World postcolonial begins as a colonized reader, querying the textual foundations of his "double consciousness." The open-mindedness Murray champions, I would argue, similarly begins with a revision of the reading process.

CHAPTER THREE. Royall Tyler's The *Algerine Captive*
and the Worthy Federal Citizen

1. Soon after these events, Napoleon would colonize most of North Africa in the name of the French. While colonization had not yet occurred, according to Said in *Orientalism*, the process of "orientalization" that would justify European incursions into local cultures had already begun (63). Throughout this crisis, Europeans and Americans imagined the North Africans as exotic and inscrutable Others.

2. By 1797 six American ships had been built. However, as Horsman has demonstrated, the Federalist administrations built these ships for reasons other than defense against the Pirates: "In 1797, the Quasi-War with France became a far more pressing problem. . . . While the administrations used the Barbary situation to obtain a Navy, actual policy in the Mediterranean followed traditional European lines" (84).

3. For titles of other American works on Algeria, see Tanselle, 142–43. With the exception of Tyler, however, they mirror the received and colonizing image of the Algerine as primitive and exotic. See Baepler for a more recent discussion of this subject.

4. The conflict was finally settled in 1815 when Stephen Decatur, under orders of President Madison, stormed Tripoli. For a more complete discussion of the entire conflict, see Ritcheson (290–304).

5. Buel discusses the increasing conflict between the Antifederalists and the French during the 1790s (170–198). However, following the stabilization of France under Napoleon, Jefferson reestablished his former affinity. William Jenks's *Memoir of the Northern Kingdom* (1808) parodies the slavishly derivative attitudes of both parties during this period. While the Antifederalists valorized France and the Federalists England, in either case, each party modeled its ideas for the country on received paradigms, not local conditions, again establishing the cultural colonialism of post-Revolutionary America.

6. Although Barlow converted to Antifederalism in the early 1790s, his actions in regard to the Algerians and certainly his poetry remained conservative rather than ex-

perimental. See Elliott and Dowling for larger discussion of the careers, both political and poetic, of this entire group.

7. Richardson demonstrates that Tyler's drama, as I suggest of his fiction, reflects a postcolonial "inevitable double-mindedness" in its similar call for the use of native materials, forms, and language. Richardson suggests that, for Tyler's drama, as I am suggesting for his fiction, the new nation is erring if it does not acknowledge both parts of its origin, both sides of its doubleness.

8. For a more complete listing of Tyler's writings, see Peladeau's *The Prose of Royall Tyler* and *The Poetry of Royall Tyler*. Tyler was also an early partner of Joseph Dennie. They wrote together as Colon and Spondee in the *Gazette of the United States* before 1796.

9. See Davidson (151–92) for a more complete discussion of American picaresque novels.

10. Distinctions between these categories were supposed to be rigid and knowable. The republicans feared chaos in both reading and society. Fliegelman's *Declaring Independence* (164–78) and Furtwangler (21–25) provide the most cogent discussions of the formulaic nature of orthodox reading and writing practices. It is my argument that such rigidity reinscribed colonial notions of literary exchange and that the texts examined in this study smudged these distinctions as part of a broader effort to resist the Anglocentric reordering of post-Revolutionary society.

11. For more information on Tyler's lifelong association with the Federalist party, see Tanselle and the Carsons. Tanselle's essential biography of Tyler comments extensively on the moderation of Tyler's Federalism. Tanselle even discusses the surprise of Tyler's Vermont neighbors at discovering that Tyler was not Antifederalist. Tyler's resistance to the narrow categories and the dogmatic rigidity of both parties in his political career, I suggest, is analogous to his work as a writer: at once a figure such as Franklin can be revered and critiqued, so one understands Tyler's skeptical perspective.

12. I refer specifically to Dennis, Davidson (240), and Engell's "Narrative Irony."

13. Besides Dwight, Federalist enemies of fiction included Samuel Miller, Ezra Stiles, John Witherspoon, and others whose power of public discourse was through the pulpit and the Federalist press. Their objection to fiction, at the most basic level, was in its ability to corrupt the purity of the republican reformulation of the post-Revolutionary personality. By invoking imagination, smudging the reliability of print, and disseminating potential national counternarratives, fiction threatened to reintroduce the anarchy of revolution. See Terence Martin's *Instructed Vision* for a more complete discussion of this subject (65–80).

14. I refer specifically to Miller's *Brief Retrospect of the 18th-Century* (1803), Kames's *Essays* (1751), and Blair's *Lectures* (1780). In these as well, there are catalogs of the genres supposedly appropriate for the transmission of respectable political and moral values.

15. In "Narrative Irony," Engell suggests that Tyler uses John Underhill to articulate the distance between the free John and the cautious and enslaved Updike. The writing and career of the real John Underhill have more recently been discussed by Nelson (12–16) and Lawson-Peebles (23–25). Both of these implicate John in the colonization of Massachusetts and in the suppression of native Americans. However, Tyler is interested more in his stature as a dissident within the colony. John was perhaps the first to embody the "double-mindedness" of the Second World.

16. Here, I allude to the work of Lester A. Cohen and others who have analyzed early republic historiography in such a way. Lawson-Peebles has similarly discussed the suppression of radical revolutionary rhetoric in the rewriting of the Revolution during the 1790s. See chapter 6 for a more extensive discussion of early republic historiography.

17. For a more extensive discussion of Updike's particular misadventures, see Dennis and Engell's "Narrative Irony." Tyler's locals are quite similar to Brackenridge's and, more likely, his own, going back to *The Contrast*. This "mob" is neither the benevolent yeomanry of Jefferson nor the revolutionary mass tending toward Jacobin self-destruction feared by so many Federalists.

18. See Buel for an extensive discussion of the Federalist condemnation of Paine's *Age of Reason* (169–70). Lawson-Peebles (61–66) also discusses how Paine represented a dangerous presence after the Revolution that was efficiently marginalized and effectively exiled.

19. Davidson's recognition that it "mostly reprises without much plot or perspective, the strange ways and religion of the Algerines" (207) epitomizes this reading. Given that Tyler was basing most of his information on the Algerines on the aforementioned propaganda, we might also say, however, that the real subject of volume 2 is these texts, not their purported subject. As such, Tyler is not implicated, as I shall show, in a colonizing Orientalism but rather emerges as a critic of it.

20. JanMohamed has held that such binaries were false categories created to purify, justify, and define the colonization in general by allowing the colonizer to dehumanize (and thus dispossess) the colonized Other. Thomas reveals that, in fact, in colonized spaces, a heterogeneous "entanglement" occurs (23). Decolonizing, in this case, would have to do with exposing the falseness of the binaries Updike champions and the Mollah defeats.

21. Davidson (210) and Engell have noted the irony of Updike's retreat to servitude so soon after his condemnation of the Englishman's slavery.

22. See Said's *Orientalism* (49–72) and Spurr (1–12). The acquisition of this gaze, particularly for a postcolonial American, would signify an aspiration to demonstrate the sameness of European and American perspectives, constructing a single, North Atlantic view of the Orient.

23. Sharp (69–91) and Steven Watts, in *The Republic Reborn* (64–77), both chart the rise in these qualities during this decade. For each, Revolutionary idealism's fading from

public view was part of the singular process that also brought about increasing materialism and nascent imperialism on both sides of the political spectrum.

CHAPTER FOUR. The Reputation of Literature and Opulence: Charles Brockden Brown's *Arthur Mervyn*

1. I am indebted to Christophersen for bringing this essay to my attention.

2. If historians and scholars of colonialism and imperialism share nothing else, it is the notion that profit motivated virtually every colonial enterprise, at least from the perspective of London. I refer specifically to Merivale (Lecture 3), Wakefield (461–69), and Said's *Culture and Imperialism* (43–60). Greene's *Pursuits of Happiness* (7–27) and Shields affirm Brown's linkage of mercantilism and colonial foundation in the British colonies of North America.

3. Economic criticism of Brown is most visible in Steven Watts, *The Romance of Real Life*, Ziff (77–82), Justus, Davidson (236–53), and Tompkins (62–93). Each has contributed to our understanding of Brown as a critic of bourgeois capitalism. More recently Hinds has commented on *Arthur Mervyn* (79–94).

4. See Warner (78–90).

5. See Wood's *Creation* (46–69), Reynolds (169–210), Ziff (100–106), and Bailyn (272–300). All of these, as well as Warner (34–72), describe republican textuality in similar terms. Patterson (xv–xxviii) and Looby (28–45) also cogently describe early republic efforts to stabilize and codify the politics of literary exchange.

6. Lawson, like most scholars of postcolonialism, refers to Memmi's colonizer/colonized binary, even though he has placed the Second World on both sides of it simultaneously. Such a simplification overlooks the complexity of British thought, especially that of England in the 1790s. Brantlinger in *Crusoe's Footsteps* (3–17) and Thomas (32) have discussed the divided nature of the imperial endeavor in England. However, Memmi has observed that the version of the metropolitan culture exported to the colonies is always "mediocre" (73) and not representative of the complexities of the metropole. Republicans then inherited and reimposed the version of British culture that had been present in the colonies since 1763.

7. See Justus, Tompkins (62–93), Warner (151–76), Grabo in *The Coincidental Art* (85–127), Steven Watts in both *The Republic Reborn* (172–88) and *The Romance of Real Life* (101–14), and Ziff (54–82).

8. See Ringe's *Charles Brockden Brown* (65–85), Russo, Berthoff, Hedges's "Charles Brockden Brown," Bell (41–61), Elliott (218–70), and Davidson (236–53).

9. Brown's many private and public references to his hope that his writing affect his readers in socially constructive ways overwhelm the ironies so many critics have noted in his fictions. In particular, see Dunlap's transcription of his undated speech to the Belles Lettres Club (18–31).

10. Previous scholars who maintain Arthur's ultimately unresolved moral condition include Brancaccio, Larson, and Spangler. All suggest that Arthur personifies the precarious moral condition of the nation in general; however, none connects this problematic ambivalence to Brown's dramatization of Arthur's development as an author.

11. See Woodmansee (87–102) and Railton (3–20) for a larger discussion of the transitional nature of late eighteenth- and early nineteenth-century authorship.

12. The only modern edition of *Arthur Mervyn* that reproduces title pages of the original editions of both volumes is Berthoff's 1962 edition for Holt.

13. For this and all other information regarding the history of *Arthur Mervyn*'s publication, I am indebted to Grabo's "Historical Essay."

14. All of Brown's biographies confirm the public knowledge of his authorship of the earlier novels. For this and all subsequent information concerning Brown's life, I have consulted Ringe's, Warfel's, Clark's, Steven Watts's, and Axelrod's biographies of Brown, as well as Dunlap's *Life of Charles Brockden Brown* (1815) and Christophersen's critical biography.

15. Virtually every novel of the early republic, to establish a utilitarian self-justification pleasing to the elite, claimed a basis in "truth" on its title page. See Petter (4–21) for a discussion of the forces that motivated this necessity. See Davis for a more complete discussion of how this practice was inherited from British models.

16. Watts in *The Republic Reborn* (177–78), Looby (158–64), and Tompkins (46–48) provide particularly illustrative discussions of Brown's use of prefaces.

17. See Jordan for a discussion on the early republic's authorization of literacy (1–26).

18. I will not attempt to trace the complexities of Arthur's story. Most existing criticism of Brown contains sufficient material on specific instances.

19. My reading of the role of fiction in a democracy has been influenced by Iser: in fiction, according to Iser, "the reader is meant to become aware of those faculties, of his own tendency to link things together in consistent patterns, and indeed the whole thought process that constitutes his relations with the world outside himself" (xiv).

20. See Larson's "*Arthur Mervyn, Edgar Huntly*, and the Critics" for a larger discussion of Brown's allusions to the critical reception of his own work.

21. See Grabo's "Historical Essay" for a review of the immediate reception of *Arthur Mervyn*.

22. See Ross's *Sentimental Novel in America* (45–62) for a larger discussion of the phraseology of sentimentality.

23. Shields's "Anglo-Jewish Elite" offers the best description of the role of Jews in eighteenth-century America.

24. Looby (193–200) has recently examined Brown's later career in greater detail.

25. Both are available in the appendixes to Dunlap's *Life*. Each was unpublished during Brown's lifetime.

CHAPTER FIVE. The Peculiar Birthright of Every
American: George Watterston's *The Lawyer*

1. I refer to Kipling's much-discussed notion of "the white man's burden." In this ideology, colonization equaled civilization, and it was the burden of the more fortunate to bring those less fortunate up to their singular, universal, and exclusive standard of civilization. Similarly, Anderson has identified the reinscription of colonial characteristics "after the revolution" as a response to violence and destruction (23).

2. I refer to Slemon's notion that Second World experience "cuts across . . . individual consciousness" (110) in "Resistance Theory," and Lawson's claim in "A Cultural Paradigm" that "the multiple perspective, the polyphony, the diachronicity" was the "birthright" (70) of Second World postcolonials. See my Introduction.

3. Warner refers to this process as "the republican paradigm" (79–85). By this phrase, Warner defines conventional authorship as presumably altruistic attempts to convey information in a way that would contribute to a homogenous national identity. In his essay "'We Hold these Truths,'" Ferguson has called this same process a literature of "consensus" (12). In both cases, Warner and Ferguson associate republicanism with the inscription of a national monovocalism, monoculturalism, and, in this case, moral monopolization.

4. Ferguson's *Law and Letters* provides a comprehensive discussion of the predominant role played by lawyers in the literature of the early republic. He argues that lawyers were trained to adhere to "universally applicable forms" (33).

5. Davidson extensively documents the role of didactic novels in the early republic (110–32). Derounian-Stodola has also observed the pervasiveness of this genre, especially as it affected female readership. I will argue, however, that Watterston carefully merged didactic and adventure genres to attract all readers, regardless of gender.

6. Neuberg has traced the emergence of chapbooks as the underground and subversive evidence for an American reading audience that deviated from the strictures of republicanism and was aware of its increasing irrelevance in American life.

7. All references to Burroughs are from the 1988 edition. See Gura's Introduction to the 1988 edition of the *Memoirs of Stephen Burroughs* for a more complete publication history.

8. See Fliegelman's *Prodigals and Pilgrims* (230–34) for a broader discussion of this subject. Fliegelman maintains that the Revolution itself did little to challenge the stability of a patriarchal community. However, he maintains, as do Arendt (13–52), Appleby in *Liberalism and Republicanism* (232–52), Bushman (235–44), and Steven Watts (2–15), that the Revolution set in motion a sequence of antiauthoritarian, and I would add anticolonial, sentiments that were gradually realized in the fifty years following the war's end.

9. All citations are from George S. Watterston, *The Lawyer; or Man as He Ought Not To Be* (1808). A limited number of copies of *The Lawyer* exist. For this study, I have consulted the one owned by the Lilly Library in Bloomington, Indiana.

10. Reynolds places *The Lawyer* in a "Romantic Adventure" tradition and overlooks the didactic pretensions of Morcell (193–94). Morcell's claims, as will be discussed below, clearly allude to the didactic tradition, not the discourse of adventure, and so suggest that *The Lawyer*'s generic assignment be reconsidered. In fact, I would argue that its resistance to generic assignment contributes to its status as a Second World text.

11. Julia Kennedy (41) connects this subtitle to English didacticist Robert Bage's *Man As He is* (1792) and *Man As He Is Not, or Hermsprong* (1796). While the allusion is clear, Watterston's replacement of "is" with "ought" complicates the subtitle's irony.

12. The most recent analysis of the spread of "moral" texts in the early republic is Richard D. Brown's *Knowledge Is Power* (65–81). Brown is concerned with how these texts constituted a means of disseminating moral conformity, a necessary perquisite for political homogeneity.

13. *Dictionary of American Biography*, s.v. "Buchanan, John."

14. Huggan (4–41) and Mancall (ii–xiv) both link cartographical technique to the establishment of North America as "empty" and connect this assignment of nullity to indigenous populations as well.

15. Along with Lawson, Boehmer (35–39) and Spurr (107–13) similarly recognize the monovocalism of the colonialist/imperialist text. By championing a monovocal morality, Morcell, like many republican authors, seeks to contain the dangerous forces of social instability unleashed by the American and French revolutions. In the process, however, he re-places his readers in a position of colonial subjecthood.

16. Masel suggests that part of the process of decolonization for settlement literatures involves confronting the lack of the kind of history presumably needed to supply materials for the construction of a national literature and identity. In this case, republicanism discourages such self-exploration by erasing the past and with it the potential for further distinguishing the new nation from its colonial past.

17. See the aforementioned *Child of Feeling*, by Watterston. In it, the most articulate character is a woman who, like Murray's Mary Vigillius, instructs and corrects the slavish and boring men.

18. I refer to Susanna Haswell Rowson's *Charlotte Temple* (1792) and Enos Hitchcock's *Memoirs of the Bloomsgrove Family* (1796). The narrative of each is repeatedly interrupted by lengthy commentary and homily on the events of the stories.

19. See Fliegelman, *Prodigals and Pilgrims* (245–47). Fliegelman holds that Burroughs's admission of guilt and lack of repentance instructed his readers to resist the early republic's patriarchs.

20. See Davidson (236).

21. See Hedges's "Charles Brockden Brown." I refer to the prefaces to nearly all of Brown's novels in which "C.B.B." instructs his reader on the interpretations he has in mind. While "C.B.B." may represent Brown's own ironic nod to convention, his initials at least represent some form of authorial presence that must be acknowledged by the reader.

22. Spurr maintains that language constructs an attitude and an imagination that then inspires and justifies more overt forms of exploitation and marginalization (1–41).

CHAPTER SIX. The Syllogistically Fatal World of Washington Irving's Diedrich Knickerbocker

1. Bryant's equation of authorship and craftsmanship is left over from the eighteenth-century, according to Woodmansee's ideas about the evolution of authorship (37–40). Nonetheless, this passage reveals the lingering prevalence of Enlightenment textuality well into the American nineteenth century.

2. For "colonial" I am borrowing Boehmer's definition: "Colonialist literature was informed by theories concerning the superiority of European culture and the rightness of empire" (3). Like all those forms addressed by writers in this study, Enlightenment historiography was geared toward legitimizing the American "empire."

3. I use the 1809 edition, ed. James Tuttleton. Like most contemporary scholars, I find this edition more interesting and, for the current discussion, more important to Irving's work in 1809 than his revised edition of 1848. For a precise discussion of the changes Irving made, see Black's "*History of New York*."

4. Gustafson offers a discussion of Irving's concept of logocracy: "The centrality of a written text and of representation in American politics did make the practice and criticism of interpretation and representation central political activities for its citizens" (21).

5. I refer specifically to Ferguson's *Law and Letters* and McWilliams (85–93). Both say Irving is reducing American history to meaninglessness. I mean to suggest his subject is the methods, not the materials, of American history writing in the republic.

6. See Lester A. Cohen's *Revolutionary Histories* (52).

7. See also Smith's *History as Argument* and Lester A. Cohen for a larger discussion of this subject. Much of the work of these chroniclers of historiography resembles White's notion that the historiographer is "indentured to a choice among contending interpretive strategies" (xii) and that early republic historians deliberately chose a past suited to their needs.

8. Hedges has produced the most consistently useful criticism on the *History*. This and subsequent references to Hedges are from his *Washington Irving*.

9. See Lester A. Cohen's discussion of the historiographic component of Scottish commonsense rhetoric (172–73).

10. See Meyer (182–91) and Kennedy (4–12) for a discussion of this subject. Other studies of American neoclassicism similarly echo their notions of the dominance of classical models on republican ideology.

11. See McLamore and Anteyles (46–58). Each charts Irving's notion of America as both colony of Europe and colonizer of the West.

12. See, in particular, Evans and Roth (114–41) as the most recent indictments of Irving's being derivately unoriginal.

13. Many explications of the *History*'s superficial narrative of the Dutch are available. The best and most recent is Jonathan Cook's. My reading confirms Cook's notion that Irving rejects the equation of America with humanity's "prelapsarian state of innocence" (512) but adds that the application of such a myth was part of a process of colonization.

14. These notices were first printed with the rest of the text in the Knickerbocker edition of Irving's Complete Works by Putnam in 1893. I use that edition here.

15. For more information on political satire in the *History*, see Black's "Political Satire" and Bowden's "Knickerbocker's *History*."

16. See Evans.

17. See Hedges's *Washington Irving* (73), for a catalogue of American histories that borrowed this technique.

18. See ibid, 58–64.

19. I will not here go into Irving's specific critique of Jefferson or an extensive discussion of his depiction of the "Yankee" tribe as nascent American, whose greed and vindictiveness could be perceived as a condemnation of early republic culture. See Roth and Hedges for explications of those subjects. Ferguson's essay on Irving in *Law and Letters* also addresses this subject.

20. See Hedges for a more detailed account of Irving's experiments with Addisonian voice (3–24).

21. Rubin-Dorsky explores Irving's extensive investigation of this subject (65–99).

22. Irving's own contributions to this revisionist historiography include *Astoria* (1836) and *The Adventures of Captain Bonneville* (1837). Antelyes's is the best study of this stage of Irving's career.

EPILOGUE: The Vagrant Inclination

1. For a more complete discussion of Irving's transitions between 1809 and 1819, see Hedges's *Washington Irving* (80–134) or Rubin-Dorsky (32–64). Volume 23 of *The Complete Works of Washington Irving* reproduces a few of the reviews and other occasional writings of this period, all of which mostly precipitate *The Sketch-Book*.

2. In 1812 Irving did, however, take up the editorship of the *Analectic Magazine*, the contents of which were largely reprints of British publications. However, these writers

often challenged the institutions of eighteenth-century thought as thoroughly as Irving had in the *History*. Moreover, Irving used the *Analectic* to rehearse sections of *The Sketch-Book*, such as the very contentious "Traits of Indian Character." See Hedges's *Washington Irving*, 107–15.

3. Woodmansee's *Author, Art, and the Market* (36–53) addresses specific transitions in artistic self-definition at the turn of the century, mostly in regard to Germany and England. Irving's awareness of these changes, however, is not colonial mimicry. Woodmansee links these transitions to localism and nationalism in European states (22–33); Irving's response was similarly based on a need to transcend classical universalism. Daniel Williams suggests that "despite his auctorial inflations, I believe Irving expressed a popular perception of writers as creators, a romantic convention that celebrated authors as inspired geniuses solely responsible for their textual creations" (265).

4. In this case of cultural lag, the republicans were outdated. Samuel Miller's catalog of acceptable forms of writing published in his *Retrospect of the Eighteenth-Century* (1802) was considered anachronistic by its British readers (Lawson-Peebles, 17).

5. In *The Empire Writes Back*, Ashcroft, Griffiths, and Tiffin write: "Postcolonial literatures would apparently demonstrate their maturity when they stopped talking about themselves and got on with more 'universal' (i.e. European) concerns" (138). In their rush to demonstrate "maturity" by eighteenth-century standards, most American writers embraced conservative forms and language.

6. My use of the term *postcolonial,* here and throughout, refers to a period when lingering colonial presences in local culture in formerly colonized places have been contained and have been integrated into the local culture to develop into a heterogeneous and hybrid combination of cultural presences, "a continuing process of resistance and reconstruction" in the words of Ashcroft, Griffiths, and Tiffin (xvii, introduction). Moreover, as Brennan has established, postcolonial nationalism often deliberately constructs itself in reactionary opposition to the departed colonizer, suggesting a "mutually constituting tension" (58). Later American writers, even nationalist figures, might still invoke the lingering British predominance in American culture, but they do so from a position of separateness, not exile.

7. Ferguson in "'We Hold These Truths'" and Furtwangler (157–164) both draw careful connections between the founders' prose style and their need for a singular and national consensus regarding certain issues of national character and identity. Warner (97–117) and Gustafson (348–71) confirm this linkage and its disintegration during the course of the early republic.

8. My comments here are indebted to Rubin-Dorsky (1–31).

9. Looby describes Irving's satire of transatlantic misperception in *Salmagundi* (78–84). Such misdescription characterized colonial writing throughout the imperial age, stretching into the twentieth century. Spurr labels such devices "exoticizations"

(43–47). Finally, Lawson-Peebles connects such stratifying descriptions to geography and landscape (39).

10. See Daigrepont for a lucid discussion of these two tales.

11. See Masel and *The Empire Writes Back* (133–45). In both studies, Second World settler writers are concerned with merging aboriginal and colonial legacies into a hybridized "indigenous" whole that would more accurately characterize local identity.

12. See Hedges, *Washington Irving* (151).

13. See Reynolds (441–82), Gilmore's *American Romanticism* (52–70), and Charvat (28–48). In regard to other uses of language in the American public sphere, Cmiel similarly traces the increasing polyvocality of the popular spoken and written media (235–50).

14. See Sharpe's "Is the United States Postcolonial?" Sharpe transfers the "postcolonial" parts of the American communities exclusively to "racial minorities and Third World Immigrants" (181), presupposing the decolonization of white Americans. However, since white American writers still seem involved in "exploring in their figures, themes, and forms, the conceptual dimensions of the act of writing itself," in the terms of Ashcroft, Griffiths, and Tiffin (137) in their book, I would suggest that postcolonialism is one of the many presences in all parts of American cultures, one that breeds a particular self-reflexivity.

15. Seelye (199–207) and Nelson (22–37) both describe American efforts to fulfill and realize the North Atlantic ideals of expansion and imperium.

16. My comments concerning link of the early republic to the American Renaissance are drawn largely from Dauber (xiii–xx), Jordan (101–9), McWilliams (15–41), Reynolds (55–64), and Gilmore's *American Romanticism* (1–15).

17. Throughout Railton provides a very helpful discussion of this subject as it affected changing modes of authorship in America. His emphasis on "performance" represents the new improvised textuality of the postcolonial literary scene.

Works Consulted

Adams, Abigail, and John Adams. Correspondence. Rpt. in *The American Reader*, ed. Diane Ravitch, 30–32. New York: Harper, 1991.

Ames, Fisher. "The Dangers of American Liberty." In *American Thought and Writing*, vol. 2, *The Revolution and the Early Republic*, ed. Russel B. Nye and Norman S. Grabo, 137–41. New York: Riverside, 1965.

———. "The Mire of Democracy." In *The Federalist Literary Mind*, ed. Lewis P. Simpson, 151–54. Baton Rouge: Louisiana Paperbacks, 1962.

Anderson, Benedict. *Imagined Communities: Reflections on the Origin and Spread of Nationalism*. Rev. ed. London: Verso, 1991.

Anteyles, Peter. *Tales of Adventurous Enterprise: Washington Irving and the Poetics of Western Expansion*. New York: Columbia Univ. Press, 1990.

Appleby, Joyce. Introduction: "Republicanism and Ideology." *American Quarterly* 37 (1985): 461–73.

———. *Liberalism and Republicanism in the Historical Imagination*. Cambridge: Harvard Univ. Press, 1992.

Arendt, Hannah. *On Revolutions*. New York: Viking, 1963.

Ashcroft, Bill, Gareth Griffiths, and Helen Tiffin. *The Empire Writes Back: Theory and Practice in Post-Colonial Literatures*. London: Routledge, 1989.

Axelrod, Alan. *Charles Brockden Brown: An American Tale*. Austin: Univ. of Texas Press, 1983.

Baepler, Paul. "The Barbary Captivity Narrative in Early America." *Early American Literature* 30, no. 2 (1995): 95–120.

Bailyn, Bernard. *The Ideological Origins of the American Revolution*. Cambridge: Belkap Press of Harvard Univ. Press, 1973.

Baron, Dennis E. *Grammar and Good Taste: Reforming the American Language*. New Haven: Yale Univ. Press, 1982.

Barrell, John. *The Birth of Pandora and the Division of Knowledge*. Philadelphia: Univ. of Pennsylvania Press, 1992.

Bayly, C. A. *Imperial Meridian: The British Empire and the World, 1780–1830.* London: Longman, 1989.

Baym, Nina. Introduction. *The Gleaner: A Miscellany,* by Judith Sargent Murray, ed. Baym, iii–xx. Schenectady: Union College Press, 1992.

———. *Novels, Readers, and Reviewers: Responses to Fiction in Antebellum America.* Ithaca: Cornell Univ. Press, 1984.

Beer, Gillian. "The Island and the Aeroplane: The Case of Virginia Woolf." In *Nations and Narration,* ed. Homi K. Bhabha, 265–90. London: Routledge, 1990.

Belknap, Jeremy. *The Foresters.* 1792. Rpt., ed. Lewis A. Turlish. New York: Scholars' Facsimiles and Reprints, 1969.

Bell, Michael Davitt. *The Development of American Romance: The Sacrifice of Relation.* Chicago: Univ. of Chicago Press, 1980.

Bennett, Charles E. "Charles Brockden Brown and the International Novel." *Studies in the Novel* 12 (1980): 62–64.

Bercovitch, Sacvan. *The Rites of Assent: Transformations in the Symbolic Construction of America.* London: Routledge, 1993.

Berthoff, Warner. Introduction. *Arthur Mervyn,* by Charles Brockden Brown, ed. Berthoff. New York: Holt, 1962.

Bhabha, Homi K. "Of Mimicry and the Man: The Ambivalence of Colonial Discourse." *October* 28 (1984): 34–51.

Black, Michael L. "*A History of New York*: Significant Revision in 1848." In *Washington Irving Reconsidered: A Symposium,* ed. Ralph M. Aderman, 48–56. Hartford: Transcendental Books, 1974.

———. "Political Satire in Knickerbocker's *History.*" In *The Knickerbocker Tradition,* ed. Andrew B. Myers, 65–87. Tarrytown, N.Y.: Sleepy Hollow Reproductions, 1974.

Blair, Hugh. *Lectures on Rhetoric and Belles Lettres.* Edinburgh, 1780.

Bloomfield, Maxwell. "Constitutional Values and the Literature of the Early Republic." *Journal of American Culture* 11 (1988): 53–58.

Bowden, Mary Weatherspoon. "Knickerbocker's *History* and the 'Enlightened' Men of New York City." *American Literature* 47 (1975): 159–72.

———. *Washington Irving.* Boston: Hall, 1981.

Brackenridge, Hugh Henry. *Modern Chivalry.* 1792–1815. Rpt., ed. Claude M. Newlin. New York: Hafner, 1937.

———. *A Brackenridge Reader, 1770–1815.* Ed. Daniel Marder. Pittsburgh: Univ. of Pittsburgh Press, 1970.

Brackenridge, Hugh Henry, and Philip Freneau. *Father Bombo's Pilgrimage to Mecca.* 1771. Rpt., ed. Michael Davitt Bell. Princeton: Princeton Univ. Press, 1975.

Brancaccio, Patrick. "Studied Ambiguities: *Arthur Mervyn* and the Problem of the Unreliable Narrator." *American Literature* 42 (1970): 18–27.

Brantlinger, Patrick. *Crusoe's Footsteps: Cultural Studies in Britain and America*. New York: Routledge, 1990.

———. *Rule of Darkness: British Literature and Imperialism, 1830–1914*. Ithaca: Cornell Univ. Press, 1988.

Brennan, Timothy. "The National Longing for Form." In *Nation and Narration*, ed. Homi K. Bhabha, 44–70. London: Routledge, 1990.

Brown, Charles Brockden. "The State of American Literature." *Monthly Magazine and American Review* 1 (1799): 1.

———. *The Novels and Selected Works of Charles Brockden Brown: The Bicentennial Edition*. 7 vols. Gen. ed. Sydney J. Krause. Kent, Ohio: Kent State Univ. Press, 1980–83.

———. "The Sketches of a History of Carsol." In *William Dunlap's The Life of Charles Brockden Brown*, ed. Paul Allen, 170–222. Philadelphia, 1815.

Brown, Richard D. "The Idea of an Informed Citizenry in the Early Republic." In *The Making of American Freedom*, ed. David Thomas Konig, 141–77. Stanford: Stanford Univ. Press, 1995.

———. *Knowledge Is Power: The Diffusion of Information in Early America, 1700–1865*. New York: Oxford Univ. Press, 1989.

Brown, William Hill. *The Power of Sympathy*. Boston, 1789.

Bryant, William Cullen. "A Discourse." In *A Century of Commentary on the Works of Washington Irving, 1860–1974*, ed. Andrew B. Myers, 3–17. Tarrytown, N.Y.: Sleepy Hollow, 1976.

Brydon, Diana. *Decolonising Fictions*. Sydney: Dangaroo, 1993.

Buel, Richard, Jr. *Securing the Revolution: Ideology in American Politics, 1789–1815*. Ithaca: Cornell Univ. Press, 1972.

Buell, Lawrence. "American Literary Emergence as a Postcolonial Phenomenon." *American Literary History* 4 (1992): 411–42.

Burchell, R. A. "The Role of the Upper Class in the Formation of American Culture, 1780–1840." In *The End of Anglo-America: Historical Essays in the Study of Cultural Divergence*, ed. Burchell, 184–212. Manchester: Manchester Univ. Press, 1991.

Burroughs, Stephen. *The Memoirs of Stephen Burroughs*. 1798. Rpt. Boston: Northeastern Univ. Press, 1988.

Bush, Sargent, Jr. "*Modern Chivalry* and *Young's Magazine*." *American Literature* 44 (1972): 292–99.

Bushman, Richard L. *King and People in Provincial Massachusetts*. Chapel Hill: Univ. of North Carolina Press, 1985.

Carson, Ada Lou, and Herbert L. Carson. *Royall Tyler*. Boston: Hall, 1979.

Charvat, William L. *The Profession of Authorship in America, 1800–1870*. Columbus: Ohio State Univ. Press, 1968.

Christophersen, Bill. *The Apparition in the Glass: Charles Brockden Brown's American Gothic.* Athens: Univ. of Georgia Press, 1993.

Clark, David Lee. *Charles Brockden Brown: Pioneer Voice of America.* Durham: Duke Univ. Press, 1952.

Cmiel, Kenneth. *Democratic Eloquence: The Fight over Popular Speech in Nineteenth-Century America.* New York: Morrow, 1990.

Cohen, Daniel A. "*Arthur Mervyn* and His Elders: The Ambivalence of Youth in the Early Republic." *William and Mary Quarterly*, 3d ser., 43 no.3 (1986): 362–380.

Cohen, Lester A. *The Revolutionary Histories.* Ithaca: Cornell Univ. Press, 1980.

Commager, Henry Steele. *Jefferson, Nationalism, and the Enlightenment.* New York: Braziller, 1975.

Cook, Don L. *The Long Fuse: How England Lost the American Colonies, 1760–1785.* New York: Atlantic Monthly Press, 1995.

Cook, Jonathan A. "'Prodigious Poop': Comic Context and Psychological Subtext in Irving's *Knickerbocker History.*" *Nineteenth-Century Literature* 48 (1993): 483–512.

Cott, Nancy F. *The Bonds of Womanhood: "Women's Sphere" in New England, 1780–1835.* New Haven: Yale Univ. Press, 1977.

Crèvecoeur, J. Hector St. John de. *Letters From an American Farmer and Sketches of Eighteenth-Century America.* 1782. Rpt., ed. Albert E. Stone. New York: Penguin, 1981.

Daiches, David. "John Witherspoon, James Wilson and the Influence of Scottish Rhetoric on America." *Eighteenth-Century Life* 15 (1991): 163–80.

Daigrepont, Lloyd M. "'Rip Van Winkle' and the Gnostic Vision of History." *Clio* 15 (1985): 47–59.

Dauber, Kenneth. *The Idea of Authorship in America: Democratic Poetics from Franklin to Melville.* Madison: Univ. of Wisconsin Press, 1990.

Davidson, Cathy N. *Revolution and the Word: The Rise of the Novel in America.* New York: Oxford Univ. Press, 1986.

Davis, Lennard. "A Social History of Fact and Fiction." In *Literature and Society.: Selected Papers from the English Institute, 1978,* ed. Edward Said, 120–48. Baltimore: Johns Hopkins Univ. Press, 1980.

Dennie, Joseph. *The Lay Preacher; or, Short Sermons for Idle Readers.* Walpole, N.H., 1796.

Dennis, Larry R. "Legitimizing the Novel: Royall Tyler's *The Algerian Captive.*" *Early American Literature* 9, no.2 (1974): 71–80.

Derounian-Stodola, Kathryn Zabelle. "The Gendering of American Fiction: Susanna Rowson to Catherine Sedgwick." In *Making America / Making American Literature,* ed. A. Robert Lee and W. M. Verhoeven, 165–82. Amsterdam: Rodopi, 1996.

Dirks, Nicholas. *Colonialism and Culture.* Ann Arbor: Univ. of Michigan Press, 1992.

Docker, John. "The Neocolonial Assumption in University Teaching of English." In *The Postcolonial Studies Reader,* ed. Bill Ashcroft, Gareth Griffiths, and Helen Tiffin, 443–47. London: Routledge, 1994.

Douglass, Elisha P. *Rebels and Democrats*. Chapel Hill: Univ. of North Carolina Press, 1955.

Dowling, William C. *Poetry and Ideology in Revolutionary Connecticut*. Athens: Univ. of Georgia Press, 1990.

Dunlap, William. *The Life of Charles Brockden Brown*, ed. Paul Allen. Philadelphia, 1815.

Dwight, Timothy. *Greenfild Hill*. New York, 1793.

Elkins, Stanley, and Eric McKitrick. *The Age of Federalism: The Early American Republic, 1788–1800*. New York: Oxford Univ. Press, 1993.

Elliott, Emory. *Revolutionary Writers: Literature and Authority in the New Republic, 1725–1810*. New York: Oxford Univ. Press, 1982.

Ellis, Joseph J. *After the Revolution: Profiles in Early American Culture*. New York: Norton, 1979.

Emerson, Ralph Waldo. "The American Scholar." In *The Portable Emerson*, ed. Carl Bode and Malcolm Cowley, 51–71. New York: Penguin, 1957.

Engell, John. "Brackenridge's *Modern Chivalry* and American Humor." *Early American Literature* 22, no.1 (1987): 43–62.

———. "Narrative Irony and National Character in Royall Tyler's *The Algerine Captive*." *Studies in American Fiction* 17, no.1 (1989): 19–32.

Evans, James E. "The English Lineage of Diedrich Knickerbocker." *Early American Literature* 10 (1975): 3–12.

Ferguson, Robert A. *Law and Letters in American Culture*. Cambridge: Harvard Univ. Press, 1984.

———. "'We Hold These Truths': Strategies of Control in the Literature of the Founders." In *Reconstructing American Literary History*, ed. Sacvan Bercovitch, 1–28. Cambridge: Harvard Univ. Press, 1986.

Field, Vena Bernadette. *Constantia: A Study of the Life and Works of Judith Sargent Murray*. Maine Bulletin 23, no.7; Univ. of Maine Studies Second Series, no. 17. Orono, 1931.

Fliegelman, Jay. *Declaring Independence: Jefferson, Natural Language, and the Culture of Performance*. Stanford: Stanford Univ. Press, 1993.

———. *Prodigals and Pilgrims: The American Revolution against Patriarchal Authority*. Cambridge: Cambridge Univ. Press, 1982.

Foster, Hannah. *The Coquette; or, The History of Eliza Wharton*. 1798. Rpt., ed. Cathy N. Davidson. New York: Oxford Univ. Press, 1986.

Franklin, Benjamin. *The Autobiography of Benjamin Franklin and Selected Writings*, ed. Larzer Ziff. New York: Holt, 1959.

Free, Willam J. *The "Columbian" Magazine and American Literary Nationalism*. The Hague: Mouton, 1968.

Furtwangler, Albert. *American Silhouettes: Rhetorical Identities of the Founding Fathers*. New Haven: Yale Univ. Press, 1987.

Gabler-Hover, Janet. *Truth in American Fiction: The Legacy of Rhetorical Idealism.* Athens: Univ. of Georgia Press, 1990.

Geertz, Cifford. *The Interpretation of Cultures.* New York: Basic Books, 1973.

Gilmore, Michael T. *American Romanticism and the Marketplace.* Chicago: Univ. of Chicago Press, 1985.

———. "Eighteenth-Century Oppositional Ideology and Hugh Henry Brackenridge's *Modern Chivalry.*" *Early American Literature* 13 (1977): 181–92.

Grabo, Norman S. *The Coincidental Art of Charles Brockden Brown.* Chapel Hill: Univ. of North Carolina Press, 1981.

———. "Historical Essay." In *Arthur Mervyn; or Memoirs of the Year 1793,* vol. 3 of *The Novels and Selected Works of Charles Brockden Brown: The Bicentennial Edition,* 464–79.

Grant, Barry K. "Literary Style as Political Metaphor in *Modern Chivalry.*" *Canadian Review of American Studies* 11 (1979): 1–11.

Grayson, William. Debates in the Virginia Convention. In *The Antifederalists,* ed. Cecilia M. Kenyon, 275–300. Indianapolis: Bobbs-Merrill, 1966.

Greenblatt, Stephen Jay. *Marvellous Possessions: The Wonder of the New World.* Chicago: Univ. of Chicago Press, 1991.

Greene, Jack P. *Imperatives, Behaviors, and Identities: Essays in Early American Cultural History.* Charlottesville: Univ. Press of Virginia, 1992.

———. *The Intellectual Construction of America: Exceptionalism and Identity from 1492 to 1800.* Chapel Hill: Univ. of North Carolina Press, 1993.

———. *Negotiated Authorities: Essays in Colonial Political and Constitutional History.* Charlottesville: Univ. Press of Virginia, 1994.

———. *Pursuits of Happiness: The Social Development of Early Modern British Colonies and the Formation of American Culture.* Chapel Hill: Univ. of North Carolina Press, 1988.

Griffiths, Gareth. "Culture and Identity: Politics and Writing in Some Recent Post-Colonial Texts." In *From Commonwealth to Postcolonial,* ed. Anna Rutherford, 436–43. Sydney: Dangaroo, 1992.

Gustafson, Thomas. *Representative Words: Politics, Literature, and the American Language, 1776–1865.* New York: Cambridge Univ. Press, 1992.

Hall, Stuart. "'When Was 'The Post-Colonial'? Thinking at the Limits." In *The Post-Colonial Question: Common Skies, Divided Horizons,* ed. Iain Chambers and Lidia Curti, 242–60. New York: Routledge, 1996.

Hamilton, Alexander, James Madison, and John Jay. *The Federalist Papers,* ed. Clinton Rossiter. New York: Mentor, 1961.

Harris, Sharon M. "Judith Sargent Murray." *Legacy* 11, no.2 (1994): 152–59.

———, ed. *American Women Writers to 1800.* New York: Oxford Univ. Press, 1996.

Hatch, Nathan O. *The Democratization of American Christianity.* New Haven: Yale Univ. Press, 1989.

Hedges, William L. "Charles Brockden Brown and the Culture of Contradictions." *Early American Literature* 9 (1974): 107–42.

———. "The Knickerbocker *History* as Knickerbocker's History." In *The Old and New World Romanticism of Washington Irving*, ed. Stanley Brodwin, 153–66. Westport, Conn.: Greenwood Press, 1986.

———. "The Myth of the Republic and the Theory of American Literature." *Prospects* 4 (1978): 101–20.

———. "The Old World Yet: Writers and Writing in Post-Revolutionary America." *Early American Literature* 16 (1981): 3–18.

———. *Washington Irving: An American Study, 1802–1832.* Baltimore: Johns Hopkins Univ. Press, 1965.

Henry, Patrick. "Speech to the Virginia Ratifying Convention: The Defects of the New Constitution." In *American Thought and Writing,* vol. 2, *The Revolution and the Early Republic,* ed. Russel B. Nye and Norman S. Grabo, 121–26. New York: Riverside, 1965.

Hinds, Elizabeth Jane Wall. *Private Property: Charles Brockden Brown's Gendered Economics of Virtue.* Newark: Univ. of Delaware Press, 1997.

Hirsch, David H. *Reality and Idea in the Early American Novel.* Paris: Mouton, 1971.

Hoffa, W. W. "Language of Rogues and Fools in Brackenridge's *Modern Chivalry.*" *Studies in the Novel* 12 (1980): 289–300.

Horsman, Reginald. *The Diplomacy of the New Republic, 1776–1815.* Arlington Heights, Ill.: Davidson, 1985.

Howard, Leon. *The Connecticut Wits.* Chicago: Univ. of Chicago Press, 1943.

Huggan, Graham. *Territorial Disputes: Maps and Mapping Strategies in Contemporary Canadian and Australian Fiction.* Toronto: Univ. of Toronto Press, 1994.

Irving, Washington. *The History of New York From the Beginning of the World to the End of the Dutch Dynasty.* 1809. Rpt. in *Washington Irving: Tales and Sketches,* ed. James Tuttleton, 363–729. New York: Library of America, 1983.

———. *The Complete Works of Washington Irving.* 30 vols. Gen. eds. Herbert L. Kleinman, Henry A. Pochman, and Richard Dilworth Rust. Boston: Twayne, 1976–86.

Iser, Wolfgang. *The Implied Reader: Patterns of Communication in Prose Fiction from Bunyan to Beckett.* Baltimore: Johns Hopkins Univ. Press, 1974.

Janiewski, Dolores. "Gendering, Racializing and Classifying: Settler Colonization in the United States, 1590–1990." In *Unsettling Settler Societies: Articulations of Gender, Race, Ethnicity and Class,* ed. Daiva Stasiulus and Nira Yuval-Davis, 132–60. London: Sage, 1995.

JanMohamed, Abdul R. "The Economy of Manichean Allegory." In *The Postcolonial*

Studies Reader, ed. Bill Ashcroft, Gareth Griffiths, and Helen Tiffin, 18–25. London: Routledge, 1994.

Jefferson, Thomas. *The Papers of Thomas Jefferson*. Ed. Julian P. Boyd. Princeton: Princeton Univ. Press, 1950–.

Jenks, William. *A Memoir of the Northern Kingdom*. Boston, 1808.

Jordan, Cynthia S. *Second Stories: The Politics of Language, Form, and Gender in Early American Fictions*. Chapel Hill: Univ. of North Carolina Press, 1989.

Justus, James H. "Arthur Mervyn, American." *American Literature* 42 (1969): 304–24.

Kames, Lord. *Essays on the Principles of Morality and Natural Religion*. Edinburgh, 1751.

Katrak, Ketu H. "Decolonizing Culture: Toward a Theory of Postcolonial Women's Texts." In *The Postcolonial Studies Reader*, ed. Bill Ashcroft, Gareth Griffiths, and Helen Tiffin, 255–58. London: Routledge, 1994.

Kelleher, James T. "Hugh Henry Brackenridge." *Dictionary of Literary Biography* 37 (1986): 45–60.

Kennedy, Julia E. *George Watterston: Novelist, "Metropolitan Author," and Critic*. Washington: Catholic Univ. of America Press, 1933.

Kennedy, Roger G. *Orders from France: The Americans and the French in the Revolutionary World*. New York: Knopf, 1989.

Kerber, Linda K. "The Republican Ideology of the Revolutionary Generation. *American Quarterly* 37 (1985): 474–95.

———. "'I have Don . . . much to Carrey on the Warr:' Women and the Shaping of Republican Ideology after the American Revolution." In *Women and Politics in the Age of Democratic Revolution*, ed. Harriet B. Applewhite and Darline G. Levy, 227–58. Ann Arbor: Univ. of Michigan Press, 1993.

———. *Women of the Republic: Intellect and Ideology in Revolutionary America*. Chapel Hill: Univ. of North Carolina Press, 1980.

Kimball, Arthur G. *Rational Fictions: A Study of Charles Brockden Brown*. McMinnville, Ore.: Linfield Research Institute, 1968.

King, Bruce. *The New English Literatures: Cultural Nationalism in a Changing World*. London: Macmillan, 1980.

Knorr, Klaus E. *British Colonial Theories, 1570–1850*. London: Cass, 1963.

Kornblith, Gary J., and John M. Murrin. "The Making and Unmaking of an American Ruling Class." In *Beyond the American Revolution: Explorations in the History of American Radicalism*, ed. Alfred F. Young, 27–79. Dekalb: Northern Illinois Univ. Press, 1993.

Kramer, Michael. *Imagining Language in America: From the Revolution to the Civil War*. Princeton: Princeton Univ. Press, 1992.

Kritzer, Amelia Howe. *Plays by Early American Women*. Ann Arbor: Univ. of Michigan Press, 1995.

Landes, Joan B. "The Public and the Private Sphere: A Feminist Reconsideration." In *Feminists Read Habermas: Gendering the Subject of Discourse*, ed. Johanna Meehan, 91–116. New York: Routledge, 1995.

Lang, Hans-Joachin. "The Rising Glory of America and the Falling Price on Intellect: The Careers of Brackenridge and Freneau." In *The Transit of Civilization from Europe to America*, ed. Wilfried Herget, 131–43. Tübingen: Marr, 1985.

Larson, David M. "*Arthur Mervyn, Edgar Huntly*, and the Critics." *Essays in Literature* 15 (1988): 207–19.

Lawson, Alan. "A Cultural Paradigm for the Second World." *Australian and Canadian Studies* 9, no.1 (1991): 67–78.

———. "Comparative Studies and Post-Colonial 'Settler' Cultures." *Australian and Canadian Studies* 10, no.2 (1992): 153–58.

Lawson-Peebles, Robert. *Landscape and Written Expression in Revolutionary America: The World Turned Upside Down*. Cambridge: Cambridge Univ. Press, 1988.

Leary, Lewis. *Soundings: Some Early American Writers*. Athens: Univ. of Georgia Press, 1975.

Lease, Benjamin. *Anglo-American Encounters: England and the Rise of American Literature*. Cambridge: Cambridge Univ. Press, 1981.

Lenz, William E. "Confidence Games in the New Country: Hugh Henry Brackenridge's *Modern Chivalry*." *Colby Library Quarterly* 18 (1982): 105–12.

Levine, Robert S. *Conspiracy and Romance: Studies in Brockden Brown, Cooper, Hawthorne, and Melville*. Cambridge: Cambridge Univ. Press, 1989.

Levy, Leonard W. *Freedom of Speech and Press in Early American History: Legacy of Suppression*. New York: Harper, 1963.

Looby, Christopher. *Voicing America: Language, Literary Form, and the Origins of the United States*. Chicago: Univ. of Chicago Press, 1996.

Maier, Pauline. *From Resistance to Revolution: Colonial Radicals and the Development of American Opposition to Great Britain, 1765–1776*. New York: Norton, 1972.

Main, Jackson Turner. *The Antifederalists: Critics of the Constitution, 1787–1788*. Chapel Hill: Univ. of North Carolina Press, 1961.

Mancall, Peter C. Introduction. *Envisioning America: English Plans for the Colonization of North America, 1580–1640*, ed. Mancall, 1–29. New York: Bedford, 1995.

Marder, Daniel. *Hugh Henry Brackenridge*. New York: Knopf, 1967.

Martin, Terence. *The Instructed Vision: Scottish Common Sense Philosophy and the Origins of American Fiction*. Bloomington: Indiana Univ. Press, 1961.

———. *Parables of Possibilities: The American Need for Beginnings*. New York: Columbia Univ. Press, 1995.

———. "Rip, Ichabod, and the American Imagination." *American Literature* 31 (1959): 137–49.

Martin, Wendy. "On the Road with the Philosopher and the Profiteer: A Study of Hugh Henry Brackenridge's *Modern Chivalry*." *Eighteenth-Century Studies* 4 (1971): 241–56.

Masel, Carolyn. "Late Landings: Reflections on Belatedness in Australian and Canadian Literatures." In *Recasting the World: Writing after Colonialism*, ed. Jonathan White, 161–89. Baltimore: Johns Hopkins Univ. Press, 1993.

Matson, Cathy, and Peter Onuf. "Toward a Republican Empire: Interest and Ideology in Revolutionary America." *American Quarterly* 37 (1985): 496–531.

McLamore, Richard V. "Postcolonial Columbus: Washington Irving and *The Conquest of Grenada*." *Nineteenth-Century Literature* 23 (1993): 26–43.

McWilliams, John P. *The American Epic: Transforming a Genre, 1770–1865*. Cambridge: Cambridge Univ. Press, 1989.

Memmi, Albert. *The Colonizer and the Colonized*. Trans. Howard Greenfield. London: Earthscan, 1990.

Merivale, Herman. *Lectures on Colonization and Colonies*. 1861. Rpt. New York: Kelley, 1967.

Meyer, Donald H. *The Democratic Enlightenment*. New York: Capricorn, 1976.

Miller, John C. *The Federalist Era, 1789–1801*. New York: Harper, 1960.

Miller, Samuel. *A Brief Retrospect of the Eighteenth Century*. 2 vols. New York, 1803.

Mitchell, W. J. T. "Postcolonial Culture, Postimperial Criticism." In *The Postcolonial Studies Reader*, ed. Bill Ashcroft, Gareth Griffiths, and Helen Tiffin, 475–79. London: Routledge, 1994.

Moore, Jack B. Introduction. In *The Algerine Captive: or, The Life and Adventures of Dr. Updike Underhill*. Facsimile ed., ed. Moore. Gainesville, Fla.: Scholars' Facsimiles and Reprints, 1967.

Murray, Judith Sargent. *The Gleaner*. 1798. Rpt. Schenectady: Union College Press, 1992.

———. *Selected Writings of Judith Sargent Murray*. Ed. Sharon M. Harris. New York: Oxford Univ. Press, 1995.

Murray, Laura J. "The Aesthetic of Dispossession: Washington Irving and the Ideologies of (De)Colonization in the Early Republic." *American Literary History* 8 (1996): 205–31.

Neal, John. *American Writers: A Series of Papers Contributed to Blackwood's Magazine (1824–1825)*, ed. Fred Louis Pattee. Durham: Duke Univ. Press, 1937.

Nelson, Dana D. *The Word in Black and White: Reading "Race" in American Literature, 1638–1867*. New York: Oxford Univ. Press, 1993.

Neuberg, Victor. "Chapbooks in America: Reconstructing the Popular Reading of Early America." In *Reading in America: Literature and Social History*, ed. Cathy N. Davidson, 81–113. Baltimore: Johns Hopkins Univ. Press, 1989.

New, W. H. "New Language, New World." In *The Postcolonial Studies Reader*, ed. Bill Ashcroft, Gareth Griffiths, and Helen Tiffin, 303–8. London: Routledge, 1994.

Newlin, Claude M. *The Life and Writings of Hugh Henry Brackenridge*. Princeton: Princeton Univ. Press, 1932.

Newton, Sarah Emily. "Wise and Foolish Virgins: 'Usable Fiction' and the American Conduct Tradition." *Early American Literature* 25 (1990): 139–67.

Nord, David Paul. "A Republican Literature: Magazine Reading and Readers in Late Nineteenth-Century New York." In *Reading in America: Literature and Social History*, ed. Cathy N. Davidson, 114–39. Baltimore: Johns Hopkins Univ. Press, 1989.

Onuf, Peter. "The Expanding Union." In *The Making of American Freedom*, ed. David Thomas Konig, 50–80. Stanford: Stanford Univ. Press, 1995.

Paine, Thomas. *Common Sense, The Rights of Man, and Other Essential Writings of Thomas Paine*, ed. Sidney Hook. New York: New American Library, 1969.

Pattee, Fred Lewis. *The First Century of American Literature*. New York: Appleton, 1935.

Patterson, Mark A. *Authority, Autonomy, and Representation in American Literature, 1776–1865*. Princeton: Princeton Univ. Press, 1988.

Paulding, James Kirke. *Koningsmarke, the Long Finne: A Story of the New World*. 1822. Rpt. Schenectady: Union College Press, 1988.

Petter, Henri. *The Early American Novel*. Columbus: Ohio State Univ. Press, 1971.

Pocock, J. G. A. *The Machiavellian Moment: Florentine Political Thought and the Atlantic Republican Tradition*. Princeton: Princeton Univ. Press, 1975.

Pratt, Mary Louise. *Imperial Eyes: Travel Writing and Transculturation*. New York: Routledge, 1992.

Radway, Janice A. *Reading the Romance: Women, Patriarchy, and Popular Literature*. Chapel Hill: Univ. of North Carolina Press, 1984.

Railton, Stephen. *Authorship and Audience: Literary Performance in the American Renaissance*. Princeton: Princeton Univ. Press, 1991.

Rakove, Jack N. "Ambiguous Achievement: The Northwest Ordinance." In *The Northwest Ordinance: Essays on Its Formulation, Privisions, and Legacy*, ed. Frederick D. Williams, 1–17. East Lansing: Michigan State Univ. Press, 1989.

Ramsay, David. *The History of the American Revolution*. Boston, 1789.

Reynolds, David S. *Beneath the American Renaissance*. Cambridge: Harvard Univ. Press, 1989.

Rice, Grantland S. "*Modern Chivalry* and the Resistance to Textual Authority." *American Literature* 67 (1995): 257–81.

Richardson, Gary A. "The Drama of Royall Tyler and William Dunlap as Post-Colonial Phenomena." In *Making America / Making American Literature*, ed. A. Robert Lee and W. M. Verhoeven, 221–48. Amsterdam: Rodopi, 1996.

Ringe, Donald A. *American Gothic: Imagination and Reason in Nineteenth Century Fiction*. Lexington: Kentucky Univ. Press, 1982.

———. *Charles Brockden Brown*. Boston: Hall, 1966.

Ringer, Benjamin B., and Elinor Lawless. *Race, Ethnicity and Society*. London: Routledge, 1989.

Ritcheson, Charles R. *Aftermath of Revolution: British Policy towards the United States, 1783–1795*. New York: Norton, 1971.

Ross, Herbert. *The Sentimental Novel in America, 1789–1860*. New York: Harper, 1940.

Roth, Martin. *Comedy in America: The Lost World of Washington Irving*. Port Washington, N.Y.: Kennikat Press, 1976.

Rubin-Dorsky, Jeffrey. *Adrift in the Old World: The Psychological Pilgrimage of Washington Irving*. Chicago: Univ. of Chicago Press, 1988.

Rush, Benjamin. *A Plan for the Establishment of Public Schools and the Diffusion of Knowledge in Pennsylvania; to Which are Added, Thoughts Upon the Mode of Education, Proper in a Republic*. Philadelphia, 1786.

———. *The Letters of Benjamin Rush*. Ed L. H. Butterfield. 2 vols. Princeton: American Philosophical Assoc., 1951.

Russo, James R. "The Chameleon of Convenient Voice: A Study of Narrative in *Arthur Mervyn*." *Studies in the Novel* 11 (1978): 381–405.

Said, Edward. *Culture and Imperialism*. New York: Vintage, 1993.

———. *Orientalism*. New York: Random House, 1978.

Samuels, Shirley. *Romances of the Republic: Women, the Family and Violence in the Literature of the Early American Nation*. New York: Oxford Univ. Press, 1996.

Schofield, Mary Anne. "'Quitting the Loom and Distaff': Eighteenth-Century Woman Dramatists." In *Curtain Calls: British and American Women and the Theater*, ed. Schofield and Cecilia Macheski, 260–73. Athens: Ohio Univ. Press, 1994.

Schulman, Lydia Dittler. *Paradise Lost and the Rise of the American Republic*. Boston: Northeastern Univ. Press, 1992.

Secor, Robert. "Ethnic Humor in Early American Jest Books." In *A Mixed Race: Ethnicity in Early America*, ed. Frank Shuffleton, 163–93. New York: Oxford Univ. Press, 1993.

Seelye, John. *Beautiful Machine: Rivers and the Republican Plan, 1755–1825*. New York: Oxford Univ. Press, 1991.

Shaffer, Arthur H. *The Politics of History: Writing the History of the American Revolution, 1783–1815*. Chicago: Precedent, 1975.

Shalhope, Robert E. "Republicanism, Liberalism, and Democracy: Political Culture in the New Nation." In *The Republican Synthesis Revisited: Essays in Honor of George Athan Billias*, ed. Milton M. Klein, Richard D. Brown, and John B. Hench, 37–90. Worcester, Mass.: American Antiquarian Society, 1992.

Sharp, James Roger. *American Politics in the Early Republic: The New Nation in Crisis*. New Haven: Yale Univ. Press, 1995.

Sharpe, Jenny. "Is the United States Postcolonial? Transnationalism, Immigration, and Race." *Diaspora* 4, no.2 (1995): 181–99.

Sherburne, Henry. *The Oriental Philosopher.* New York, 1800.

Shields, David S. "Cosmopolitanism and the Anglo-Jewish Elite in British America." In *A Mixed Race: Ethnicity in Early America,* ed. Frank Shuffleton, 143–62. New York: Oxford Univ. Press, 1993.

———. *Oracles of Empire: Poetry, Politics, and Commerce in British America, 1690–1750.* Chicago: Univ. of Chicago Press, 1990.

Shuffleton, Frank. Introduction. *A Mixed Race: Ethnicity in Early America,* ed. Shuffleton, 3–16. New York: Oxford Univ. Press, 1993.

Simpson, David. *The Politics of American English, 1776–1850.* New York: Oxford Univ. Press, 1986.

Slaughter, Thomas. *The Whiskey Rebels.* New York: Norton, 1990.

Slemon, Steven. "Unsettling the Empire: Resistance Theory for the Second World." *World Literature Written in English* 30, no.2 (1990): 30–41.

Slemon, Steven, and Helen Tiffin. Introduction. *After Europe: Critical Theory and Post-Colonial Writing,* ed. Slemon and Tiffin. Sydney: Dangaroo, 1989.

Smith, William Raymond. *History as Argument.* The Hague: Mouton, 1966.

Spangler, George M. "Charles Brockden Brown's *Arthur Mervyn*: A Portrait of the Young American Artist." *American Literature* 52 (1981): 578–92.

Spengemann, William C. *The Adventurous Muse: The Poetics of American Fiction, 1789–1900.* New Haven: Yale Univ. Press, 1977.

Spivak, Gayatri. *The Postcolonial Critic: Interviews, Strategies, Dialogues.* London: Routledge, 1990.

Spurr, David. *The Rhetoric of Empire: Colonial Discourse in Journalism, Travel Writing, and Imperial Administration.* Durham: Duke Univ. Press, 1993.

Stasiulus, Daiva, and Nira Yuval-Davis. Introduction: "Beyond Dichotomies—Gender, Race, Ethnicity and Class in Settler Societies." *Unsettling Settler Societies: Articulations of Gender, Race, Ethnicity and Class,* ed. Stasiulus and Yuval-Davis. London: Sage, 1995.

Sterne, Laurence. *The Life and Opinions of Tristram Shandy, Gentleman.* London, 1759–67.

Stonum, Gary Lee. "Undoing American History." *Diacritics* 11 (1981): 3–12.

Tanselle, G. Thomas. *Royall Tyler.* Cambridge: Harvard Univ. Press, 1967.

Taylor, Alan. "From Fathers to Friends of the People: Political Personas in the Early Republic." In *New Perspectives on the Early Republic: Essays from* The Journal of the Early Republic, *1981–1991,* ed. Ralph D. Gray and Michael Morrison, 139–63. Urbana: Univ. of Illinois Press, 1994.

———. *William Cooper's Town: Power and Persuasion on the Frontier of the Early American Republic.* New York: Vintage, 1995.

Thacher, Samuel Cooper. "An Original American Poetry." In *The Federalist Literary Mind*, ed. Lewis P. Simpson, 154–55. Baton Rouge: Louisiana Paperbacks, 1962.

Thomas, Nicholas. *Colonialism's Culture: Anthropology, Travel, and Government*. Princeton: Princeton Univ. Press, 1994.

Tiffin, Helen. "Postcolonial Literature and Counter-Discourse." In *The Postcolonial Studies Reader*, ed. Bill Ashcroft, Gareth Griffiths, and Helen Tiffin, 95–98. London: Routledge, 1994.

———. "Transformative Imageries." In *From Commonwealth to Postcolonial*, ed. Anna Rutherford, 428–35. Sydney: Dangaroo, 1992.

Tompkins, Jane. *Sensational Designs: The Cultural Work of American Fiction, 1790–1860*. New York: Oxford Univ. Press, 1986.

Trumbull, Benjamin. *A General History of the United States of America*. New York, 1810.

Tyler, Royall. *The Algerine Captive; or, The Life and Adventures of Dr. Updike Underhill*. 1797. Rpt. Facsimile ed. Gainesville, Fla.: Scholars' Facsimiles and Reprints, 1967.

———. *The Poetry of Royall Tyler*. Ed. Marius B. Peladeau. Montpelier: Vermont Historical Society, 1969.

———. *The Prose of Royall Tyler*. Ed. Marius B. Peladeau. Montpelier: Vermont Historical Society, 1972.

Unrue, Darlene Harbour. "Brackenridge's *Modern Chivalry*: A Reassessment." In *History and the Humanities*, ed. Francis X. Hartigan, 271–83. Las Vegas: Univ. of Nevada Press, 1989.

Van Anglen, K. P. *The New England Milton: Literary Reception and Cultural Authority in the Early Republic*. Univ. Park: Pennsylvania State Univ. Press, 1993.

Wakefield, Edward Gibbon. *England and America: A Comparison of the Social and Political State of Both Nations*. New York: Harper, 1834.

Wales, Samuel. "The Dangers of Our National Prosperity and the Way to Avoid Them." In *Political Sermons of the American Founding Era, 1730–1805*, ed. Ellis Sandoz, 835–64. Indianapolis: Liberty, 1990.

Warfel, Harry. *Charles Brockden Brown: American Gothic Novelist*. Gainesville, Fla: Univ. of Florida Press, 1949.

Warner, Michael. *The Letters of the Republic: Publication and the Public Sphere in Eighteenth-Century America*. Cambridge: Harvard Univ. Press, 1990.

Watt, Ian. *The Rise of the Novel: Studies in Defoe, Richardson, and Fielding*. Berkeley: Univ. of California Press, 1957.

Watterston, George. *The Child of Feeling*. Washington, D.C. 1809.

———. *The Lawyer; or, Man as He Ought Not To Be*. Pittsburgh, 1808.

Watts, Emily S. *The Poetry of American Women from 1632 to 1945*. Austin: Univ. of Texas Press, 1977.

Watts, Steven. *The Republic Reborn: The Birth of the Liberal Republic, 1790–1820.* Baltimore: Johns Hopkins Univ. Press, 1987.

———. *The Romance of Real Life: Charles Brockden Brown and the Origins of American Culture.* Baltimore: Johns Hopkins Univ. Press, 1994.

Webster, Noah. Selections from *Dissertations on the English Language.* In *American Thought and Writing,* vol. 2, *The Revolution and the Early Republic,* ed. Russel B. Nye and Norman S. Grabo, 281–87. New York: Riverside, 1965.

White, Hayden. *Metahistory.* Baltimore: Johns Hopkins Univ. Press, 1973.

Wiebe, Robert H. *The Opening of American Society: From the Adoption of the Constitution to the Eve of Disunion.* New York: Vintage, 1985.

Wilkins, Kirsten. "The Scribblings of a Plain Man and the Temerity of a Woman: Gender and Genre in Judith Sargent Murray's *The Gleaner.*" *Early American Literature* 30, no.2 (1995): 121–44.

Williams, Daniel E. "Authoring the Author: Heroes and Geeks." *Early American Literature* 30, no.2 (1995): 264–74.

Williams, Stanley T. *The Life of Washington Irving.* 2 vols. New York: Octagon, 1971.

Winthrop, James. The Letters of Agrippa. In *The Antifederalists,* ed. Cecilia M. Kenyon, 131–60. Indianapolis: Bobbs-Merrill, 1966.

Wood, Gordon S. *The Creation of the American Republic, 1776–1787.* Chapel Hill: Univ. of North Carolina Press, 1969.

———. *The Radicalism of the American Revolution.* New York: Vintage, 1993.

Woodmansee, Martha. *The Author, Art, and the Market: Rereading the History of Aesthetics.* New York: Columbia Univ. Press, 1994.

Youmans, Gilbert, and Greg Stratman. "American English: The Transition from Colonialism to Independence." In *The End of Anglo-America: Historical Essays in the Study of Cultural Divergence,* ed. R. A. Burchell, 137–59. Manchester: Manchester Univ. Press, 1991.

Young, Robert R. C. *Colonial Desire: Hybridity in Theory, Culture, and Race.* London: Routledge, 1995.

Ziff, Larzer. *Writing in the New Nation: Prose, Print, and Politics in the Early United States.* New Haven: Yale Univ. Press, 1991.

Index

Adams, Abigail, 52, 177–78, 190 n.7
Adams, John, 10, 11, 52, 57, 104, 124, 177–78, 191 n.22
Adams, John Quincy, 22
Addison, Joseph, 60, 69, 165, 190 n.8, 200 n.20
Algerine Captive, The, (Tyler) 6, 21, 25, *73–94,* 177. *See also* Tyler, Royall
Algerine Crisis, 74–90, 192 nn.2 & 4, 194 n.19
Alien and Sedition Acts, 30
"American in Algiers," 74
American Law Journal, 169
American Philosophical Society, 36, 43
American Revolution, 4, 13, 15, 20, 52, 54, 60–61, 98, 123, 132, 141, 153, 163, 171, 185 n.30, 190 n.12, 191 n.16, 198 n.15
Ames, Fisher, 14, 16, 74, 124, 182 n.7, 184 n.28, 188 n.19, 189 n.27
Anderson, Benedict, 3, 10, 181 nn.2 & 3, 183 n.18, 187 n.6, 190 n.14, 197 n.1
Anteyles, Peter, 149, 200 n.11
Anticolonialism, 10, 16, 17, 50, 60, 141
Antifederalism, 2, 4, 19, 30, 39, 44, 74, 181 n.1, 192 nn.5 & 6
Appleby, Joyce, 183–84 n.19, 190 nn.12 & 13, 197 n.8
Arendt, Hannah, 10, 181 n.3, 183 n.18, 187 n.6, 197 n.8
Aristotle, 161
Arthur Mervyn (Brown), 6, 25, *95–121,* 195 n.3, 196 n.12. *See also* Brown, Charles Brockden

Ashcroft, Bill, 18
Authorship, 12–14, 18, *20–24,* 41, 63–67, 79–80, 110, 117, 159, 169–71, 175, 196 n.10
Axelrod, Alan, 196 n.14

Baepler, Paul, 192 n.3
Bailyn, Bernard, 7, 182 n.12, 183 n.14, 195 n.5
Bancroft, George, 166
Barlow, Joel, 61, 75, 192 n.6
Baron, Dennis E., 187 n.7
Barrell, John, 187 n.8
Bayly, C. A., 7, 181 n.2, 182 n.13, 183 n.14
Baym, Nina, 190 n.6, 191 nn.19, 20, & 21
Beer, Gillian, 184 n.25
Belknap, Jeremy, 61, 187 n.14
Bell, Michael Davitt, 195 n.8
Bercovitch, Sacvan, 18, 20
Berthoff, Warner, 195 n.8, 196 n.12
Bhabha, Homi K., 16, 28, 181 nn.2 & 5, 182 n.8, 184 n.25, 186 n.4, 190 n.6
Bible, 155
Bird, Robert Montgomery, 119
Black, Michael L., 199 n.3, 200 n.15
Blair, Hugh, 147, 193 n.14
Bleeker, Anna Eliza, 51
Boehmer, Elleke, 4, 13, 162, 165, 181 n.5, 182 n.9, 198 n.15, 199 n.2
Bowden, Mary Weatherspoon, 200 n.15
Brackenridge, Hugh Henry, 6, *27–50,* 60, 65, 72, 82, 97, 107, 110, 131, 139, 142, 145, 171, 176,

Brackenridge—*continued*
177, 179, 186 nn.1 & 5, 187 nn.10 & 11, 188
nn.20 & 21, 194 n.17; and democracy, 39;
and federalism, 47-51; "Incidents of the
Insurrection," 33; *Modern Chivalry*, 6, 21,
27–50, 145; political career of, 32–34; "To a
Dissenting Assemblyman," 188 n.17; "Trial
of Mamachtaga," 50–51, 188 n.15, 189 n.29
Brancaccio, Patrick, 196 n.10
Brantlinger, Patrick, 14, 184 n.27, 195 n.6
Brennan, Timothy, 201 n.6
British literature, 13–14, 129, 171–74, 187 n.8;
and the early republic, 9–15, 21, 22, 52, 165
Brown, Charles Brockden, 6, 21, 22, 25, 40, 82,
94, 95–121, 122–23, 127, 129, 139, 151, 159, 160,
170, 171, 178–79, 185 n.29, 195 n.9, 196 n.14;
"Alcuin," 63, 115, 134; *Arthur Mervyn*, 6, 21,
22, 25, 40, 95–121; and authorship, 98–99,
103; and capitalism, 95; *Clara Howard*,
119; and colonialism, 105, 111; *Edgar Huntly*,
106, 107, 108, 110; and feminism, 112, 115;
Jane Talbot, 119; and literacy, 103–104; "On
the State of American Literature," 95; *Or-
mond*, 99, 100, 110; and professionalism,
110, 111, 113, 117; and readership, 95, 102, 105,
116–119; "The Sketches of a History of
Carsol," 119–20; *Wieland*, 21–22, 99, 100,
108, 110
Brown, Richard D., 30, 185 n.34, 198 n.12
Brown, William Hill, 63, 101, 187 n.14
Bryant, William Cullen, 144, 199 n.1
Brydon, Diana, 8
Buchanan, John, 129–30, 198 n.13
Buel, Richard, Jr., 192 n.5, 194 n.18
Buell, Lawrence, 5, 26, 128, 182 n.11, 185 n.33
Bunyan, John, 80, 98
Burchell, R. A., 124
Burke, Edmund, 8
Burns, Robert, 138
Burroughs, Stephen, 119, 125–26, 136–37,
141–43, 169, 197 n.7, 198 n.19
Bush, Sargent, Jr., 188 n.22
Bushman, Richard L., 7, 182 n.12, 197 n.8

Butler, Samuel, 44
Byron, George Gordon, Lord, 128

Caleb Williams (Godwin), 106
Calvinism, 124, 137
Carey, Mathew, 74
Carlyle, Thomas, 148
Cervantes, Miguel de, 40, 77
Charvat, William L., 176, 202 n.13
Chaucer, Geoffrey, 144
Christopherson, Bill, 97, 195 n.1, 196 n.14
Clark, David, 196 n.14
Classicism, 12–13, 40, 60, 84–85, 146–47, 152,
155–56, 161–62, 188 n.24, 200 n.10
Cmiel, Kenneth, 12, 187 n.7, 202 n.13
Cohen, Daniel A., 194 n.16
Cohen, Lester A., 147, 199 nn.6, 7, & 9
Colonialism, 3, 5, 9, 13, 15, 20, 105, 132, 144, 153,
156–57, 171, 181 n.5, 182 n.8, 183 n.14; and re-
publicanism, 9–15, 117, 183 n.16, 184 n.24,
194 n.20, 199 n.2; and writing, 14, 24, 46,
118, 195 n.2. *See also* Decolonization
Commager, Henry Steele, 184 n.24, 188 n.19
Connecticut Wits, 75, 84, 188 n.24
Constitution, U.S., 2, 171, 181 nn.1 & 4
Cook, Don, 7, 182 n.13
Cook, Jonathan A., 200 n.13
Cooper, James Fenimore, 48, 167, 173
Cott, Nancy F., 54, 72
Crèvecoeur, J. Hector St. John de, 19–20

Daiches, David, 185 n.29, 190 n.11
Daigrepont, Lloyd M., 149, 174, 202 n.10
Darwin, Erasmus, 154
Dauber, Kenneth, 97, 185 n.29, 190 n.10, 202
n.16
Davidson, Cathy N., 52, 78, 89, 127, 138–39,
184 nn.21, 22, & 28, 186 n.3, 187 n.9, 189 n.2,
190 n.6, 191 nn.16 & 25, 193 nn.9 & 12, 194
nn.19 & 21, 195 nn.3 & 8, 197 n.5, 198 n.20
Davis, Lennard J., 129, 196 n.15
Decatur, Stephen, 192 n.4
Declaration of Independence, 167

Decolonization, 2, 5–6, *15–19*, 20, 22, 49, 61, 71, 87, 94, 96, 99, 101, 108, 120–21, 125, 139, 143, 145–46, 158, 160, 166–68, 169–79, 182 nn.7 & 9, 191 n.19, 194 n.20

Democracy, 12, 15–19, 39, 60, 71, 108, 142, 170–72; and writing, 63, 175–78

Dennie, Joseph, 193 n.7

Dennis, Larry R., 193 n.8, 193 n.10, 194 n.17

Derounian–Stodola, Kathryn Zabelle, 189 n.4, 197 n.5

Didacticism, 56–57, 62–63, 93, 102, 117, 123, 126, 129, 134, 140, 191 n.25, 197 n.5, 198 n.10

Dido, 66

Digges, Thomas Alonzo, 77

Dirks, Nicholas, 104, 181 n.2

Docker, John, 6

Douglass, Elisha P., 10

Dowling, William C., 12, 184 n.23, 188 n.24, 193 n.6

Dunlap, William, 17, 97, 195 n.8, 196 n.25

Dutch settlement (New Amsterdam), 150–153, 156, 158, 162–63, 200 n.13

Dwight, Timothy 14, 84, 184 n.28, 187 n.14, 193 n.13

Elkins, Stanley, and Eric McKitrick, 51

Elliott, Emory, 14, 27, 34, 48, 53, 124, 179, 184 n.21, 185 n.35, 186 nn.39, 2, 3, & 5, 190 n.9, 193 n.6, 195 n.8

Ellis, Joseph J., 185 n.31, 187 n.11, 189 n.27

Eloquence, 12, 111, 123

Emerson, Ralph Waldo, 5, 176, 182 n.7, 187 n.12

Empire Writes Back, The, (Ashcroft, Griffiths, and Tiffin), 18, 24, 145, 167, 175, 181 n.5, 186 n.37, 201 nn.5 & 6, 202 nn.11 & 14

Engell, John, 78, 89, 186 n.3, 187 n.9, 188 n.16, 193 n.12, 194 nn.15, 17, & 21

Evans, James E., 200 nn.10 & 16

Federalism, 3, *47–51*, 73–75, 78, 80, 192 n.5, 193 n.11; and writing, 87, 194 n.17

Ferguson, Robert A., 12, 108, 124, 139, 182 n.6,

185 n.31, 197 nn.3 & 4, 199 n.5, 200 n.19, 201 n.7

Field, Vena Bernadette, 190 n.7, 191 n.21

Fielding, Henry, 22, 27, 129

First World, 8, 10, 18, 118, 183 n.15, 186 n.37

Fliegelman, Jay, 59, 186 n.38, 191 n.22, 193 n.10, 197 n.8, 198 n.19

Franklin, Benjamin, 7, 82–83, 85–86, 87, 90, 97, 102–4, 108, 114–19, 132, 185 n.29

Free, Willam J., 14, 185 n.29

French Revolution, 74, 198 n.15

Freneau, Philip, 32

Freud, Sigmund, 131

Furphy, Joseph, 31

Furtwangler, Albert, 181 n.4, 190 n.10, 191 n.22, 193 n.10, 201 n.7

Geertz, Cifford, 10, 183 n.18

Gilmore, Michael T., 176, 202 nn.13 & 16

Gleaner, The (Murray), 6, 24, *51–72*, 76, 94, 190 n.7, 191 n.19. *See also* Murray, Judith Sargent

Goldsmith, Oliver, 14

Gordon, William, 147

Gothic, 106–7, 109, 115, 127

Grabo, Norman S., 100, 195 n.7, 196 nn.13 & 21

Grant, Barry K., 37

Grayson, William, 19

Greenblatt, Stephen, 95

Greene, Jack P., 7, 181 n.5, 182 n.12, 183 n.14, 195 n.2

Gura, Philip, 197 n.7

Gustafson, Thomas, 13, 53, 105, 184 n.22, 186 n.39, 190 n.9, 199 n.4, 201 n.7

Habermas, Jurgen, 55

Hall, John E., 169, 174

Hall, Stuart, 1–2

Hamilton, Alexander, 11, 16, 41, 43

Harris, Sharon M., 190 n.6, 191 nn.17, 19, & 21, 192 n.26

Hatch, Nathan O., 52, 189 n.5

Hawthorne, Nathaniel, 127, 178–79

Hazard, Ebenezar, 147
Hedges, William L., 101, 147, 149, 195 n.8, 199 nn.21 & 8, 200 nn.17, 19, 20, & 1, 201 n.2, 202 n.12
Henry, Patrick, 2–5, 10, 18, 176
Herbert, Xavier, 177
Hesiod, 155
Hirsch, David H., 187 n.9
History of New York, (Irving), 6, 25, *144–68,* 177. *See also* Irving, Washington
Hitchcock, Enos, 136–37, 198 n.18
Hoffa, W. W., 27, 186 nn.2 & 3
Homer, 162–63, 166
Howard, Leon, 188 n.24
Howells, William Dean, 120
Huggan, Graham, 8, 16, 130, 150, 183 n.15, 198 n.14
Hume, David, 8, 146
Humphreys, David, 61, 74, 75, 78, 79, 91

Imperialism, American, 1, 11–12, 33, *176–78,* 181 n.1, 186 n.5, 192 n.1
Imperialism, British, 3, 4, 7–9, 30, 130–31, 178, 181 nn.2 & 5, 182 n.13, 183 n.14
Irving, Washington, 6, 21, 23, 25, 82, 90, 142–43; *144–68,* 169, 179, 201 nn.2 & 9; *Analectic Magazine,* 200 n.2; *Astoria,* 200 n.22; *Captain Bonneville,* 200 n.22; *The History of New York,* 6, 21, 25, 144–68, 177; "The Legend of Sleepy Hollow," 148, 165, 174–75; "The Oldstyle Papers," 165; "Rip Van Winkle," 148, 165, 174–75; *Salmagundi,* 76, 82, 120, 148, 170; *The Sketch-Book of Geoffrey Crayon,* 165, 172–175, 200 n. 1
Irving, William, 172
Iser, Wolfgang, 196 n.19
Islam, 89–92

James, Henry, 173
Janiewski, Dolores, 8, 156–57, 183 n.15
JanMohamed, Abdul R., 34, 187 n.13, 194 n.120
Jefferson, Thomas, 7–8, 10, 33, 41, 43, 74, 114, 151, 153, 183 n.16, 188 n.20, 194 n.17, 200 n.19

Jenks, William, 19–20, 192 n.5
Jordan, Cynthia S., 184 nn.20 & 22, 186 n.3, 187 n.9, 190 n.6, 196 n.17, 202 n.16
Jung, Carl, 131
Justus, James H., 195 nn.3 & 7

Kames, Lord, 81, 147, 193 n.14
Katrak, Ketu H., 51, 189 n.1
Kelleher, James T., 186 n.3
Kennedy, Julia E., 127, 140, 198 n.11
Kennedy, Roger G., 12, 184 n.24, 188 n.19, 200 n.10
Kerber, Linda K., 54, 72, 189 n.2, 190 n.13, 191 nn.16 & 19
Kickapoo tribe, 39
King, Bruce, 181 n.3, 183 n.14, 186 nn.37 & 4, 190 n.14
Kipling, Rudyard, 197 n.1
Knorr, Klaus E., 7, 182 n.13, 183 n.14
Kramer, Michael, 12, 123, 181 n.4, 184 n.20, 185 n.35, 187 n.7
Kritzer, Amelia Howe, 191 n.17, 192 n.26

Landes, Joan B., 191 n.18
Larson, David M., 196 nn.10 & 20
Lawson, Alan, 8, 9, 10, 16, 17, 21, 29, 93, 97, 108, 123, 177, 183 n.15, 192 n.28, 195 n.6, 197 n.2, 198 n.15
Lawson-Peebles, Robert, 11, 93, 108, 122, 186 n.3, 187 n.6, 188 n.15, 194 nn.15, 16, & 18, 201 n.4, 202 n.9
Lawyer, The (Watterston), 6, 25, *122–43,* 198 n.9. *See also* Watterston, George
Lawyers, 124–26, 131–34, 137, 197 n.4
Leach, James, 74
Leary, Lewis, 186 nn.1 & 5
Lenz, William E., 29, 186 n.5
Lewis, Sinclair, 120
Lippard, George, 119, 123
Livy, 42
Looby, Christopher, 12, 28, 123, 184 nn.20 & 22, 185 n.35, 189 n.26, 190 n.8, 195 n.5, 196 nn.16 & 24, 201 n.9
Lowell, James Russell, 70

Lucian, 40
Lyrical Ballads (Wordsworth and Coleridge), 171

Madison, James, 104
Maier, Pauline, 7, 182 n.12, 183 n.14
Main, Jackson Turner, 181 n.1
Mancall, Peter C., 130, 198 n.14
Marder, Daniel, 187 nn.10 & 12
Mark Twain (Samuel Clemens), 141
Martin, Terence, 188 n.15, 190 n.11, 193 n.13
Martin, Wendy, 186 n.1
Mary, Queen of Scots, 66
Masel, Carolyn, 175, 198 n.16, 202 n.11
Massachusetts Magazine, 56–60, 65
McLamore, Richard V., 149, 174, 182 n.11
McWilliams, John P., 166, 199 n.5, 200 n.11, 202 n.16
Melville, Herman, 1, 48, 120, 127, 131, 141, 167, 178–79
Memmi, Albert, 9, 178, 181 n.5, 183 n.16, 184 n.25, 188 n.20, 195 n.6
Merivale, Herman, 95, 183 n.14, 195 n.2
Metafiction, 19–24, 31
Meyer, Donald, 12, 184 n.24, 188 n.19, 200 n.10
Miller, John C., 75
Miller, Samuel, 14, 81, 124, 152, 184 n.28, 189 n.27, 193 n.14, 201 n.4
Milton, John, 61, 75
Mitchell, W. J. T., 6
Modern Chivalry (Brackenridge), 6, 21, 24, *27–50*, 76, 77, 94, 177, 186 n.3; and the author–narrator, 23, 27–28, 30–31, 34, 58. *See also* Brackenridge, Hugh Henry
Morse, Jedediah, 147
Morton, Sarah Wentworth, 57, 68, 71
Murray, John, 52, 56
Murray, Judith Sargent, 6, 24, *51–72*, 82, 96, 97, 103, 123, 134, 139, 160, 171, 179, 189 n.2, 191 n.21, 192 n.28; and drama, 68–69; *The Gleaner*, 51–72; and male voice, 55–56; and slavery, 72; and women's education, 62–66
Murray, Laura J., 28–29, 182 n.11, 185 n.33

Naipaul, V. S., 173
Napoleon Bonaparte, 192 n.1
Neal, John, 167, 173
Nelson, Dana D., 11–12, 176, 183 nn.16 & 17, 188 n.20, 194 n.15, 202 n.15
Neuberg, Victor, 197 n.6
New York Evening Post, 150
New York Historical Society, 151
Newlin, Claude M., 187 n.12
Newton, Isaac, 147
Newton, Sarah Emily, 190 n.8, 191 n.24
Nord, David Paul, 124, 185 n.31

Paine, Thomas, 7, 10, 32, 194 n.18
Patterson, Mark A., 105, 186 nn.36 & 3, 195 n.5
Paulding, James Kirke, 167, 173
Peladeau, Marius, 193 n.8
Petter, Henri, 127, 186 n.1, 196 n.15
Pindar, Peter, 86
Plato, 155, 161
Plutarch, 66, 82
Pocock, J. G. A., 7, 104, 182 n.13, 183 n.19
Poe, Edgar Allen, 48, 127–28, 178–79
Postcolonialism, 1–2, 5, 6, *16–19*, 26, 98, 128, 149, 150, *171–76*, 181 n.3, 182 nn.8, 9, & 10, 183 n.15, 185 n.32, 187 n.6, 190 n.14; and women, 51, 54, 189 n.1, 191 n.15, 198 n.16. *See also* Decolonization
Pratt, Mary Louise, 91, 181 n.2
Prescott, William, 166–67
Pythagoras, 155

Radway, Janice A., 191 n.25
Railton, Stephen, 179, 196 n.11, 202 n.17
Rakove, Jack N., 122–23
Ramsay, David, 146–48, 151–54, 158, 167
Readership, 12–14, 26, 42, 53, 77, 105, 116, 119, 122, 125, 129–31, 135–37, 145
Republicanism, 2–6, *9–15*, 24, 175, 190 n.12; and Anglocentrism, 5, 13, 16, 18, 23, 74, 76, 170, 187 n.8; and education, 125, 132; and elitism, 52, 56, 64, 67, 70, 105, 151, 184 n.19, 185 n.30, 188 n.16; and ethnicity, 117, 160; and history, 146–49; and morality, 78, 81,

Republicanism—*continued*
123–24, 129, 140–41; and the public sphere, 20, 30, 44, 99, 127, 144, 175; and writing, 6, 12, 20, 30, 40, 41, 44, 52, 55, 115, 122, 125–26, 185 n.35, 193 n.10, 197 n.3
Reynal, Abbé, 147
Reynolds, David S., 97, 123–24, 127, 176, 195 n.5, 198 n.10, 202 nn.13 & 16
Rice, Grantland S., 27–28, 31, 186 n.5
Richardson, Gary A., 17, 166, 182 n.11, 185 n.33, 193 n.7
Richardson, Samuel, 22, 123
Ringe, Donald A., 195 n.8, 196 n.14
Ringer, Benjamin B., and Elinor Lawless, 9, 183 n.17
Ritcheson, Charles R., 74
Ross, Harold, 196 n.22
Roth, Martin, 144–45, 170, 200 nn.12 & 19
Rousseau, Jean–Jacques, 71
Rowson, Susanna Haswell, 74, 136, 198 n.18
Rubin–Dorsky, Jeffrey, 200 nn.21 & 1, 201 n.8
Rush, Benjamin, 12, 125, 130, 152, 184 n.28
Russo, James R., 195 n.8

Said, Edward, 3, 33, 91, 95, 181 n.2, 187 n.6, 190 n.14, 192 n.1, 194 n.22, 195 n.2
Schofield, Mary Anne, 68–69, 192 n.27
Schulman, Lydia Dittler, 12
Scottish rhetoric, 14, 188 n.18, 199 n.9
Second World, 8–9, 10, *15–19*, 20–21, 37–39, 64, 76, 78, 93, 97, 120, 123, 126, 132, 145, 150, 157, 167, 176–77, 183 nn.15 & 16, 185 n.33, 186 n.37, 187 nn.6 & 12, 195 n.6, 197 n.2, 202 n.11
Secor, Robert, 37
Seelye, John, 11–12, 33, 176, 186 n.5, 187 n.11, 202 n.15
Seneca Falls convention, 167
Shaffer, Arthur H., 146–47
Shakespeare, William, 79
Shalhope, Robert E., 16
Sharp, James Roger, 10, 11, 15, 20, 23, 194 n.23
Sharpe, Jenny, 155, 176, 202 n.14
Shays's Rebellion, 122, 154

Sherburne, Henry, 76
Shields, David S., 181 n.5, 195 n.2, 196 n.23
Shuffleton, Frank, 160
Simpson, David, 5, 12, 184 n.20, 187 n.7, 190 n.10
Sketch-Book of Geoffrey Crayon, The (Irving), 169–72. *See also* Irving, Washington
Slaughter, Thomas, 189 n.25
Slavery, 11–12, 42, 72, 86, 88–92, 188 n.15
Slemon, Steven, 8, 16, 17, 24, 28, 46, 121, 123, 132, 178, 182 n.10, 183 n.15, 197 n.2
Smith, Adam, 8
Smith, William Raymond, 199 n.8
Smollett, Tobias, 129, 154
Spangler, George M., 196 n.10
Spectator, 85.
Spenser, Edmund, 144
Spivak, Gayatri, 16, 54, 181 nn.2 & 5, 189 n.1, 191 n.15
Spurr, David, 14, 91, 181 n.2, 183 n.14, 184 n.27, 194 n.22, 198 n.15, 199 n.22, 201 n.9
Stead, Christina, 173
Sterne, Laurence, 22, 27, 47
Stonum, Gary Lee, 22, 153
Swift, Jonathan, 27, 40, 165

Tanselle, G. Thomas, 192 n.3
Taylor, Alan, 3–4, 190 n.12
Thacher, Samuel Cooper, 4–5, 15, 182 n.7, 184 n.23
Third World, 10, 16, 181 n.5, 183 n.15, 185 n.32, 189 n.1, 191 n.15
Thomas, Nicholas, 16–17, 181 n.3, 185 n.32, 187 n.8, 194 n.20, 195 n.6
Thompson, George, 123
Thoreau, Henry David, 141
Tiffin, Helen, 8, 18, 19, 178, 182 nn.9 & 11, 183 n.15, 185 n.32
Tocqueville, Alexis de, 124, 181 n.8
Tom Jones (Fielding), 106
Tompkins, Jane, 195 nn.3 & 7, 196 n.16
Trumbull, Benjamin, 147, 148, 164
Trumbull, John, 45, 61

Tuttleton, James, 199 n.3

Tyler, Royall, 6, 17, 25, *73–94*, 95, 107, 122, 151, 164, 166, 171, 179, 192 n.3, 193 n.7; and *The Algerine Captive*, 6, 17, 25, 73–94, 100; and the Algerine Crisis, 25, 73–78, 79, 88–92; and Christianity, 89–92; and classicism, 84–85; and the Connecticut Wits, 75–79, 84; *The Contrast*, 92, 194 n.17; and decolonization, 87, 94; and federalism 73–75, 78; and language, 88; and Orientalism, 74–75; political career of, 74–76; and slavery, 86, 88–92; and Updike Underhill, 76–93

Underhill, John, 77, 83–84, 87, 90, 92, 194 n.15

Unrue, Darlene Harbour, 187 n.9

Van Anglen, K. P., 12

Virgil, 66, 84

Wakefield, Edward Gibbon, 5, 95, 182 n.8, 183 n.14, 195 n.2

Wales, Samuel, 190 n.5

Warfel, Harry, 100, 196 n.14

Warner, Michael, 4, 12, 13, 29, 53, 96, 115, 184 nn.20, 21, & 22, 185 n.35, 186 n.39, 190 nn.7 & 9, 195 n.4, 5, & 7, 197 n.3, 201 n.7

Warren, Mercy Otis, 51, 61, 69–70, 71, 190 n.7

Washington, George, 43, 175

Watt, Ian, 14, 31, 52

Watterston, George, 6, 21, 23, 25, 94, *122–143*, 151, 170; and authorship, 125–29; biographical information, 127–28; "The Child

of Feeling," 127, 142, 170, 198 n.17; and didacticism, 123–29; *The Lawyer*, 6, 21, 25, 94, 122–143; and the legal profession, 124–26, 131–34; and Morcell, 40, 124–42; and readers, 122, 125, 135–37; and republican textuality, 125–26

Watts, Emily S., 189 n.2

Watts, Steven, 15, 168, 187 n.9, 194 n.23, 195 nn.3 & 7, 196 n.16, 197 n.8

Webster, Noah, 30, 182 n.7

Wheatley, Phillis, 51

Whiskey Rebellion, 47–48, 122, 189 n.25

White, Hayden, 199 n.7

White, Patrick, 177

Whitman, Walt, 141

Wilkins, Kirsten, 189 n.3, 191 n.20

Williams, Daniel E., 201 n.3

Winthrop, James, 4

Wollstonecraft, Mary, 69, 191 n.16

Wood, Gordon S., 7, 10–11, 15, 20, 23, 75, 182 n.12, 183 nn.14 & 19, 185 n.30, 190 nn.12 & 13, 195 n.5

Woodmansee, Martha, 14, 170, 174, 185 n.29, 196 n.11, 199 n.1, 201 n.3

Yellow fever, 101

Youmans, Gilbert, and Greg Stratman, 30, 170

Young, Robert J. C., 184 nn.25 & 26

Ziff, Larzer, 97, 168, 184 n.22, 186 nn.38 & 39, 195 nn.3, 5, & 7